Economic Concepts for the Social Sciences

The primary purpose of this book is to present some of the key economic concepts that have guided economic thinking in the last century and to identify which of these concepts will continue to direct economic thought in the coming decades. This book is written in an accessible manner and is intended for a wide audience with little or no formal training in economics. It should also interest economists who want to reflect on the direction of the discipline and to learn about concepts and achievements in other subfields. The author imparts his enthusiasm for the economic way of reasoning and its wide applicability. Through the abundant use of illustrations and examples, the author makes concepts understandable and relevant. Topics covered include game theory, the new institutional economics, market failures, asymmetric information, endogenous growth theory, general equilibrium, rational expectations, and others.

Todd Sandler holds the Robert R. and Katheryn A. Dockson Chair of International Relations and Economics at the University of Southern California. He was a NATO Fellow for 1998–2000 and an Institute of Policy Reform Senior Fellow for 1990–94. Professor Sandler has written, edited, or coauthored fifteen other books, including *The Political Economy of NATO* (with Keith Hartley, Cambridge University Press, 1999), *Global Challenges: An Approach to Economic, Political, and Environmental Problems* (Cambridge University Press, 1997), *Collective Action: Theory and Applications* (1992), *The Economics of Defense* (with Keith Hartley, Cambridge Surveys in Economic Literature, 1995), *Handbook of Defense Economics* (with Keith Hartley, 1995), and *Theory of Externalities, Public Goods, and Club Goods* (with Richard Cornes, second edition, Cambridge University Press, 1996). He has published widely on economics and international relations.

Economic Concepts for the Social Sciences

TODD SANDLER

University of Southern California

CAMBRIDGE
UNIVERSITY PRESS

PUBLISHED BY THE PRESS SYNDICATE OF THE UNIVERSITY OF CAMBRIDGE
The Pitt Building, Trumpington Street, Cambridge, United Kingdom

CAMBRIDGE UNIVERSITY PRESS
The Edinburgh Building, Cambridge CB2 2RU, UK
40 West 20th Street, New York, NY 10011-4211, USA
10 Stamford Road, Oakleigh, VIC 3166, Australia
Ruiz de Alarcón 13, 28014 Madrid, Spain
Dock House, The Waterfront, Cape Town 8001, South Africa

http://www.cambridge.org

First published 2001

Printed in the United States of America

Typeface Times New Roman 10/12 pt.   *System* QuarkXPress [BTS]

A catalog record for this book is available from the British Library.

Library of Congress Cataloging in Publication data
Sandler, Todd.
Economic concepts for the social sciences / Todd Sandler.
p.   cm.
Includes bibliographical references and index.
ISBN 0-521-79262-2 – ISBN 0-521-79677-6 (pb.)
1. Economics – History – 20th century.   2. Social sciences – History – 20th century.
I. Title.
HB87.S234   2001
330 – dc21   2001025637

ISBN   0 521 79262 2   hardback
ISBN   0 521 79677 6   paperback

To the memory of Mancur Olson, whose writings enlightened me and whose kindness will always be remembered. His insights, generosity, and energy meant so much to so many.

Contents

Table and Figures

Preface

One morning I awoke to find that I had changed. Although I had not grown a shell and turned into a beetle, as in Kafka's story, I had experienced a fundamental metamorphosis in my views of economics and my role as an economist. I could no longer fathom why I had followed my fellow economists in making my writing accessible to so few. I realized that economics had taken root because the writings of Adam Smith and David Ricardo could be read by any educated person, including policy makers. So I decided then and there to write more general-interest pieces and to communicate more widely. If I succeeded, then maybe even my brothers and sisters would finally understand what I study and do. I began this task with *Global Challenges: An Approach to Environmental, Political, and Economic Problems*, which showed how basic game theory could enlighten us on a host of exigencies confronting humankind. This book opened doors previously shut to me, thus reinforcing my revelation that being understood by people in international organizations, students in universities, and others among the general population had its rewards. But *Global Challenges* was only a halfway house, because many of the game concepts remained abstruse.

The success of *Global Challenges* emboldened me to go further with my venture. Thus, I coauthored *The Political Economy of NATO* with Keith Hartley. This book was written for an interdisciplinary audience that included political scientists. Aided by its publication at the start of NATO's bombing campaign against Serbia, this book has also done well.

In the current book, *Economic Concepts for the Social Sciences*, I take an even larger step in my crusade to be read and to enlighten. This book is intended for a wide audience with no formal training in economics. My purpose is simple – to present the key economic concepts that have influenced economic thinking in the twentieth century and to identify those concepts that will continue to guide economic thought in the years to come. I am especially interested in identifying how economic concepts interface with those of the other social sciences and how these concepts can be applied to advantage.

By illustrating concepts with amusing examples, I wish to make this book enjoyable and interesting. I want to share my love for economics and to convince readers that the economic way of thinking has something to teach us all. This book is also intended to demonstrate to other economists that economics can be made exciting and understandable even to nonspecialists. By examining a broad range of concepts and putting them in perspective, this book is also aimed at economists who might like to relax their focused study and contemplate new directions in economic thought – to consider "what a long strange trip it has been," in the words of the Grateful Dead. Many economists never take time from their overcommitted schedules to stay current with what is happening in other areas of economics.

In understanding the revolution in economics, a reader should be aware of five themes of the "new" economics that surface throughout the book. First, economics now incorporates strategic behavior in which the interaction of choices among agents (for example, consumers, firms, governments) is highlighted. How one should behave depends on how others *are expected to react.* These expectations are based on what one thinks others know. This way of reasoning reflects the influence of game theory. Second, there is the message that markets do not always perform ideally and that, at times, a public sector is needed to guide resources to their best use. Since the end of World War II, the growth of the public sector has characterized all industrial economies. The notion of market failure is pivotal to modern economic thought and the understanding of the public sector. Third, economics now takes less as given, so that institutional arrangement, tastes, and even knowledge become integral considerations in economic representations. Fourth, economics is becoming more multidisciplinary in its methods, topics, and outlook. Branches of economics are incorporating techniques, knowledge, and concepts from other disciplines in the social and natural sciences. Fifth, dynamic considerations are playing a greater role, as economists study the process and pathways of change, not just final resting points.

I owe a tremendous debt of gratitude to Carol Sandler and Jon Cauley, who read the entire manuscript and provided excellent editorial comments. I also appreciated their constant encouragement. I have also profited from insightful comments provided by four anonymous reviewers. As in the case of my last three Cambridge University Press books, I have received encouragement and excellent counsel throughout the writing of the book from Scott Parris, the economics editor. This interaction and his friendship have made the process special. I appreciate the efforts of the production staff at the Press, who transformed the typescript into a book. I also have benefited greatly from the skills, care, and patience of Christie Rainey, Ann Hrbek, and Sue Streeter, who typed the myriad drafts of the chapters. Of course, the project would not have succeeded without the support of my wife, Jeannie, and my son, Tristan, who always bear much of the true cost of my books. Many mornings at 4:30 they were awakened by my stirrings as I set out to write or research this book.

Los Angeles　　　　TODD SANDLER
January 2001　　　*Robert R. and Katheryn A. Dockson Professor*
　　　　　　　　　of International Relations and Economics,
　　　　　　　　　University of Southern California

1   Economics without Apology

On the dubious date of 1 April 1971, after two and a half years of study, I successfully defended my dissertation in economics. Although the 2000–01 academic year marks my thirtieth year of teaching economics since the fall of 1970, I am no less enthusiastic about the subject. To impart my excitement about economics to a fresh group of students is a recurring challenge that I confront most fall semesters as I rush to my large 8 A.M. section of economic principles on the other side of campus. It must be my perverse sense of humor, or else self-punishment, that I would place before myself the supreme challenge of interesting 250–300 students in a large, overheated lecture theater with its uncomfortable seats at such an ungodly hour. As I walk down the aisle to a sea of whispers as the students give me the once-over, I ask myself if I am pre-pared for this. At the front of the room, I pull up my blue jeans and take a deep breath. I attach the remote microphone to my shirt, switch on the infrared receiver, remove the laser pointer from my pocket, and then my eyes scan the youthful faces before me. Every semester it is the same story: of the 300 or so pairs of eyes, no pair is looking at the same spot, and no pair is looking at me – not a one! From this nadir, I must accom-plish my task – to somehow get these students to understand and appre-ciate the power, importance, and prevalence of economic concepts in the modern-day society that we inhabit. While I cannot claim to get through to all of them, I do manage, I believe, to convince a large percentage that economic principles have influenced our lives greatly during the last century and will have a more pronounced effect in the twenty-first century. Economics not only provides insights into social phenomena that we experience daily – for example, how prices and wages direct resources to their most valued uses – but also plays an active role in guiding policy.

   In this book, I take up the same daunting task of convincing my reader that economic thinking has much to offer and remains a driving force in society today. Its influence will grow in the new century as resource scarcity increases. Economics not only can explain how nations can collectively address the deterioration to the oceans, groundwater, rivers, forests, and atmosphere, but also can enlighten us on how best to assist developing countries.[1] A knowledge of economics can guide intergenerational choices on how decisions today affect the choices available tomorrow. Additionally, economics can help to explain the decay of urban centers, the breakdown of cartels, the need for governments, the design of contracts, the decline of trade unions, and the pitfalls of minimum wages. Economics can promote informed decisions about sustainability, globalization, and the transition to capitalism. If you choose to be ignorant about economics, then you are governed in many aspects of your daily existence by forces beyond your control that remain a mystery. With a basic understanding of economics, these forces can be harnessed to advantage.

If I were pressed to say why economics has held my attention for so many years, five things would top the list. First and foremost is its relevancy in explaining the real world. I can understand why many social interactions assume the forms that they do by applying economics and, in so doing, I am able to profit from an ability to anticipate outcomes. Second, I love the way that economics combines alternative ways of reasoning as it borrows from so many disciplines. Third, there is its beauty and elegance of expression. When economics is executed by a skilled mind, its formulation is clever and pregnant with applications. Fourth, economics is interdisciplinary in its orientation. As an offspring of moral philosophy and physics, economics requires both sides of the brain, owing to its philosophical, analytical, and visual underpinnings. Finally, and no less important than the other reasons, economics is logically rigorous. Even when it merely conceptualizes a problem, there is a rigorous framework to the argument. Given its reliance on well-reasoned and well-expressed arguments, it is no wonder that economics is an excellent pre-law degree. There is almost universal agreement among economists on the important basic postulates upon which economics rests.

Economics was perfected by Adam Smith, David Ricardo, John Stuart Mill, and Thomas Robert Malthus, from earlier writings dating back to Aristotle, in order to influence policy decisions. Smith and Ricardo were especially concerned with practices – the Corn Laws – that restricted international trade, as advocated by the mercantilists, who mistakenly believed that a nation's wealth was tied to its accumulated money and

---

[1] On these global problems see Helm (1991), Kaul, Grunberg, and Stern (1999), and Sandler (1997, 1998); on foreign assistance see Kanbur, Sandler, and Morrison (1999) and World Bank (1998).

gold reserves. This monetary treasury could be augmented by running trade surpluses (that is, exporting more than was imported) and placing payments for exports, not covered by imports, into the monetary reserves. The larger the trade surplus, the greater the growth of the treasury. Smith showed that the true wealth of a nation was dependent on its productive capacity and not on its monetary reserves, while Ricardo formulated trade theory and the poignant principle, no less true today, that free trade can improve everyone's well-being.[2] If a nation's trade surplus *limits* the buildup of its productive capacity, as it would if the money pool were not put to productive advantage, then mercantilist doctrine would lead to the decline of a nation. Free trade ensures that goods are available at the lowest price, with inefficient enterprises being driven out of business and replaced by more profitable ones. With these two intellectual giants and their theories, modern economics was born. Although economics has progressed greatly over the last 200 years, it remains a policy-oriented study. Young and talented economists must not lose sight of economics' concern for, or obsession with, policy.

This last century has witnessed significant refinements and advances in economic thought.[3] Much of the revolution in economic thinking during the twentieth century was in terms of the enhanced awareness of how markets are tied together. *General-equilibrium* analysis, whereby market interdependence is taken into account, has displaced the practice of examining isolated markets.[4] Policy prescriptions involving trade, foreign assistance, taxation, government spending, the environment, and labor practices now must recognize the influence that actions in one market have on other markets. Another important innovation is economics' enhanced emphasis on strategic behavior, whereby economic agents (for example, firms, individuals, governments) anticipate the responses of others to their own actions. For example, a firm that lowers its price must judge this decision in light of the expected reactions of others. A government that installs metal detectors in airports should not be surprised when terrorists respond by abducting hostages at other

---

[2] When extolling the virtues of free trade I emphasize that it "may" improve everyone's well-being, which is different from saying that it will make everyone better off. The gains from trade are often unevenly distributed and can impoverish some in sweatshops while adding to the wealth of the rich. Globalization and the increased trade that it brings may skew incomes, thereby accentuating inequality. It is this perceived widening income gap that has brought demonstrations against the World Trade Organization, the World Bank, the International Monetary Fund, and multinational firms (for example, Starbucks Coffee) to the streets of Seattle, Washington, D.C., Geneva, and elsewhere.

[3] For up-to-date and excellent treatments of the history of economic thought, see Blaug (1997) and Heilbroner (1986).

[4] On the importance of general-equilibrium analysis, see Starr (1997) and Arrow (1974a).

venues. Similarly, neighborhoods taking actions against the sale of crack cocaine should anticipate that dealers will relocate to the nearest neighborhood not taking action. With the importance of strategic behavior comes an increased interest in information. To anticipate other agents' actions, you must know not only what they know about themselves, but also what they know about you, and even what they know that you know about them. Information is no longer assumed to be costless and pervasive. Another crucial innovation in economic thought involves the role of institutions. Once regarded as given and outside of economics, institutions are now viewed by economists as an integral part of the analysis. The design of institutions can affect allocative efficiency, the distribution of income, growth, and stability – all four basic economic problems.

The purpose of the current chapter is to set the stage for the rest of the book. Thus, I am interested in addressing the role of economics in modern-day society. In particular, I want to identify the pressing issues of the day and how modern economics can enlighten us on these issues. This chapter also introduces some exciting and influential economic concepts that will be studied in greater detail in the later chapters. A crucial question involves which of these concepts and methods will have staying power and why.

ECONOMICS AND SOCIETY

We live in a world of contrasts. A few nations have accumulated vast wealth in the form of physical and human capital, while the majority have relatively little. In 1997, the richest fifth of all nations earned 86% of world income, leaving about 14% for the other 80% of nations.[5] Some of these poor nations possess tremendous natural resource wealth, but have little means to exploit this wealth. Many nations' environments are severely polluted, while others are still pristine. Select societies are technological marvels, while others have not progressed much beyond the Iron Age. Some countries dream of colonies in space and journeys to neighboring planets, while others do not dream at all, worrying instead about how to feed their teeming populations today and tomorrow. The most technologically sophisticated countries can easily protect their people against most disease-causing viruses, which can decimate less-developed countries; while these same advanced countries can be stopped in their tracks by insidious computer viruses, which have little impact in less-developed countries. Even among the rich countries, contrasts are dramatic – for example, the importance of

---

[5] United Nations Development Program (1999) and other years of the *Human Development Report*.

the military-industrial base, the percentage of gross domestic product (GDP) devoted to research and development (R & D), the size of the public sector, the rate of unemployment, and the nature of institutions. These contrasts, and many others, pose interesting questions about income distribution, resource allocation, and growth that economics can help to explain. When economics addresses such issues, it assumes a relevancy.

Economics is often unfairly characterized as the "dismal science," because some early classical economists warned of worsening conditions for humankind. For example, Malthus hypothesized that population grows at a geometric rate while the food supply grows at a much slower arithmetic rate, thus portending famine and pestilence – not a promising destiny. Fortunately, his calculations were faulty and, most important, technological advances in agriculture have continued to ward off these scenarios, except in the poorest countries. Ricardo's theory of rent predicted that landlords would assume an ever-increasing share of income as population pressures made us turn to less productive land – surely a depressing prediction to everyone but landowners! This hypothesis also was never realized because of technological advances in agriculture that have allowed an acre to feed ever-greater numbers of people. Landlords now receive a small share of national income – just one-half of one percent in the United States in 1993.

Economics not only can warn of pending crises, it also can lead to the sought-after result of lessening the effects of these crises or forestalling them completely. Modern economics not only identifies when intervention may be needed, but also indicates when policy is not required: in some instances, incentives may mean that the problem is self-correcting. Medicine identifies diseases, some of which can be cured and others not; but medicine is not labeled dismal. Economics is particularly promising when it helps guide society to better outcomes, such as full employment without inflation – an outcome thought impossible twenty years ago, but which has characterized the prosperity of the United States during the 1990s and beyond. While some of this prosperity may be serendipity, economic principles have been applied by the Federal Reserve to raise interest rates at appropriate points, so that inflation has not taken off during these halcyon times.

Sometimes, slight alterations in institutions and their implied incentives can have extremely favorable consequences with only modest costs. Economics' new focus on institutions and their incentive structures has allowed its methods to be applied to an ever-widening set of social and economic problems. Consider the behavior of political officeholders. A relatively new field of economics, known as public choice, views these politicians as acting to pursue their own well-being, sometimes to the detriment of their constituents' welfare.[6] In order to win and maintain office, politicians cater to special interests, trade votes or logroll, ignore long-term consequences of their decisions, and assume centrist positions. Changes to campaign financing, term limits, election procedures, and information dissemination can influence these practices and, by so doing, can make politicians more responsive to the electorate.

As a discipline that studies optimizing behavior in the face of constraints (for example, getting the most satisfaction from your budget), economics lends itself to the study of a wide variety of social interactions and problems. Economic methods can be applied to questions in sociology (for example, group formation and actions), political science (for example, the behavior of parties in elections), history (for example, the profitability of slavery), and ecology (for example, biodiversity and species preservation). With their large bag of theoretical and empirical tools, economists are particularly adept at infiltrating other fields. This extension of economics to diverse areas has led some to complain about an economic imperialism. Edward Lazear (2000) defends this imperialism and attributes economics' successful invasion to its emphasis on rational behavior, equilibrium, and competition. Recent economic insights and methods should further the application of economic ideas to issues in other disciplines.

ISSUES OF THE DAY

We inhabit a "brave new world" where allocative decisions today can have consequences that transcend political and generational boundaries. For example, the lamp beside you that illuminates this book may use electricity generated by a nuclear power plant, whose by-products include plutonium that can pollute the planet for millennia to come. Genetic engineering raises a host of issues that range from ownership of genetic codes to inefficiencies stemming from the benefits and costs of unintended side effects. Even the choice by doctors of how often to prescribe antibiotics has an intergenerational consequence, as their use allows bacteria to acquire a tolerance, leading to more virulent forms that can threaten current and future generations. Increasingly, technologies place in our hands consumption goods that affect the unborn, who have no say in these far-reaching decisions. A related notion concerns the now-popular concept of economic sustainability, whereby the current generation's actions do not limit the options available to subsequent generations.[7] Are generations sufficiently motivated through altruism or

---

[6] The classic works in public choice include Black (1958), Buchanan and Tullock (1962), and Downs (1957). The field is surveyed by Mueller (1989).

[7] On sustainability, see the World Commission on Environment and Development (1987), Solow (1986), Howarth (1995), Pearce and Atkinson (1995), and Doeleman and Sandler (1998).

other interests to achieve sustainable development? The answer to this question is not very promising.

From an economic viewpoint, political borders are losing their importance. This is also true from a security perspective. Technologies have created goods and bads, whose benefits and/or costs slip through political borders. Thus, coal-fired power plants produce sulfur and nitrogen oxide emissions that travel to downwind countries and fall as acid rain or dry deposits. Coolants in refrigerators and air conditioners can release chlorofluorocarbons (CFCs) that migrate to the upper stratosphere and thin the ozone layer, which protects humans and animals from harmful ultraviolet radiation.[8] The burning of fossil fuels releases carbon dioxide (CO_2), which accumulates in the atmosphere and results in a greenhouse effect, as trapped solar energy heats up the Earth. The inhospitality of Venus is due, in large part, to elevated temperatures caused by a runaway greenhouse effect. Myriad transboundary pollutants at the regional and global levels are of current concern. In the case of health, disease-causing bacteria and viruses cross borders at will, aided by modern transport. The security of national frontiers is called into question, not only because of diseases and pollutants that travel without passports, but also because of terrorism, civil unrest, criminal activities, and revolutions that traverse borders with disastrous consequences. This increased prevalence of transnational interdependencies is traceable to more than just new technologies; it is also due to expanding populations, the breakup of nations, and accumulated stresses to our planet. We are more aware of these interdependencies because we are better able to spot them using newly developed means to monitor the environment and society.

An important question of the day concerns changing from one economic system to another. In particular, the breakdown of communist regimes from 1989 to 1991 has led to "transition economies," which are in the process of introducing a greater reliance on markets. Such transition can be accomplished all at once – the so-called "big bang" – by relinquishing government controls and fiats to all transactions. Opening up the country to international trade permits world prices to discipline domestic exchange, but often at the price of great hardship to domestic industries. This wholesale institution of markets requires an infrastructure – property law, enforcement of contracts, and a banking system – that must be set up quickly at tremendous expense. An alternative pathway of transition involves more gradual changes – myriad options exist. The nature of the best transition pathway is subject to much current debate.

Another important issue involves the architecture of institutions. Consider the firm, one of the essential agents in any economic system.

[8] See de Gruijl (1995) and Environmental Protection Agency (1987a, 1987b).

Standard economic analysis – the "neoclassical" theory – does not present an explicit theory of the firm's structure and merely assumes that firms of an unspecified nature control many economic decisions. Thus, we have little guidance in choosing between, say, the Western corporate form or the less hierarchical form of the Japanese firm.[9] What should replace the Chinese large-scale state-owned enterprises, if anything, is of considerable interest. Institutional design permeates almost every current economic problem – for example, the form of environmental treaties to address transfrontier pollution problems, the design of non-market structures to address market failures, and the proper structure of government decision making to limit participants' pursuit of their self-interest.

Another area of interest concerns whether or not people really act according to the rational-choice models that dominate the landscape of economic thought. Modern-day tools and analyses – for example, game theory, rational expectations, portfolio theory, and public choice – assume a great deal of rationality by participants. Recent analyses may allow for ill-informed agents or even mistaken behavior, but these agents are still driven to seek their own self-interest and to respond in predictable and appropriate ways to changes in constraints. Recent Nobel Prizes awarded to some of the strongest proponents of rational-choice models (for instance, Amartya Sen, Robert Lucas, Ronald Coase, James Mirrlees, Gary Becker, William Vickrey, and John Harsanyi) reflect the profession's continued faith in (obsession with) the usefulness of this paradigm. Of course, the opposite case of completely irrational (mad) behavior with no predictable pattern would leave virtually nothing for economists to study. Some unpredictability or bounded rationality can be accommodated, as some recent advances in game theory demonstrate, but predictable aspects must also remain – that is, madness or restricted capabilities must have enough predictability to allow modeling to be applied, if economics is to cast some light on these kinds of behavior.

EXCITING ECONOMIC CONCEPTS FROM THE TWENTIETH CENTURY

The obvious first place to turn to predict what economic concepts will rule thought in the twenty-first century is to identify influential and exciting concepts from the last century, especially during its last quarter. As mentioned earlier, the dominant paradigm of economics during the

---

[9] The background for this statement comes from Aoki (1984, p. v). The form of the firm was first systematically analyzed by Williamson (1975). Also see Cauley and Sandler (1992).

previous century was that of general equilibrium, accounting for the interrelationship of markets. By far, the most Nobel Prizes in economics were awarded for studies of the interrelationship of markets; Nobel recognition was given to contributions that analyzed its foundation (John Hicks and Paul Samuelson), its existence (Kenneth Arrow and Gerard Debreu), its linear representation (Wassily Leontief and Leonid Kantorovich), its application to specific economies (Lawrence Klein), its growth (Simon Kuznets and Robert Solow), and its trade representation (Bertil Ohlin). A recent and noteworthy extension to general-equilibrium analysis concerns systems that include economic and noneconomic phenomena. For example, bioeconomic models involve biological interactions within economic systems and have been applied to study the management of renewable resources (for example, fisheries and forests – see Chapter 11).[10] Similarly, the study of environmental economics has begun to include hydraulics, atmospheric relationships, and stochastic factors.

Much interest has been shown in the role of information in economic systems. Classical economics gave little thought to information, since everyone was assumed to be perfectly well-informed. Information was also assumed to be costless. In recent years, information has come to be considered a factor to be reckoned with, and one that may be costly to acquire. Knowledge, and who possesses it and when, is an important determinant of economic outcomes (see Chapter 7). Consider investors in a stock market who foresee or have reliable information about the future prospects of a corporation. Once this knowledge is acquired, investors will act on it and, in so doing, cause stock prices quickly to reflect these prospects. When some months later the prospect is realized, the stock price hardly budges, having already incorporated the anticipated event's influence on the value of the company. A particularly fascinating analysis involving information occurs when one party to a transaction knows more than the other. This situation of "asymmetric information" is pervasive in social and economic contexts. For instance, a terrorist group knows its own true strength, while the targeted government must decide how to respond to a bombing campaign based on signals picked up from the group's actions and the manner in which the government processes these signals. Surely, a government would capitulate to the terrorists' demands if it knew immediately that the terrorists' resources were sufficient to make the political and associated costs of giving in less than those of holding firm.

The terrorist example reminds us that game theory – the study of strategic interactions – has come to dominate economics over the last

---

[10] The seminal work on bioeconomics is by Clark (1985).

two decades (see Chapter 3). In economics, the application of game theory is so ubiquitous that even policy decisions are often represented as strategic interactions among policy makers and other economic agents. Sometimes, these policy interactions involve addressing market failures (see Chapters 2 and 4), and, at other times, they include agents bent on influencing decisions for their own gain (see Chapter 5). Thanks to economics, governments are no longer viewed as benevolent institutions whose actions always further societal welfare. Moreover, government interventions do not necessarily remedy market shortcomings; in fact, government failures may stem from the very same factors that lead to market failures.

In a perfect economic environment in which every activity has a price, property rights are assigned, and competition is rigorous, independent agents' pursuit of their own self-interest leads to the betterment of everyone. This result was dubbed "the invisible hand" by Adam Smith. Markets fail when this pursuit results in an inefficient allocation in which resources do not gravitate to their most valued use, so that a reassignment can improve society's well-being. Market failures are associated with externalities, public goods, open-access resources, and increasing returns to scale. An *externality* is an interdependency among two or more agents that is not taken into account by a market transaction. If running your car pollutes the environment, and if, moreover, you are not charged for the resulting damage, then an externality exists. In the absence of this charge, car owners can be expected to drive too much from a social viewpoint.

Market failures may also be associated with public goods. Publicness here does not necessarily refer to government provision; rather, it means that the good's benefits possess two properties that distinguish these goods from those that can be traded in markets. First, a pure public good's benefits are nonexcludable, with both payers and nonpayers gaining from the good once it is provided. Since the provider cannot keep others from consuming the good's benefits, consumers have a natural incentive to take advantage of the public good without paying for it, which leads to a *free-rider* problem and an anticipated underprovision of the public good. If I put on a fireworks display at the city park and then request a donation from anyone who comes to watch, my collection would surely be meager no matter how spectacular the pyrotechnics. Second, the benefits of a public good are nonrival in the sense that one user's consumption of these benefits does not detract, in the least, from the consumption opportunities still in store for others. Consider the cleanup of a polluted lake and those who visit its shores or use its waters. Once the lake is cleansed, the benefits from the cleaner environment for one visitor do not diminish those available for another visitor.

Market failures may also arise from property rights (or ownership claims) that are either undefined or owned in common with unrestricted access. There is little incentive to acquire a good if your ownership rights are not recognized or protected. Suppose that there were no property rights to houses, so that all were considered open to the public. Clearly, there would be no reason to purchase one only to share it with any uninvited guest. For open-access resources – fisheries, hunting grounds, orbital slots – where users cannot be restricted, exploitation becomes wasteful as users ignore the effects of their actions on others. If more fishing vessels ply a fishing ground, then greater effort must be expended by each crew to land the same catch, so that actions by one vessel adversely affect the catch of others. As individuals see the resources grabbed by others, they accelerate their own grabbing until, in some instances, nothing remains.[11]

Yet another cause of market failures is attributable to *increasing returns to scale*, whereby a doubling of all inputs results in more than a doubling of output. With increasing returns, the cost per unit of production falls with an increased scale of output. There is thus a motive for ever-larger output levels within a single firm. In fact, the presence of increasing returns can lead to a *natural monopoly*, in which a single firm provides the output at a lower unit cost than multiple competitors. To ensure that such a monopoly does not restrict output and exploit its market power through high prices, governments have imposed regulatory regimes.

Market failures are discussed in greater detail in Chapters 2, 4, 5, 7, 10, and 11. Research on such failures has been a high spot in economics in the last quarter century. To appreciate markets and when they work, one must understand market failures. When markets fail, a natural question to ask is what can be done about it. The public sector with its provision of some goods and services is one alternative, but market failures are many and varied, as are their suggested remedies. Devising these remedies, while accounting for the environment of policy makers (see Chapters 4, 5, and 12), has increasingly occupied the attention of economists. What is new is the representation of this environment in terms of the policy makers' motivation, information, and strategic interactions. This new perspective is nothing short of a revolution in the study of public finance, or the way in which governments allocate resources,

---

[11] On externalities and public goods, consult Cornes and Sandler (1996); on open-access resources, see Ostrom (1990).

redistribute income, and stimulate growth. With the realization that regulators may not be benign welfare maximizers with the requisite information, there is now less enthusiasm for government controls, even in the case of monopolies.

Another revolution may be called *endogenizing*, whereby a variable, previously taken as given, is now determined *within the model*. For example, efforts to explain the form of economic institutions, such as the firm, represent this endogenizing revolution (see Chapter 6). Another instance involves endogenous growth and the attempt to identify which economic variables, determined by the model, can themselves stimulate growth (see Chapter 14).[12] Thus, externalities associated with technological advances can promote growth. For example, the creation of the laser and the computer had an impact on myriad industries and stimulated long-run growth. This was also true of the steam engine. Additionally, the education of women can foster growth by giving women more say over childbearing decisions. By putting off childbearing until later years, women benefit from their human-capital investment, while helping to limit population expansion and the demands for resources that this expansion entails. The end result can be faster growth and a higher standard of living.

Another noteworthy break with economic tradition involves the available procedures by which theories are tested or subject to scrutiny against the facts. I am not referring here to the tremendous refinements in econometrics (that is, the statistical representations of economics); rather, I have in mind the use of new testing procedures. Foremost among them is experimental economics, where economic theories are tested in a controlled laboratory environment (see Chapter 9).[13] Experimental economics has many advantages, since it can, for example, permit researchers to generate data rapidly without having to wait years for market-generated data. In an experimental framework, the desirability of alternative institutional arrangements, some of which may have no real-world counterpart, can be analyzed. Another novel testing procedure is the contingent valuation or survey approach, which constructs hypothetical markets in the minds of the respondents.[14] The procedure is particularly useful in situations where market data are not available. If, for instance, a society wanted to determine the impact that a planned power plant would have on hikers in a remote wilderness, the only way

---

[12] For a careful and up-to-date treatment of endogenous growth, see Aghion and Howitt (1998).

[13] See, for example, Kagel and Roth (1995) on experimental economics.

[14] A good source on contingent valuation methods is Cummings, Brookshire, and Schulze (1986).

to ascertain such information would be to design a survey that would enable the hikers to indicate their willingness to pay to avoid losses in visibility, as presented by simulated pictures of such a planned plant's emissions. There is obviously no other way to value such a hypothetical contingency – data just do not exist.

A final revolution in economic reasoning that is worth singling out is the incorporation of time and space into economics.[15] Many economic decisions have a time dimension, which can show up in terms of which agent goes first (leads) and which goes second (follows) in an economic interaction. The sequence of moves can have a profound influence on an outcome, as any child who has played tic-tac-toe knows. With the recognition that time matters should come the realization that the intertemporal consequences of transactions matter. Unquestionably, any explanation of economic growth or economic sustainability must account for the sequence of decisions (see Chapters 10 and 14). But with the insight that time matters should come the recognition that space also matters. Surely, the manner in which an idea spreads temporally *and* spatially is important. In the last century, spatial considerations have begun to be included in economic analysis.

WHICH IDEAS HAVE STAYING POWER?

This book is intended, in part, to answer this question. Any answer offered can be no more than an educated guess, backed by research, careful thinking, and intuition. I, however, make no claim for the universality of my views. I have no doubt that many economists, who work in areas that I do not single out as having staying power, will find displeasure with my choices and dismiss them summarily. No matter what my thoughts on staying power may be, I will alienate more economists than I win over; nevertheless, I offer these views here and throughout the book without apology.

Simple concepts and theories tend to stay around and influence thinking. For many years, the ruling paradigm in growth theory was that of Harrod-Domar, which relates growth to two easy-to-measure variables – the savings rate and the capital-output ratio.[16] The former is the proportion of annual income saved, while the latter is the number of units of capital, on average, required to produce a unit of output. Even though sophisticated refinements came along, one could get a good fix on a country's growth potential by ascertaining the ratio of these two values. Mancur Olson's (1965) seminal work, *The Logic of Collective Action*, which seeks to explain how groups form and achieve common

---

[15] See Faden's (1977) interesting work on the economics of space and time.
[16] On Harrod-Domar growth models, see Aghion and Howitt (1998) and Wan (1971).

objectives, is also based on a simple model with some easy-to-remember maxims – for example, larger groups are more difficult to form and, when formed, achieve less efficient results when compared to smaller groups.

Yet another example of a simple theory with staying power is contained in George Akerlof's (1970) brilliant paper on "the market for lemons" (see Chapter 7). The paper shows how asymmetric information, where sellers of used cars are well informed about the cars' quality while potential buyers are not, drives down the price of all used cars. Insofar as people with lemons – cars with chronic problems – are apt to trade them in, there are a disproportionately large number of lemons in the used-car market. Buyers, who cannot distinguish a car's quality, discount their offers as though all cars were lemons. The prophecy is self-fulfilling, as the resulting low price does not warrant trading in a good car, so that these cars are held onto or else sold to friends or family. This "adverse-selection" problem, where the bad risks drive the good out of the market, applies to many other economic scenarios, such as insurance markets.

To have lasting interest, economic theories or concepts must be applicable to a wide range of relevant situations. Again consider Olson's theory of collective action. The need for collective action, where two or more agents must join forces for a mutual gain, characterizes important concerns in virtually every field of economics: unions in labor economics, cartels in industrial organizations, alliances in defense economics, public good provision in public economics, interest groups in public choice, and pollution control in environmental economics. Many of the pressing issues of today – global warming, transnational terrorism, and control of ethnic conflict – are collective action problems. *Broad-based relevancy* is crucial for lasting power. If an economic theory affects disciplines beyond economics, as Olson's concept of collective action influenced sociology, political science, and anthropology, then its staying power is further enhanced.

Another ingredient for staying power is *testability* – that is, whether the theory can be tested, either against real-world data or in an experimental environment. Theories and hypotheses that can be tested can be judged periodically for relevancy and their ability to explain social and economic phenomena. When a theory is either too abstract to test or without real-world counterparts, it may not spread much beyond the initial formulators and their devoted disciples. Opportunities for outside funding are limited if the researcher cannot demonstrate that the concept being developed explains economic phenomena. While new theories can survive for a time and be developed for the sheer fun of it, lasting theories must eventually be judged against the standard of explaining behavior. Theory-for-theory's-sake can carry a new economic paradigm only so far.

A final requirement for endurance is that the concept be truly *novel*. To be novel, an economic theory must be more than a formalization of standard insights. In fact, too much formalization can severely limit the audience and may become an obstacle in applying the theory. Novel findings have an element of surprise to them. While all good new theories are "obvious once understood," a point sadly misunderstood by some unimaginative journal referees, the theory's message must *at first* appear almost counterintuitive to be truly a step forward.

Of the concepts analyzed in this book, collective action possesses staying power because it fulfills all of the criteria put forward. Other theories and paradigms with staying power to direct economics in the new century include, among others, the new institutional economics, intergenerational economics, experimental economics, and spatial economics. These choices are justified in later chapters.

INTENDED AUDIENCE AND PURPOSE OF THE BOOK

This book is intended for a wide audience with no formal training in economics. I hope that it will also interest economists, especially those who like to stop and think about what we are really doing in economics and what we are likely to do in the future. A self-evaluation is therapeutic from time to time. To illustrate economic concepts, I rely on a large number of examples, which highlight the subject's applicability to a wide range of social situations. As the book's title indicates, concepts that are useful to many social sciences are emphasized in hopes of making the book of interest to readers in related disciplines. Although this book touches on a broad set of economic concepts, some restraint had to be exercised in its coverage. Preference is given to concepts that either have been recognized by the Nobel Prize committee or have been allocated a disproportionate amount of journal space. These are the concepts that have driven economic thinking. Concepts likely to receive Nobel recognition are also highlighted. In some cases, this focus is understandably influenced by my own expertise in public economics, even though I have tried not to let this be a guiding factor.

The primary purpose of this book is to present some of the key economic concepts that have influenced economic thinking in the last century and to identify which of these concepts will continue to direct economic thought in the new century. In some instances, concepts that are either not currently in vogue or just coming on the scene are offered as likely candidates to steer economic thought. In making these predictions, a secondary purpose is served by taking stock of and evaluating the contributions of economics in the twentieth century. How has economics contributed to society during the last century? How is it likely to contribute during the twenty-first century? Which economic ideas will maintain their hold and which will be replaced by new ones? These and similar questions are addressed. Another purpose is to impart in some small way the excitement that I find in economics. This is accomplished by showing its far-reaching application beyond economics and the beauty of its logical consistency. Economic thinking will be an important tool for surviving in the twenty-first century. It is my intention to choose a sufficient number of interesting and, at times, unusual examples to make the book both enjoyable and informative.

2   Back to the Future: Political Economy

Suppose that the bodies of three great political economists – Adam Smith, Thomas Robert Malthus, and David Ricardo – had not decayed into dust, but had instead been frozen and preserved through the ages. How would these three philosophers view economic thought and methods today if they were reincarnated? It would be an amusing sight to see Adam Smith wandering a modern campus muttering to himself, clad in Reeboks, blue jeans, and a baseball cap, rather than his usual buckle shoes, knee breeches, and beaver hat.[1] Ricardo and Malthus would delight in seeing one another and renewing their lifelong debate over the principles of political economy, now by e-mail. As a gifted businessman and stock trader, a reincarnated Ricardo would be apt to exercise his astute business acumen and amass a fortune as an entrepreneur of space technology or as a day trader. Malthus would look at the growth of population in the less-developed countries (LDCs) and feel partly vindicated. For advanced industrial countries, he would point to the second edition of his *Essay on the Principle of Population as It Affects the Future Improvement of Society*, in which he recognized the exercise of moral restraint from marriage and childbearing.[2] Nevertheless, he would marvel at the Earth's ability to support six billion people, about six times the world population at the time of the first edition of Malthus's essay in 1798.[3]

Each of these great economists would have to reassess some of his key predictions and policy prescriptions. Smith would wonder about the growth of the public sector, which even in a capitalist economy like

---

[1] Insights into the character and dress of these economists come from Heilbroner's (1986) *The Worldly Philosophers*.
[2] See Newman, Gayer, and Spencer (1954, pp. 170–7).
[3] According to the UN Population Fund (1994), population first reached one billion around 1800 and reached six billion in 1999.

the United States constitutes about a third of gross domestic product (GDP).[4] In the time of Smith, competition disciplined markets to a larger extent, so that the need for government intervention in the economy was much less than for current economies, with their large enterprises controlling significant market shares. Mergers in the oil industry, the defense sector, the pharmaceutical industry, the airline industry, and elsewhere have decreased competition in recent years. These three economists would be bewildered by the profession's concerns over the last seventy years with market failures, including failures (such as externalities) of a kind that they had never considered. Unlike Malthus, who foresaw the possibility of gluts where products sat on store shelves, Smith did not foresee recessions and would ponder our preoccupation with business cycles and the prospect that the economy does not always progress to new heights.[5] Ricardo would be shocked that the tenets of free trade are still being debated and that protectionism is often an issue in national elections. Recent demonstrations against free trade might make him include its distributional implications.

Malthus and Ricardo would surely consult the income distribution to ascertain whether or not landowners had acquired the lion's share of annual income earnings as they had predicted. Their theory of rent or the return to land hypothesized that, as populations expanded, land of poorer and poorer quality would have to be pressed into cultivation.[6] With population expansion, society has indeed brought marginal land into cultivation, including forests and environmentally sensitive tracts. The *difference in earnings* between the most marginal, or least productive, tract of land and another better piece of land represents the better parcel's *rent*. For example, suppose that the marginal tract earned nothing beyond its opportunity cost (or foregone earnings) and the cost of cultivation, while another parcel netted $100 after costs. The latter plot is then said to earn a rent of $100. With the growth of population, Ricardo predicted that the rent for the better land would rise as the margin of cultivation is pushed out. This increase in land rents would lead to higher grain prices, which would raise wages, leaving the capitalists in an ever-worsening squeeze and the laborers in a struggle for subsistence to pay

---

[4] For a chart of the share of GDP devoted to government expenditures in the United States, see Bruce (2001, p. 8). For the United States, Canada, the United Kingdom, Germany, France, Italy, and Japan, this share averaged over 40% (Bruce 2001, p. 7).

[5] The differences between Malthus's and Smith's views of the progress of economies is addressed in Heilbroner (1986, pp. 94–100).

[6] The theory of rents is discussed by Blaug (1997), Heilbroner (1986, pp. 96–100), and Newman, Gayer, and Spencer (1954).

for dearer food, as the higher wages would merely maintain subsistence. According to Ricardo's depressing predictions, landlords would acquire an ever-greater share of national earnings, leaving less for everyone else. A look at income distribution over time paints a much different picture: wages account for about three-quarters of earnings, with the remaining quarter going to the profits of capitalists, the interest payments of lenders, and the rents of landowners. Both profits and rents tend to fluctuate yearly, with rents typically constituting a very modest share of earnings. More important, there has been no upward trend in this latter share over time.

If Malthus and Ricardo were to delve into why their prediction had proved wrong, though their theory was fine, they would discover that they had greatly underestimated the importance of technological advances. For example, the recent Green Revolution and its advances in cultivation methods have vastly increased land's productivity, giving significant returns to the capital applied to the land and raising the living standards of workers. Genetic engineering and the increased application of science to agricultural practices are leading to the next increase in land's productivity. Before the Green Revolution, the application of capital – tractors and fertilizers – also allowed for the rapid rise in land's productivity that warded off the gloomy prophecy of Malthus and Ricardo regarding population growth, food supply growth, and the changing income distribution. The dynamics of technology and its influence on a host of economic phenomena remain today a poorly understood process, one that can cause the predictions of well-reasoned theories to go far wide of the mark.

If these men were to spend time in catching up on the key contributions written since the publication of Smith's *The Wealth of Nations* in 1776, or Ricardo's or Malthus's *Principles of Political Economy* in 1817 and 1820 respectively, they would encounter a rather technical, and often demanding, body of work. Much of this work is highly mathematical, drawing from a wide range of mathematical fields. They would undoubtedly be pleased to see the broad scope of applications of economics, ranging from traditional topics to the study of the environment, health care, urban centers, and outer space. Much of the literature of the second half of the twentieth century would be beyond their limited mathematical and statistical backgrounds. No doubt, Ricardo, who enjoyed abstraction and tried to distill the essential structure of the economic system, would defend this heightened abstraction of economics to his skeptical, complaining colleagues. These economic pioneers would discover a discipline that is much less preoccupied with moral philosophy, though some work in the fields of social choice, the economics of justice, and related topics carry on these philosophical pursuits. But even this work requires abstraction and analytical reasoning.[7]

A major disappointment to these pioneers would be the fading interest now shown in the history of economic thought, which allows each new generation of economists to understand the roots of modern economic reasoning. Although undergraduate economics majors are usually required to take a history of thought class, this is usually not the case any longer for graduate degrees. This lack of perspective and appreciation of the discipline's foundations is apt to lead many academic economists to rediscover old insights, thinking them to be new.

Perhaps Adam Smith's and his colleagues' greatest disappointment would be to learn how a sizable amount of economic literature consists of abstraction-driven modeling exercises without much in the way of policy application. Another portion of the literature is more concerned with the behavior of individual agents – consumers and firms – than with the implications of their collective behavior on the economic system. During the last couple of decades, many economists seem to have lost sight of the political economy roots from which the discipline sprung. Economics should and does have much to say about policy. Economists who have become well known in recent years (for example, Paul Krugman, Joseph Stiglitz, Lester Thurow) continue to practice political economy and to nurture the roots of the discipline.

This chapter investigates why economics is still a policy-oriented study of issues of political significance. Recent events may be increasing the need for political economy. A secondary purpose of the chapter is to introduce the reader to some important economic concepts, to which we turn first.

MARKETS AND MARKET FAILURES

Markets can be a thing of beauty when they function properly. Through a series of impersonal signals in the form of prices, profits, wages, and interest rates, resources are directed to their most valued use. For example, as business schools' enrollments increased during the last decade, the resulting shortage of accounting and finance professors raised the salaries offered to Ph.D.'s with such specialties relative to other specialties. More individuals responded to these relatively high remunerations, so that the number of people getting Ph.D.'s in these areas increased. If differential wages could not be offered, then the adjustment to the shortage would take longer, and some slots would remain open in the interim. Another example of markets responding to price signals concerns oil.

---

[7] Good sources on social choice, justice, and related topics include Kelly (1988) and Sen (1979).

When the members of the Organization of Petroleum Exporting Countries (OPEC) voluntarily restricted their output in 1973, OPEC countries managed to quadruple the price of a barrel of crude oil and earned massive profits. These profits, however, set off exploratory efforts that significantly added to known oil reserves. By the late 1990s, the world was awash in oil and the real price (adjusted for inflation) of a barrel of crude oil was below the price at the start of the 1970s. With the oil price rise in 2000, a new wave of exploration and conservation should ensue. Well-functioning markets respond to changes in tastes and technologies through a mechanism that coordinates the actions of buyers and sellers. This coordination is automatic – no social planner needs to send directives to sellers as to what to produce and when.

A key element in the operation of markets consists of property rights or recognized claims of ownership, written or implicit, to a good's benefits. If property rights are neither recognized nor enforced, there may be little incentive to acquire the particular good. A market is a mechanism or place for the voluntary exchange of property rights. Without these property rights, there can be no market.

Pure public goods, which were briefly introduced in Chapter 1, possess property rights that cannot be traded or protected. Suppose that you have the means to limit the accumulation of carbon dioxide (CO_2) in the atmosphere by planting fast-growing tree plantations in the tropics as a means to sequester carbon. This sequestration provides benefits for everyone, none of whom can be excluded. Asking for voluntary payments after you perform the service would yield little in sequestration revenues. The inability to exclude nonpayers from the good's benefits, once the public good is provided, leads people to free ride and to use their budgets to acquire other goods whose services can be withheld unless a payment is made. Regulating payment before providing the public good would result in many people claiming to have little or no interest, while hoping that others will be more honest about their true gains from the good. Again, little would be collected. Furthermore, the nonrivalry-of-benefits property of a pure public good makes it inefficient to deny access to anyone who gains, because extending consumption to another user creates benefits that lose society nothing owing to nonrivalry. Thus, blocking someone from seeing a fireworks display eliminates that person's pleasure without gaining anything for society. Letting the person enjoy the show creates no necessary congestion or cost, and, as such, society is benefitted if the person can see the display.

To address the underprovision of public goods, governments step in and provide some of these goods. Thus, central governments supply national defense, remove pollution, subsidize basic research, interdict drug traffickers, thwart terrorism, and control diseases. Surely, no individual – not even Bill Gates – would spend the trillions of dollars needed to develop and deploy the US strategic nuclear weapons and delivery systems. Public goods are supplied by governments at the local, state, and national levels. Public provision raises its own concerns – for example, how do public officials know the social optimal or best level of the public good to provide when tastes differ among constituents who may not honestly reveal their true interests when asked?[8] Economists are becoming more aware that turning tasks over to governments is not necessarily a recipe for achieving an ideal outcome or an efficient amount of the public good (see Chapter 5) – this insight differs from that of the classical economists. For instance, weapon producers that profit from defense contracts may lobby for large production runs, which may not be in the nation's interest. In other instances, public goods, whose benefits are partially rival and excludable at a reasonable cost, may be provided by marketlike club arrangements, as discussed in Chapter 4. Thus, a telephone network, whose benefits are excludable to nonsubscribers and whose access can be monitored, can have its use sold like a commodity in a market. Our monthly phone bill illustrates this. Private schools, private toll roads, parks, garbage collection, and theaters are other examples where some types of public goods are traded in quasi-market arrangements.

Even though Adam Smith was a champion of laissez faire, or the absence of government interference in markets, he still appreciated the need for some public goods – defense, schools, courts, and public works. Some of Smith's public goods consist of the very infrastructure or foundation required for the functioning of markets per se. Courts are needed to protect property rights and adjudicate property rights disputes – activities needed to protect and enforce ownership to transactions. How have public goods changed since Smith's era? Public goods abound today. Technology continues to create novel forms of these goods, never dreamed possible in the late 1700s, including discoveries from space telescopes, methods to curb ozone shield depletion, atmospheric monitoring devices atop Mauna Loa in Hawaii, crisis management squads, weather satellites capable of seeing into hurricanes, and antibiotics. Each new public good *may* create its own need for a market intervention. Compared to the high-technology, complex, and ever-changing society of today, the world of the classical economists had few public goods to divert their attention from what markets do best – trade private goods, whose benefits are excludable and completely rival.

---

[8] There is a vast literature on public goods. This concept is explained in simple terms in Sandler (1997) and in more complicated terms in Cornes and Sandler (1996). Some classic papers are Davis and Whinston (1967a) and Samuelson (1954, 1955).

Another important market failure, first encountered in Chapter 1, is that of externality or uncompensated interdependency, where the action of one agent imposes consequences on other agents, and these consequences are not accounted for by a market transaction or price. With externalities, something of positive or negative value is exchanged without consent or compensation. If, for example, a tannery disposes of toxic substances in a nearby stream or pool, the cost of the leather product is being kept down by placing a cost on current and future inhabitants of the region. This cost assumes the form of the health risks from the hazardous waste. It is conceivable that the cost of proper disposal is much less than the health costs associated with dumping. By narrowly focusing on final outputs and ignoring side effects, classical economists missed spotting externalities. Surely, Glasgow and London had their externalities in the form of horse manure, unpleasant noises, sewage, and smoke; nevertheless, the analysis of externalities had to wait until A. C. Pigou (1920) published his masterpiece, *The Economics of Welfare.*

Externalities are market failures in two related senses. First, a market for an activity (say, smoke from a power plant) does not exist, since there is no price assigned.[9] If a price could be assigned, the actions of those who cause the externality would be affected. As the price of gasoline rises to reflect the damage that our driving does to the environment, we may well eliminate needless trips. Second, an externality gives a recipient an additional constraint – an amount of someone else's activity – outside of the recipient's control. Additional constraints limit choices, which can result in less desirable outcomes. The negative impact of a constraint can be aptly illustrated by a simple example. Suppose that you were asked to choose the smallest and largest number from a list of integers from one to ten. In the absence of constraints, you would obviously choose the numbers one and ten, respectively. If, instead, the smallest choice is constrained to be even and the largest to be odd, then you would pick two and nine. Constraints that are effective – restrict choice[10] – lead to larger minima and smaller maxima. As their name implies, constraints limit what you can achieve, which is bad news.

There are many means for correcting an externality. For those involving lots of people, as in the case of many pollutants, a government can impose a tax on the activity. Ideally, this tax should equal the

---

[9] This sense comes closest to Arrow's (1970) view of externalities as an absence of markets. See also Heller and Starrett (1976), Hurwicz (1999), and Cornes and Sandler (1996, pp. 46–51).

[10] If, instead, the constraints require the smallest choice to be odd and the largest to be even, then they are not effective, because they do not really restrict the choice in this example. Such constraints are then not binding.

incremental harm imposed on outside parties to the transaction.[11] The proposed "carbon" tax on fossil fuels is an example and is intended to reflect the harmful effects of global warming coming from CO_2 emissions. By raising the price of a product to account for these third-party costs, such taxes are intended to engineer a price that is more representative of the private and social costs associated with burning fossil fuels. For activities conferring benefits on third parties, a subsidy or payment to the externality generator acts to encourage the activity by adjusting for the incremental benefits to third parties, not reflected in the current price. These adjustments to price through taxes and subsidies are designed to reduce (augment) activities with harmful (desirable) side effects.

In some instances, the externality is addressed through direct actions by governments to police harmful side effects and promote beneficial ones. Thus, the Environmental Protection Agency (EPA) sets and enforces pollution regulations. Myriad governmental agencies interfere to control activities with externalities; for example, the Federal Aviation Agency (FAA) is charged with keeping the skies safe for commercial and private airplanes. To foster the positive side effects associated with education at all levels, governments subsidize schools through tax revenues. In some states, such as Iowa, even private colleges receive state funds.

There is, however, a tendency to turn to government too quickly to correct problems with externalities. It is important never to lose sight of the fact that interventions cost society resources, which, at times, may be more expensive than the value of the allocative improvement achieved by the actions. Suppose that you build a strip mall, frequented by 100 customers' cars at peak times. Further suppose that ten noncustomers typically park in your lot. It might be cheaper to provide 110 parking spaces and forget about expending the resources to police the lot.[12] If, however, an inexpensive sign that threatens freeloaders with being towed deters free riders by half, then the cheap sign and 105 spaces might be the best means for addressing the externality.

Next suppose that an exhibitionist moves next door to a prude of the opposite sex. Not surprisingly, the former has no window shades and insists on undressing nightly in front of an illuminated window. This externality can easily be fixed by the prude's keeping his or her shades tightly drawn. If, instead, the neighbor is not prudish and enjoys the view, he or she might encourage a more optimal level of exhibitionism

---

[11] These taxes and/or subsidies are known as Pigouvian corrections (see Cornes and Sandler 1996, Chapter 4; Mishan 1971).

[12] This is the message contained in Demsetz (1964).

by sending the exhibitionist brighter bulbs! Next, suppose that one rancher's ostriches stray into a neighbor's soya bean crop, causing damage. These neighbors may be able to correct the externality through negotiations and actions. Fencing may be just the fix. How the cost of this fencing is shared depends on the farmer's and rancher's negotiating skills. If the neighbors cannot resolve their difficulty, the case may be brought before a judge, who would then assign property rights or liability as appropriate. No matter how these rights are assigned, the neighbors would be expected to come to an efficient arrangement.[13] If, for example, the rancher is responsible for crop damage, then he will restrict the roaming birds through fencing, herd size, or other means until the cost of further restraint matches the damages that result. It would be senseless to spend $100 reinforcing the fencing when the cost of the damage inhibited by this extra effort, for which the rancher is liable, is only $80. The rancher is, of course, better off not providing the extra reinforcement and compensating instead for the $80 worth of damage. If, however, the cost of the damage were $120, the extra effort would be advisable. These kinds of corrections through either liability assignment or face-to-face bargaining are best suited to externalities involving a small number of people, where the cost of addressing the problem is small.

Another class of market failures can arise when resources are owned in common and people have open access. The blue whale was hunted nearly to extinction in the open oceans, where harvesters did not take into account what their catch implied for the harvesting costs of others or to the species' chance for survival. The same kind of problem is being addressed in national parks, where signs instruct us not to pick the flowers or to remove rocks, and to stay on the path. Common ownership can work if access to outsiders is restricted; for example, native tribes have been known to pass forest tracts from one generation to the next in an undiminished condition.[14] Hunting and fishing grounds can be properly managed if the common owners can reap the rewards from their management efforts without the exploitation of poachers from outside.

The smooth operation of markets depends on a host of implicit assumptions, such as the absence of externalities, public goods, and prohibitively high *transaction costs*, which involve resources needed to

---

[13] This result is known as the Coase Theorem, named after Ronald Coase, who won the Nobel Prize for this insight and his work on why firms exist. See Coase (1960).

[14] On open access resources and common property resources, see Hardin (1968), Libecap (1989), Lueck (1993), and Ostrom (1990).

accomplish an exchange. Suppose that a pound of garbage gives you a dollar's worth of displeasure to dispose of – say, by burying it in your backyard or incinerating it. If an entrepreneur offers to collect your garbage for 80¢ a pound, you are better off engaging in this market exchange. When, however, this exchange costs 25¢ per pound to consummate in addition to the 80¢, these transaction costs, *which are greater than the net gain of 20¢ per unit exchanged*, inhibit the market from forming. Transaction costs are an important economic consideration introduced by Coase, Arrow, Demsetz, and others during the twentieth century. A more recent concern for the operation of markets involves the role of information. Unlike the theories of the classical economists, modern economics no longer takes information for granted. Information is not perfect or costless, as becomes clear when you leave the interstate to refuel your car and suspect that the service stations near the exit are overpriced. If you knew for sure that a mile closer to town there were a cheaper station, then your choice to go into town would be an easy one. This lack of information and the required cost to resolve the uncertainty about the cheapest gas limit competition and allow the price differences to persist. Such difference can be expected to be larger the farther the town's center is from the interstate.

When we turn to government as a savior from a market failure, we must remember that governments may fail for precisely the same reasons that markets fail. For example, governments may have no means for truly ascertaining the demand of the constituency for a pure public good. Without knowing the demand, the government cannot be expected to supply the appropriate level of the public good, since it can only guess at what people really want. Government actions may create their own externalities – the production of nuclear warheads to deter the Soviet Union during the Cold War has created radioactive sites that will require tens of billions of dollars or more to clean up. Elected officials pursue some of their own objectives to the detriment of those who put them in office.

Political economy is a far more complex subject today than ever presupposed by the classical economists. We inhabit an intricate mixed economy that depends on both markets and judicious interventions in these markets. If Smith and the others could be resurrected today, it would be enlightening to learn to what extent they would advocate market interventions. Would Smith want to take a sabbatical at the University of Chicago, where market intervention is not encouraged, or at Harvard, where it is more appreciated? Whatever these founders of economics would suggest in terms of actual policy, they would clearly see a continued role for economics in directing policy in the form of political economy.

POLITICAL ECONOMY IN THE TWENTY-FIRST CENTURY

Political economy today involves far-reaching concerns: economic and political problems now transgress national and generational frontiers. Despite the years since Ricardo's appeal for free trade in the early 1800s, the world still struggles with the liberalization of trade. Although the excuses are "modern," nations still engage in trade wars, as the recent flaps between the United States and the European Union (EU) over such things as bananas, mad cow disease, and genetically altered foods demonstrate. What is different today is the creation of institutions and rules – the World Trade Organization (WTO) and the General Agreement on Tariffs and Trade (GATT) – to oversee this liberalization. Technological advances have promoted the globalization of markets, which has increased the flow of goods, capital, ideas, and institutional arrangements. This globalization can augment world income through greater commerce and the spread of knowledge. For example, developing countries can acquire new technologies embodied in foreign direct investment, which also provides much-needed savings for these countries.[15]

But globalization also has a dark side. Instabilities in financial institutions half a globe away can send shock waves across US stock exchanges and, in so doing, wipe out billions of dollars in value within minutes. The health of economies now depends on sound financial practices not only at home but also abroad; but most nations have little or no say regarding such practices abroad and, as a consequence, may suffer greatly from actions beyond their control. As goods and capital markets become more intertwined worldwide, financial and economic crises are apt to display a greater contagion and volatility. Globalization can exacerbate the worsening gap between the richest and poorest nations: nations at the bottom of the income distribution are apt to fall ever further behind because they do not have the requisite human capital and know-how to profit from new technologies. A mere ten developed countries account for 84% of research and development worldwide and have controlled 95% of US patents during the last two decades.[16] In many LDCs, a large share of national income has to be directed toward feeding and clothing a rapidly expanding population. Another sizable share must provide these LDCs' cities with urban infrastructure. By the year 2000, urban population had reached half of the world's total, with some three hundred cities with populations of a million or more in the

---

[15] See Coe and Helpman (1995).

[16] On the concentration of patents and research and development, see UN Development Program (1999).

LDCs alone.[17] The required large-scale investment in housing, sanitation, schools, police, and transportation will divert funds in LDCs from private investment for the foreseeable future and, in so doing, will stifle economic growth and the ability of these countries to close the poverty gap with the rich countries.

Is globalization welfare-improving? This question may not be so simple to answer, even though most developed countries will prosper from their ability to get products more cheaply and to sell their own exports in new markets. Nevertheless, this new openness limits the security afforded by political boundaries by exposing countries to greater financial instabilities from shocks (political or natural) and economic downturns abroad. For example, Midwestern pork producers' reliance on Asian markets meant that the recession in Asia depressed these producers' income at a time when the US economy was healthy. These pork producers had expanded their operations greatly as the Asian markets had opened up and were thus vulnerable to the Asian economic crisis. Things got so bad that one Iowan pork farmer tried to sell permits to "hunt" his free-roaming pigs – hardly a sporting event with a domesticated animal – a sale that the state authorities had the good sense to block on humane grounds. In return for the larger incomes that derive from globalization, developed countries must assume a greater risk of instability and an enhanced susceptibility to externalities from abroad. It is still an unanswered question whether or not the increased instability and insecurity associated with globalization are outweighed by the larger resulting incomes. This is a political economy question for the twenty-first century. Dani Rodrik argues that there is little convincing evidence that a greater openness, in general, promotes economic growth and well-being in LDCs.[18] To prosper from globalization, according to Rodrik, LDCs must engineer a sound domestic investment strategy and develop "appropriate institutions to handle adverse external shocks" (Rodrik 1999, p. 1). There is no substitute for devising a competent development strategy with sensible policies and institutions; globalization by itself will not sweep nations to prosperity.

To support globalization, the world community needs to institute a supranational infrastructure, not unlike the infrastructure that augments market performance and transactions at the national level.[19] This supranational infrastructure must, at a minimum, enforce and protect

---

[17] UN Population Fund (1994). On urbanization and its effects on urban planning, see Rabinovitch and Leitman (1996).

[18] See Rodrik (1999) for a fuller discussion.

[19] Supranational infrastructure is addressed in Sandler (2000).

property rights at the supranational level – for example, an enforcement mechanism for contracts involving transnational exchange. Supranational market failures involve the provision of public goods (curbing global warming, maintaining world peace, stemming acid rain), the correction of externalities (controlling organized crime), and the problem of open-access common property resources (the oceans, the electromagnetic spectrum, geostationary orbital spaces). In the form of treaties, norms, institutions, and other linkages, a supranational infrastructure needs to address these market failures. The provision of such an infrastructure poses greater obstacles at the supranational than at the national level, where subnational governmental units institutionally accept that they must subject their authority on some issues to a central government that attempts to correct market failures. At the supranational level, however, nations vigorously protect their autonomy and are loathe to sacrifice their revenue collecting, policy-making, or security operations to a higher authority.

As new political economy concerns move beyond the nation-state to involve collectives of nations, the essential issues remain the same and include the four basic economic problems of allocative efficiency, stability, the distribution of income, and economic growth. The solutions to these problems are, however, more complicated and touch a larger set of agents at the national and transnational levels. Currently, the global community addresses transnational issues in an ad hoc fashion when the associated costs escalate. Thus, a treaty on ozone depleters is devised only after dire consequences are evident from an enlarged ozone hole in the stratosphere that has developed because nothing was done.[20] A more systematic approach is required, where steps are taken before the problem has progressed too far. The current lack of progress on global warming underscores the fact that this message has not yet been heeded. International externalities and the misallocation of resources that results are getting greater attention in the media, which may have an eventual effect on policy makers from pressures of voters. New technologies, and the furtherance of globalization that they support, facilitate the transfer not only of capital, goods, laborers, and ideas, but also of diseases, political revolutions, recessions, and economic pessimism.

Political economy in the twenty-first century will increasingly address actions and policies that affect multiple generations, both present and not yet born. In the twentieth century, social security became an important intergenerational policy issue, addressing the question of how to link generations so as to support the elderly generation during its retirement

---

[20] On ozone diplomacy and the ozone hole, see Benedick (1991), Barrett (1998, 1999), de Gruijl (1995), Murdoch and Sandler (1997), and Toon and Turco (1991).

from savings during its productive years.[21] Schemes were devised whereby the younger generation supported the older generation through forced contributions to a fund in return for the promise that it will be supported during its own retirement. The financing and maintenance of the social security system remain a crucial concern owing to demographic changes in many advanced industrial countries (for example, the United States and Japan) in which a relatively small working generation must support a larger retired generation. Additionally, intergenerational resource allocation issues will continue to surface as a growing population inhabits the Earth. Decisions today may impact many generations to come; for example, the building of a dam – say, to flood the Grand Canyon – can cause irreversible damage to places of scenic wonder, leaving future generations to admire pictures and imagine what it was really like to stand buffeted by the wind on the canyon's rim, watching a bird of prey glide on the canyon's updrafts. Simple acts like washing our hands with antibacterial soap may lead to new, more virulent bacteria, as existing strains acquire an immunity, thereby jeopardizing our children's welfare.

With the notable exception of population growth, the classical economists addressed few political economy questions with an intergenerational dimension. Surely, Earth's resources must have seemed very plentiful in those halcyon days. No wonder that it would be a century later before political economists became interested in the environment or in resource management. The issue of how much of the environment should be passed between generations was of no concern back in the early 1800s. The classical economists' fixation with measuring all value in terms of labor, a practice that would later form the foundation of Marxism, underscores the fact that the crust of the Earth was assigned little importance in those days. With this realization, there should have been little surprise to see the sorry state of the environment in the once-communist countries of Eastern Europe that observers from the West encountered at the start of the 1990s. Today's practice of not including the depreciation of the country's natural assets in our national income accounts suggests that our awareness of intergenerational allocations is not so farsighted as we might like to believe.

A RETURN TO POLITICAL ECONOMY

During the twentieth century, economists focused on perfecting the foundations of economics and showed an obsession with theoretical developments. There were times when academic economists seemed to be pursuing economics for its own sake, with relatively little concern for the

---

[21] The logic and theory of social security is carefully addressed in Meyer and Wolff (1993).

study of political economy. Economists interested in political economy were viewed as outside of the mainstream. Of course, there was an interest in economic policy – monetary and fiscal policy to stabilize employment and prices – but even here the profession was experiencing a nihilistic tendency, as economists worried whether such policy really promoted stability or only exacerbated cycles by being applied at the wrong time. With the end of the millennium, there has been a return to economics' roots in political economy that would put smiles on the faces of our classical forefathers. During the last decade, the top journals have devoted more pages to the application of economics to topics of political significance, which include the study of insurrections, defense spending, treaty making, foreign aid, globalization, policy reform, transition economies, common markets, monetary unions, and tropical deforestation. Many stars in economics – Paul Krugman, Dani Rodrik, Jeffrey Sachs, Joseph Stiglitz, Partha Dasgupta, and Lawrence Summers – have turned their attention to political economy issues. Recent developments in game theory, information economics, and public choice theory can readily be applied to pressing political problems. In a supporting role, innovations in econometrics allow for the testing of many theoretical breakthroughs against real-world data.

Perhaps one way to gauge the growing preoccupation with political economy is to note that in the last few years economics departments have begun advertising for political economists in the *Job Openings for Economists*. In a parallel fashion, political science departments at major universities are advertising for economists interested in researching political economy. There is a convergence in some subareas of economics and political science, a convergence that is long overdue.

There is certainly no dearth of topics to analyze in political economy. They include issues such as the design of more effective foreign aid, so that the recipient countries acquire the requisite knowledge and interest to sustain their own development programs.[22] Why can some countries use a few billion dollars to embark on a pathway to sustained development, while others can take many times that amount and make little progress? The growing inequalities both within and among countries must also be scrutinized with the tools of political economy. Another topic of current concern involves the design of supranational structures (for example, monetary unions, trading blocs, military alliances, pollution pacts, treaties) in a world of growing transnational

---

[22] In the last fifty years, the hundreds of billions of dollars of foreign assistance has met with mixed success. There is an interest in reassessing how to improve the effectiveness of foreign aid. Relevant studies include Gwin and Nelson (1997), Kanbur, Sandler, and Morrison (1999), van de Walle and Johnston (1996), and World Bank (1998).

interdependency. In this century, political economists will tackle inter-generational problems involving biodiversity, the oceans, the climate, hunger, inequality, and environmental sustainability.

As economics returns to its roots, it acquires a greater relevancy. Economics is meant to enlighten society about how to manage its scarce resources that are under greater pressure, creating many of the most critical problems facing humankind today. Smith, Ricardo, and Malthus would delight in tackling the exigencies that confront our planet if they were alive today. After a remedial course or two in game theory and mathematics, they would be leading a new generation of economists.

3   In Another's Shoes: Games, Strategies, and Economics

Open any modern-day textbook in economics and you will see game boxes and game trees used to explain the strategic interaction among diverse economic agents. It matters not whether it is a macroeconomics text addressing policy making, or a public finance text analyzing how people voluntarily contribute to a public good. This methodological revolution has swept economics during the last two decades. When I completed my doctorate in 1971, game theory had barely been mentioned, and when it had been discussed, the reference had usually been disparaging. My first exposure to this tool came in the early seventies when, as an assistant professor at Arizona State University, I took mathematics classes from Albert Tucker and Evar Nering. These great mathematicians had been at Princeton University during the days when game theory was being developed as a mathematical tool for the social sciences. There had been high hopes during the 1940s and early 1950s that this development would provide all of the social sciences with a unifying theoretical base, from which great insights would spring.[1] A driving force behind this development was a brilliant mathematician – perhaps the brightest of the twentieth century – named John von Neumann. This self-absorbed, totally focused individual first developed his game-theoretic ideas in papers published in 1928 and 1937.[2] His quickness and brilliance were legendary, but then so was his single-minded dedication to his work. Albert Tucker, his ex-colleague at Princeton, once illustrated von Neumann's consuming and humorless focus with the following story. Von

---

[1] These hopes and even euphoria are mentioned by Luce and Raiffa (1957, p. 10) and Kreps (1990a, p. 1).

[2] Apparently von Neumann's (1928, 1937) papers, published in German, were not the first on game theory. Maurice Fréchet (1953) credits Emile Borel with the first work on psychological games in the early 1920s. Of course, Cournot's (1838) work on strategic interactions by oligopolists predated these forerunners of game theory by over eighty years!

Neumann had come to Tucker for a name for John's latest monograph on an esoteric geometry that contained no points. Tucker, who had named the Prisoners' Dilemma as well as Luce and Raiffa's (1957) book *Games and Decisions*, was the logical person to consult. After some reflection, Tucker offered the title "Pointless Geometry" – to which von Neumann stormed off, never to return for similar advice.

In the 1940s, the pathbreaking work in game theory was von Neumann and Morgenstern's (1944) *The Theory of Games and Economic Behavior*, a massive book that addressed noncooperative and cooperative games in two-player and many-player settings. Although the book was intended for social scientists, understanding it posed a formidable challenge for many of its intended readers. A more accessible treatment did not come along until over a decade later with the publication of Luce and Raiffa's *Games and Decisions*, which still serves as a useful starting place for learning game theory.

During World War II and shortly thereafter, game theory was developed, in part, under defense contracts in military applications. It was used to calculate, for example, how to engage in dogfights or aerial duels where each pilot must choose when to fire and the appropriate maneuvers to avoid being shot down, with the goal of killing the opponent without being annihilated first. Much of the initial effort went into the development of *zero-sum games*, in which one player's gain comes at the expense of the other player. As a result, the payoffs from any combination of strategies by the opponents add to zero.[3] Splitting a prize, gaining yardage on a gridiron, reallocating moneys in a university, or acquiring points in a match-play golf tourney are examples of zero-sum games. If, however, we reflect on the kinds of strategic interactions that we face in economics and elsewhere, the players' interests are not typically diametrically opposed. In fact, the most famous game of all – the Prisoners' Dilemma – is not a zero-sum game. There are myriad games for which a coordination of efforts can improve both players' well-being, leading to *nonconstant-sum games*. Upon further reflection, we must conclude that zero-sum games are rather special and relatively rare.

If such games are so special, then why the preoccupation with these games by the originators of game theory? This preoccupation has done much to divert game theory from its prophecized goal of establishing a science of economics, as foreseen on the book cover of *Theory of Games and Economic Behavior*. The answer is simple: zero-sum games possess

---

[3] It is *not* essential that the sum be zero; rather, the crucial feature is that the sum be constant, so that the players' interests are diametrically opposed. Any constant-sum game can be transformed into a zero-sum game with a simple transformation of payoffs that does not affect the solution.

an elegant mathematical structure that results in a unique and easy-to-find solution in terms of the *maximin* (or *minimax*) theorem, which assumes that a player chooses a counterstrategy to leave the opponent as little as possible, so that one needs to fix on a strategy that provides the largest of these sorry outcomes. The maximin theorem tied together game theory, linear programming, and nonlinear programming, the second of which was also formulated by von Neumann. Even the initial work on cooperative games (for example, voting games to form election-winning coalitions) focused on a zero-sum game played by opposing coalitions. Ironically, this obsession with zero-sum games greatly diminished the relevancy of the new method to the very discipline for which it had been developed. The military/Rand involvement with zero-sum games also tainted game theory and helped to divert interest in this new method.

But there were other factors that limited economists' and social scientists' interest in game theory for over two decades. Initially, game theory often did an inadequate job in explaining *dynamic* strategic interactions.[4] In particular, it frequently ignored the sequence or timing of strategic interactions, so that too little thought was given to the internal consistency of the interactions among players. Would players, for example, really threaten an action that they would never carry out in order to provoke a desired outcome?[5] Game theory started off "flat" and "timeless." If the sequence of moves is unimportant, then please let me go second in a game of rock–paper–scissors for $1,000! Once your choice is indicated, I will cover your rock, or smash your scissors, or cut your paper, and walk off with the prize. At first, game theory did not concern itself with the information possessed by the participants. In practice, economic agents are differentially informed based not only upon the sequence of moves (or the "history" of the game) but also upon the starting endowments of these agents. If game theory had first been invented by economists, then it might from the beginning have addressed a more interesting and germane set of dynamic interactions and not vanished from orthodox economic analysis for two decades.

During the last twenty years, the application of game theory to economics, political science, sociology, and related disciplines has expanded rapidly. As game theory now better accounts for the underlying

---

[4] According to Kreps (1990a, p. 41), "The great successes of game theory in economics have arisen in large measure because game theory gives us a language for modelling and techniques for analyzing specific dynamic competitive interactions."

[5] The threat by major league umpires to resign prior to the 1999 World Series if their contracts were not renegotiated early indicates that sometimes people do make foolish threats that can cost them dearly. Some knowledge of modern game theory could have kept the umpires from making such a costly mistake.

dynamics and rests on more internally consistent solution concepts, economists have applied it to advantage to some fascinating issues – treaty making, negotiations with terrorists, arms races, technology races, voting behavior, and union actions. These interesting applications cannot be emphasized enough in explaining the phenomenal growth, which is nothing short of a revolution, in interpreting economic and political behavior in terms of strategic notions of game theory. Not surprisingly, these applications do not involve zero-sum games. However, the problem of dynamic consistency has not disappeared, as some accepted equilibrium concepts require players to behave in ways that experimental subjects rarely display – for example, the ability to reason backward from a long series of future moves. The purpose of this chapter is to explore the game theory revolution and display its power, potential, and shortcomings. Will it continue to be a driving force in economic analysis during the new century? This question and others are addressed.

A CASE FOR GAME THEORY

Strategic behavior, the hallmark of game theory, involves how one agent (person, nation, firm, government, or institution) behaves when its choices depend on those of others. Interactive choices that cause players' payoffs to be interdependent are viewed as strategic. If what I choose to do is not affected by what another does, then my choice is not strategic. For example, suppose that my choice gives me the same payoff no matter how others choose their strategies. There is then nothing strategic about my decision, and the choice is not in the realm of game theory. When, however, my choice and its resulting payoff are dependent on those of another, there is a strategic interdependence. Strategic behavior also involves a recognition of this interdependence; one player thinks that the opponent(s) will behave in a certain manner and acts on this presumption. Similarly, the opponent anticipates the other player's belief-based actions and chooses a strategy based on this belief, and so it goes. Each player is putting herself in the other's shoes and basing her own behavior on how her counterpart would act in these circumstances, knowing that each is trying to anticipate the other's optimizing actions. If this sounds far-fetched, then imagine yourself at a chessboard poised to move out your queen in a bold attack. What goes through your mind as you lift the queen? For most people, it is how will my clever opponent counter this play. Skillful players are known to anticipate a number of moves ahead, always assuming that the opponent will counter so as to leave the least advantage. This insight leads to another characteristic of strategic behavior and thinking: namely, your opponent is considered to be a worthy one, equally capable of insightful ratiocination.

In a game with a temporal dimension involving multiple periods, strategic behavior requires a complete plan of action in the face of all possible contingencies.

Game theory is so vital for economics because strategic interactions, where what I do depends on what someone else does, permeates nearly all fields of economics. If I am a jeweler in a small town, my Christmas advertising budget depends on my competitors' expected advertising spending. Whether or not to raise my price in an oligopoly hinges on the anticipated price responses of other firms in the industry. In a cartel where two or more firms collude to raise prices, my output decisions depend on those of the other members, quota or no quota. Two adjoining neighborhoods confronting a similar crack cocaine problem must be aware that efforts by one neighborhood to purge dealers will likely move them next door if similar actions are not taken there as well. Games are played between similar and/or diverse economic agents. In the latter case, strategic interactions characterize, for instance, the way that the federal and state governments address poverty or choose their tax instruments. Procurement of weapons involves a sophisticated game among the Department of Defense, the Congress, and defense contractors, all of whom have different objectives.[6] For similar agents, the adoption of an industry standard in a new consumer technology – mini-disks, DVDs – represents a coordination decision among the potential suppliers, since it is in everyone's interest to adopt the *same* standard to attract more consumers, even if one's own standard is not adopted. International environmental agreements constitute games played among nations and their representatives seeking to curb transnational pollutants.[7]

Game theory is ideal for providing a unifying framework for economics, which investigates optimizing behavior in the face of constraints such as resource scarcity, because game theory is also based on optimization. Thus, the underlying motives of economics and game theory are the same: do the best that you can under the circumstances. In addition, modern game theory forces economists to be vigilant about the consistency of beliefs. Earlier economic theories assumed that agents could act without anticipating the responses that their actions might elicit from others, so that crucial feedbacks and the reactions to these feedbacks were ignored. These earlier theories rested on an inconsistent set of beliefs and, as such, offered a partial analysis; game theory provides a sounder general-equilibrium framework. Given its emphasis on the

---

[6] On such games, see McAfee and McMillan (1986), Rogerson (1990, 1991), and Sandler and Hartley (1995).

[7] International environmental agreements in a game framework are analyzed by Barrett (1994, 1999), Murdoch and Sandler (1997), Sandler (1998), and Sandler and Sargent (1995).

consistency of beliefs, the application of game theory is more than an extension of existing economic thinking, which, like some of the first forays into game theory, was rather flat. By this I mean that agents were not viewed as individuals who gave much thought to others, and especially to how others might respond to their actions.

To explain how game theory has engendered this revolution, I must first introduce some essential concepts. One way to analyze a game is to study its underlying strategic structure with a simple game box containing the respective players' payoffs. This box representation is known as the *strategic* or *normal form* of the game and indicates the players, their strategies, and the resulting payoffs – the three ingredients defining many games. Readers familiar with these concepts should skip the next section, while others should brace themselves and bear with me for this short analytical interlude.

SOME IMPORTANT CONCEPTS OF GAME THEORY

There are two branches of game theory: cooperative and noncooperative games. The former refers to agreed-upon actions that are enforceable and result in net gains to all players who are party to the agreement. By contrast, noncooperative games involve situations where such agreements are not achieved and players consequently act only in their own self-interest. Arguably, the most famous cooperative game is the voters' game where a group of players or a *coalition* agrees to support or not support a candidate (for example, the "alliance" in the television show *Survivor* that agreed to vote out all of the members of the other tribe). In the voters' game, the winning coalition institutes policies that give it the maximum payoff to divide among members. The most famous example of a noncooperative game is the Prisoners' Dilemma, for which this independent pursuit ends in a disappointing outcome where both players could do better if only a self-enforcing agreement could be reached. This result is very much against the prediction of Adam Smith's invisible hand, according to which individuals' pursuit of self-interest improves everyone's welfare.

A story line behind the Prisoners' Dilemma goes as follows. Two individuals in a car are stopped for suspicious behavior in the vicinity of an armed robbery. As luck would have it, not only do the suspects appear to match eyewitnesses' vague descriptions, but a search of their vehicle also turns up an unregistered handgun. The district attorney knows that she has insufficient evidence to convict them of the armed robbery, despite the gun and the eyewitnesses, unless she can get a confession. Without a confession, she can only convict them of carrying an unregistered handgun, which carries a one-year sentence. She separates the two suspects and offers each of them the following deal. If just one of them confesses, then the confessor walks free, while the nonconfessor serves the maximum five-year sentence for the robbery. If, however, both confess, then they each receives a reduced three-year sentence.

In Figure 3.1, the relevant payoffs for the two suspects – prisoners *A* and *B* – are displayed in the four cells of the game box where each prisoner has two strategies: confess or not confess. There are four possible strategy combinations for the suspects: both confess (cell *a*), just prisoner *A* confesses (cell *b*), just prisoner *B* confesses (cell *c*), and neither confesses (cell *d*). The first payoff (or prison sentence) in each of these four cells of the game box is that of prisoner *A* or the row player, whereas the second payoff is that of prisoner *B* or the column player. To examine the strategic dilemma from *A*'s viewpoint, we must compare his payoffs from his two strategies. When prisoner *B* confesses, prisoner *A* gets a lighter sentence of three years by confessing as compared to the five-year sentence for not confessing. If, however, prisoner *B* does not confess, prisoner *A* is still better off by confessing, since he gets to walk rather than serve a one-year sentence for not confessing. Thus, when prisoner *A*'s payoffs in one row are compared with the corresponding payoffs in the second row, *his payoffs are always better in the confess row*. A strategy such as confessing that provides a greater payoff regardless of the other player's action is a *dominant strategy* and should be played. Similarly, a strategy whose payoffs are less than some other strategy's corresponding payoffs is said to be a *dominated strategy* and should not be chosen. In Figure 3.1, prisoner *B*'s dominant strategy is also to confess when the corresponding payoffs in the two columns are compared – that is, a three-year sentence is better than five years, and walking free is more desirable than a one-year term. When both players employ their dominant strategies, the outcome is cell *a* with the three-year sentences. Surely, keeping silent would be an outcome that both would prefer.

The true culpability of our hapless suspects is immaterial to this anticipated outcome. Let us for a moment assume them to be innocent. The

A's Strategy \ B's Strategy	Confess	Do not confess
Confess	NASH *a* 3 years, 3 years	*b* 0 years, 5 years
Do not confess	*c* 5 years, 0 years	*d* 1 year, 1 year

Figure 3.1. Prisoners' Dilemma

district attorney's deal would still result in their seeing the irresistibility
of confessing, especially because each knows that his or her friend faces
the same temptation (dominant strategy) to confess. Next, suppose that
the prisoners speak just before they are separated and agree not to
confess to anything. Given the dominant strategy placed before his or
her buddy, neither prisoner can be sure what the other will do – promise
or no promise. In fact, if prisoner *A* knows that *B* will not confess, so that
A must choose between cell *b* and cell *d*, prisoner *A* is better off confessing and playing his friend for a sucker if conscience does not affect
the payoffs! Each player is a prisoner of his or her own dominant
strategy, which results in a poor outcome.

The mutual confession strategy denotes a *Nash equilibrium*, a concept
uncovered by John Forbes Nash, at the age of twenty-one, in his brilliant
twenty-seven-page doctoral dissertation.[8] This concept is a generalization of the maximin theorem and serves as a solution for all noncooperative games. By the age of thirty, Nash had made fundamental
contributions to game theory, the bargaining problem, geometry, and
artificial intelligence. Just prior to receiving his professorship at MIT, he
lost his sanity and for the next thirty or so years was gripped by para-
noid schizophrenia (Nasar 1998). When he miraculously awoke from his
delusions, he received the 1994 Nobel Prize in economics, forty-four
years after introducing his pathbreaking Nash equilibrium. At such an
equilibrium, each player is choosing his or her best strategy as a counter
to the other player's best response or strategy. A Nash equilibrium is a
collection of strategies – one for each player – such that no player would
unilaterally alter his or her strategy. This can be seen by focusing on cell
a in Figure 3.1, which is the Nash equilibrium of the Prisoners' Dilemma.
If, at cell *a*, player *A* (or *B*) alone changes to not confessing or with-
drawing the confession, then this player's payoff is worsened by the addition of two years of jail time and will not change his or her strategy. That
is, for player *A*, compare the left-hand payoffs in the first column, which
holds *B*'s strategy fixed at confessing; and for player *B*, compare the
right-hand payoffs in the first row, which holds *A*'s strategy fixed at confessing. Neither player has an incentive in cell *a* to change strategy *given*
the other player's strategy.

There are many examples of the Prisoners' Dilemma, including an
arms race, a tariff war, an advertising duel, or price cutting. In all of
these instances, playing one's dominant strategy (for example, escalate
the level of arms, raise tariffs) leads to a Nash equilibrium in which both
players can do better if they *both* change their strategies. The distin-

---

[8] These facts about his life come from Nasar's (1998) biography of Nash. Nash's concept
of an equilibrium appeared in his 1951 paper.

guishing features of a Prisoners' Dilemma can be identified by rank ordering the payoffs from best to worst. The best payoff (the walk-free sentence) is assigned a 4, the next best (the one-year sentence) is given a 3, and so on. In Figure 3.2, ordinal ranks have been accordingly assigned to the payoffs of the game box of Figure 3.1. Any two-person game box of payoffs that possesses the same ordinal payoff array as in Figure 3.2 is a Prisoners' Dilemma. In Figure 3.2, the dominant strategy is to confess, since *A*'s ordinal payoffs of 2 and 4 are greater than the corresponding payoffs of 1 and 3 in the bottom row. Similarly, player *B*'s dominant strategy is to confess, and the Nash equilibrium occurs when both players confess. Other payoff configurations – and there are seventy-seven other distinct alternatives – constitute a different game. The ordinal depiction captures the essential strategic features of the game, including the presence of dominant strategies, dominated strategies, and Nash equilibrium(s).

Imagine an arms race where two enemies can either increase arms by ten percent (escalate) or disarm by the same amount (limit arms). The best payoff comes from escalating when the opponent limits arms, since this results in a gain in arms superiority. The next-best payoff comes from mutually limiting arms, insofar as each country saves money and is no less secure. The next-to-worst payoff comes from engaging in an arms race that is costly but makes neither country any more secure. Obviously, the worst payoff arises from unilateral disarmament. By filling in the four cells for the corresponding game box, one can confirm that this is a Prisoners' Dilemma with the Nash equilibrium at the mutual escalation cell. Thus, the Prisoners' Dilemma does, indeed, have real-world counterparts. But one must be cautious not to give too much weight to the Prisoners' Dilemma as the underlying game form. The Prisoners' Dilemma is just one of seventy-eight distinct 2 × 2 game forms, many of which can apply to social interactions (Rapoport and Guyer 1966). In related disciplines, such as political science, there has been an obsession with the Prisoners' Dilemma that has only recently been broken.

A's Strategy \ B's Strategy	Confess	Do not confess
Confess	NASH *a* 2, 2	*b* 4, 1
Do not confess	*d* 1, 4	*c* 3, 3

Figure 3.2. Ordinal form of Prisoners' Dilemma

It is essential to emphasize that a Nash equilibrium characterizes games other than the Prisoners' Dilemma. Moreover, the presence of dominant strategies is not required for there to be a Nash equilibrium. While many games have no dominant-strategy equilibrium, all games have at least one Nash equilibrium.

NASH EQUILIBRIUM AS A SOLUTION CONCEPT

A Nash equilibrium is a solution for a competitive interaction between two or more rational individuals who act independently.[9] Such an equilibrium addresses the "he thinks that I think that he thinks . . ." thought exercise posed by a strategic interaction, by assuming that a player needs only to choose the best counter to the best responses of the other players when placed in a similar position. Nash's strategic notions differ in a couple of fundamental ways from those of von Neumann and Morgenstern (1944). First, Nash was not concerned per se with zero-sum games, and, second, he did not eliminate the independence of agents by assuming that two opposing coalitions would form when more than two players interact. Although coalition formation is an important consideration for some situations – treaties, alliances, and cartels – von Neumann and Morgenstern's method of analyzing *n*-person games in terms of coalition formation lost much of the intrinsic competitiveness underlying these games. Furthermore, the precise nature of this coalition formation was left a mystery.

Even though Nash did not set out to solve a zero-sum game, the maximin solution to such games is a Nash equilibrium in which neither player can unilaterally improve his or her well-being. A payoff matrix for a zero-sum war game is displayed in Figure 3.3, where the attacker (*A*) can attack by flanking left, going down the center of the front, or flanking right. As a counter, the defender (*B*) can reinforce the left side, center, or right side of the front. The payoffs given are just those of the attacker, since the defender's payoffs are merely the negative of those displayed, because the game is zero-sum. To the right of each row, the minimum in each row is indicated. This payoff is relevant if the attacker assumes that the defender foresees the attack strategy and takes the best counter to it. The attacker will then want to choose the maximum of these worst-case outcomes. For the defender, the maximum payoffs for the columns are listed on the assumption that the attacker anticipates the adversary's defense and chooses the offense that hurts the defender the most. The defender then limits this damage by choosing the defense that yields the smallest such maximum or gain for the attacker. From

---

[9] Myerson (1999) examines how the Nash equilibrium fits into the history of economic thought.

B's Strategy / A's Strategy	Reinforce left flank	Reinforce center	Reinforce right flank	Min
Flank left	-3	2	10	-3
Center	8	Maximin 6	9	6
Flank right	5	4	-2	-2
Max	8	6	10	

Figure 3.3. A zero-sum game with a maximin solution

both sides' viewpoints, the same outcome results: the offender launches an attack down the center and the defender anticipates correctly by reinforcing this portion of the front. The maximin choice of the offense then coincides with the minimax choice of the defense. At this maximin solution, neither side wants on its own to switch to an alternate strategy. The maximin solution is indeed a Nash equilibrium and assumes that one's opponent is smart enough to minimize the gain resulting from any strategic choice taken. In applying maximin, there is a logical inconsistency insofar as each player plans a response as though the other player's action were already revealed.[10] This kind of strategic thinking is used to identify the maximin solution, thereby tainting this solution concept.

Even though the Nash equilibrium can coincide with maximin, this equilibrium concept does not imply this temporal inconsistency. Nevertheless, criticisms of a different nature have been leveled against the Nash equilibrium.[11] Perhaps one of the strongest criticisms has to do with the many such equilibria that may result and the need to choose among them. To illustrate this multiplicity, consider a two-player game of chicken, whose ordinal or rank-ordered payoffs are depicted in Figure 3.4. This game derives its name from two individuals who are attempting to gain peer respect by proving their bravery. Players *A* and *B* are in cars speeding toward one another from opposite directions down the middle of the road. Neither driver wants to be the first to swerve out of the pathway of the other vehicle. Of course, the worst payoffs (the 1s) result if neither driver chickens out and a head-on collision results. The

[10] Consult Myerson (1999, p. 1072).
[11] See Dixit and Skeath (1999, pp. 213–14), Kreps (1990a), and Myerson (1999).

B's Strategy / A's Strategy	Do not swerve	Swerve
Do not swerve	*a* 1, 1	NASH *b* 4, 2
Swerve	NASH *c* 2, 4	*d* 3, 3

Figure 3.4. Chicken game in ordinal form

best payoff follows from not swerving when the other driver swerves. But even here, the swerver is better off alive and wimpy than dead; hence, the ordinal payoff of 2 instead of 1. If both swerve, then the payoffs are below the best but above those associated with swerving first and being the chicken, or being in a crash.

Even though the ordinal payoffs in the chicken game only differ from the Prisoners' Dilemma by having the 2s and 1s switched, the strategic implications are quite different. First, there is no dominant strategy: from either player's viewpoint, there is no strategy that gives a higher payoff regardless of the other player's choice. For example, swerving gives 2 or 3, payoffs which do not *both exceed* the corresponding payoffs of 1 and 4, respectively, of holding one's path. Second, there are two Nash equilibria in which one driver swerves and the other holds the path. At cells *b* and *c* in Figure 3.4, neither player gains by altering his or her strategy alone, since 4 > 3 and 2 > 1.

This multiplicity of equilibria can be addressed in a number of ways. Thomas Schelling speaks of a focal equilibrium, where through common culture, shared perceptions, or historical conventions the players will gravitate to one of many equilibria.[12] Suppose, for example, that two neighbors face a common pest that only one individual needs to take action against in any given period to eliminate. Moreover, no action at all is disastrous. This scenario would correspond to a chicken game with Nash equilibria where just one of the neighbors needs to act. Common culture may well lead the neighbors to alternate between periods as to who will eradicate the pest. In other situations, one equilibrium may be focal because it yields the greatest payoffs, as illustrated by Figure 3.5. This two-person, three-strategy game has seven Nash equilibria, as indicated. The equilibrium where player *A* plays down and *B* moves right may be focal, because both players receive their highest

---

[12] Schelling's (1960) work contains many ideas that have influenced modern game theory.

A's Strategy \ B's Strategy	Left	Center	Right
Up	NASH 0, 0	NASH 2, 0	3, −1
Middle	NASH 0, 2	NASH 2, 2	NASH 4, 2
Down	−1, 3	NASH 2, 4	NASH 4, 4

Figure 3.5. Game with many Nash equilibria

payoffs.[13] Another means to focus among equilibria is through pregame communication or cheap talk, whereby players signal to one another how to coordinate their actions. This kind of private coordination through discussion could be replaced by public coordination, whereby a central authority or leader directs the players to better payoffs by coordinating how often the participants play their strategies.[14]

Yet another means for culling equilibria is to introduce a temporal dimension into the game, so that players move sequentially, and then eliminate strategies that involve incredible threats or promises that players would never carry out if their bluffs were called. Suppose that as an encumbent firm I threaten any potential entrant with a ruinous price war that will cost me greatly, as a ploy to deter entry. If an entrant still comes in, a rational encumbent would then reevaluate the costs of the price war and would be expected not to go through with it. A prospective entrant is expected to look ahead and realize the incredibility of the encumbent's threat and then enter. If the game is displayed in a game box or normal form, two Nash equilibria are present: (1) the prospective entrant enters and the encumbent does not engage in a price war, and (2) the prospective entrant stays out because the encumbent will carry out a price war had the entrant not stayed out (Sandler 1992, pp. 84–6). The second equilibrium is duly removed by the Nash refinement that looks ahead and removes equilibria based on noncredible threats. Solving a game *backwards* by finding the best move at each decision

[13] This is an interesting game because the method of successive elimination of weakly dominated strategies would remove the three equilibria with the greatest aggregate payoffs.

[14] Such correlated equilibria are discussed in Arce (1997), Arce and Sandler (2001), and Aumann (1974, 1987).

point (or subgame) that makes up the game is the refinement of Nash equilibria known as subgame perfection.[15] The encumbent firm example is essential to understanding how modern game theory tries to address dynamic competitiveness in a consistent fashion. In the study of international relations, the behavior of nations in responding to threats from other nations, including the initiation of conflict, can be investigated with this notion of subgame perfection. It also applies to the study of labor disputes, the introduction of new technologies, and the international community's confrontation with a rogue nation.

We can take this example a step further to consider the impact of other factors, such as reputation. If the encumbent realizes that a failure to carry through on its threat would encourage additional entrants and a continuing loss of market share, then the cost of the price war may not look as bad as that of acquiescing, which, when reputation is included, results in even worse payoffs. As a consequence, an encumbent who is aware of these reputational effects may fight, insofar as the short-run losses may be less than the long-run gains from deterring future entry. Analogously, a superpower may have to carry out an ultimatum (for example, the bombing of Iraq in 1991 or of Serbia in 1999) even if it is costly, because of the threat to its reputation of a failure to act. Other refinements for culling Nash equilibria in dynamic settings have been proposed. For example, a "trembling hand" equilibrium even allows for a tiny possibility of an opponent's error at some move.[16] And still others permit uncertainty about the type of opponent being confronted: either an encumbent firm obsessed with its reputation, or a wimp with no stomach for a fight. Suffice it to say, methods exist to address in some fashion the issue of multiple Nash equilibria, but no refinement is completely compelling.

Another potential problem with the concept of Nash equilibrium is that no such equilibrium may exist in terms of a strategic combination that is always played. Consider the game of matching pennies, where each of two players must simultaneously choose whether to display the coin with heads or tails facing up. Suppose that player A wins a penny from B if a match occurs, while player B wins a penny from A on a nonmatch. Because of one's ignorance of the opponent's choice, there is no strategic combination of always displaying heads or always displaying tails that results in a Nash equilibrium. For such games, a Nash equilibrium can be found by randomizing the strategy of displaying heads or tails so that each is chosen 50% of the time. This same kind of situation can occur when opponents can do best when their strategies are kept

---

[15] On subgame perfect equilibrium, see Selten (1965, 1975) and Kreps (1990a, pp. 56–72).
[16] Selten (1975) is the originator of a trembling hand equilibrium.

secret,[17] which is certainly true of how terrorists randomize their targets and modes of attack. Surely, in poker, it is best not to be known for always bluffing or always folding; hence, if you win a hand after everyone drops out, it is wise not to reveal your cards.

Another concern about Nash equilibrium involves whether people really end up at a Nash equilibrium in practice. A large experimental literature has devised games played in an experimental setting where players do not necessarily follow their Nash-equilibrium strategies.[18] If, however, players are allowed to gain experience by playing the game repeatedly, then the Nash equilibrium shows up more frequently in some kinds of games, such as contributing to a public good. These experiments must be evaluated carefully as to whether they truly reflect the game that they are testing. If they pass muster, then the experimental design and results need to be checked carefully. In those cases where the experiments cannot be faulted, one must contemplate whether some other consideration – for example, risk attitudes – is subtly altering how the payoffs are perceived by the subjects. Valuable lessons can be learned from these cases, the most important being the ability to identify a reasonable alternative to Nash equilibrium.

EVOLUTIONARY GAMES AS A NEW DEFENSE FOR A NASH EQUILIBRIUM

Evolutionary game theory studies the population dynamics of a game played over and over again – a repeated game. Each player type is hard-wired or programmed with a strategy that directs his or her play. Evolutionary game theory predicts that the "fittest" strategy choices, as determined by their resulting payoffs, will survive, multiply, and characterize a population. If a population with a single type of strategy results, then the population is *monomorphic*.[19] Consider a population of defectors (who always defect) who are invaded by some cooperators (who always cooperate). Suppose that a Prisoners' Dilemma is played in each period. Cooperators who appear earn low payoffs by being played for suckers by defectors. Over time, cooperators will reproduce less rapidly because of these smaller payoffs, and their numbers will dwindle, so that a defector population can withstand such an invasion. That is, a defector population is stable against an invasion by cooperators. For other scenarios, the proportion of the various types in the population makes a difference with respect to which invasions can be withstood.

---

[17] See Dixit and Skeath (1999, pp. 125–36).

[18] A good source for such experimental results is Kagel and Roth (1995).

[19] Monomorphic population is analyzed by Bergstrom (1995), Bergstrom and Stark (1993), and Maynard Smith (1982).

Evolutionary stability requires that any small band of individuals employing a strategy different from that of the larger population will not do as well over time as population members who employ the prevailing strategy.[20] That is, the population will be able to maintain its dominance. Evolutionary stable strategies represent a refinement of Nash equilibrium, because all such strategies are Nash equilibria, but not the other way around. If an *evolutionary stable strategy* (ESS) were not a Nash equilibrium for the repeated game, then a contradiction would follow. Suppose that there is a strategy that yields more than the ESS when played against it, so that the ESS is not a Nash equilibrium. Any mutant playing such a strategy will perform better than nonmutant population members, and this enhanced fitness will allow it to reproduce faster and invade successfully. Thus, the alleged ESS cannot be stable. For a Nash equilibrium to be an ESS, *it must be a Nash equilibrium when played against itself* – all players must be employing an identical strategy. In a chicken game, its Nash equilibria, where one player is swerving and the other is holding his ground, are not ESS, because the same equilibrium strategy is *not* being played against itself. Population dynamics provide a justification for Nash equilibrium strategies, because a Nash equilibrium can result in resilient populations.

Thus far, monomorphisms, where a single type of player takes over, have been represented as ESS. An ESS that involves more than one type of a player is a *polymorphism*. Skyrms (1996, pp. 12–14) indicates an interesting polymorphism in a cake-splitting game where the cake is divided only when a bargain uses up 100% or less of the cake. If more than a whole cake is demanded, the paired players walk away empty-handed. Suppose that the population is made up of one-third modest types who ask for a quarter of the cake, and two-thirds greedy persons who ask for three-quarters. Two-thirds of the time, given population proportions, greedy players meet one another and walk away with nothing. When modest demanders are paired, a bargain is consummated and each leaves with a quarter of the cake. For heterogeneous pairings, which occurs a third of the time, a bargain results in a 25:75 split. Thus, the modest demanders always get their quarter, while the greedy demanders get their three-quarters but only a third of the time, for an average payoff of just a quarter. A stable population of both types ensues because each is equally fit, receiving an expected payoff of one quarter of the cake per period. Thus, more than one type of player can coexist in a stable population dynamics. This is intuitively appealing when one observes such heterogeneous populations in the real world.

---

[20] Evolutionary stable strategies are discussed in Dixit and Skeath (1999), Skyrms (1996), and Weibull (1995).

A cultural interpretation has players' strategies being learned or acquired by imitation of the successful strategies of their neighbors rather than being hardwired. The analysis of evolutionary games can then provide an explanation for cultural norms. For example, the norm of fair division, observed in many societies, can be shown to be an ESS against more unequal divisions.[21] Thus, the game theory of population dynamics can address how conventions develop and enable individuals to choose among Nash equilibria.

SUCCESSES OF GAME THEORY

Game theory has much going for it that has allowed it to "invade" the population of economic methods in recent years. In the social sciences, the success of game theory is dependent on a number of factors.[22] First, it gives social scientists a means for conceptualizing strategic and dynamic interactions. Although individuals may act independently, the best choice of action and the resulting payoffs are not necessarily independent of the actions of others. Second, game theory forces us to think about credible threats and promises. An agent must be willing to carry out a threat when its bluff is called if such threats are to warrant serious consideration. Third, game theory results in the construction of logically consistent theories that no longer examine an optimizing choice of an isolated agent as though other agents were passive and unable to try to gain a similar advantage. Fourth, game theory creates the need to consider each player's knowledge and how the player can process information over time to strategic advantage. Fifth, game theory provides a formal language and structure for predicting and understanding competitive interactions. Sixth, it can further our knowledge of institutions, conventions, and social norms. In many ways, the rules governing an institution define a game played among its participants. Seventh, game theory can lead to more informed policy making.

This last advantage can be illustrated by some work on "games" played between terrorists and a government. In the early 1970s, terrorists targeted US embassies as a protest against US support of Israel and other US foreign policies. These attacks usually involved spraying machine-gun fire at the embassy's walls or throwing small bombs into the compound – damage and casualties were typically minimal. As a reaction to such attacks, the United States began a process of fortifying its embassies. While the number of attacks declined greatly, assassinations of embassy

---

[21] See Skyrms (1996, pp. 3–16). The Skyrms book is a fascinating treatment of social conventions, based on evolutionary game theory.

[22] Some of these successes are presented in Kreps (1990a, Chapter 4), while others are my own.

personnel when they ventured from secure grounds increased significantly.[23] Obviously, the policy decision to fortify the embassies did not anticipate the terrorists' likely response, and, as a consequence, more costly attacks replaced less costly ones. If terrorists are expected to substitute in a strategic fashion among attack modes, then informed policy either engineers a substitution to less damaging attacks by deterring multiple kinds of attacks, or, better yet, reduces terrorists' resources so as to limit all attacks.

A different example concerns a terrorist group that targets one of two countries. As one country augments its deterrent efforts, the threat may merely be displaced to the other country as terrorists respond to risks. If targeted countries do not coordinate their efforts, overdeterrence may result, with governments spending too much on transferring the problem abroad. Suppose that the two governments have two policy-coordination decisions: deterrence spending and sharing information about terrorists' preferred targets. Partial cooperation that involves only one of these policy instruments can make both governments worse off. For example, sharing intelligence without coordinating deterrence can escalate overspending on deterrence, as informed countries capitalize on their knowledge about terrorists' intended targets by spending even more on deflecting attacks abroad. Such insights follow from a game-theoretic analysis.[24]

MORE ON NONCOOPERATIVE AND COOPERATIVE GAMES

When dynamic situations are analyzed, an extensive form or game tree representation of the game is appropriate. Solution concepts can involve looking ahead and solving the game backward, known as backward induction, or looking forward at a sequence of moves to anticipate what both players may do from some vantage point on, known as forward induction. In Figure 3.6, a game between a central government (C) and a lower-level government (L) is depicted. Initially, C determines whether to augment its militia or allow for free elections. Following this decision, which is known to the lower government, the latter must decide whether or not to ask C for help to maintain order if no election is allowed, or to conduct its own elections if free elections are permitted. The first number at the four end points of the tree indicates C's payoff, and the second denotes L's payoff. Backward induction involves starting at the end of the game and first determining L's best strategy at its two decision points. On the top branch, L is better off asking for help, since 20 > 10, while on the bottom branch, L is better off conducting local

---

[23] The underlying empirical analysis is presented in Enders and Sandler (1993).
[24] Sandler and Lapan (1988) contains the underlying game-theoretic analysis.

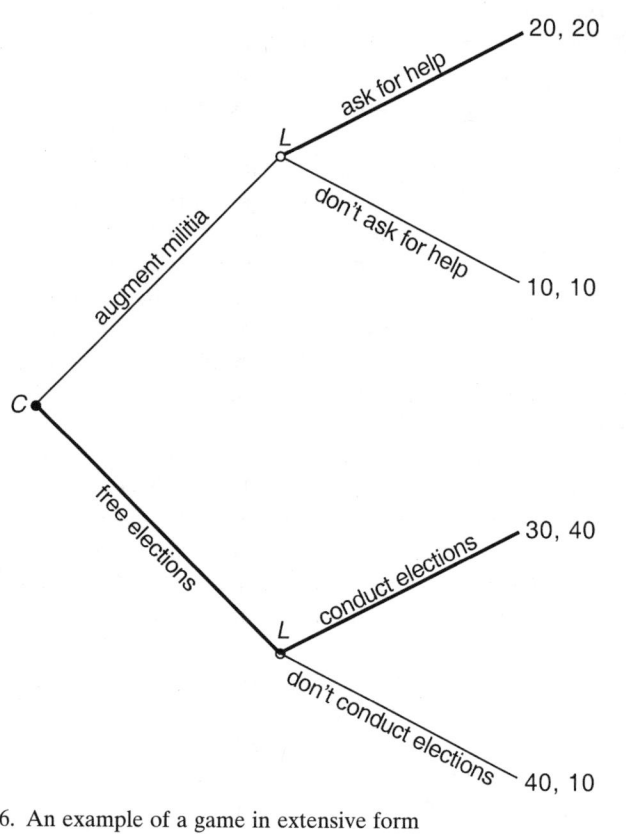

Figure 3.6. An example of a game in extensive form

elections, since 40 > 10. These two branches are changed to boldface to indicate that *L* is expected to move in these ways at its respective decision nodes. *C* must then decide, given *L*'s anticipated subsequent decisions, whether it wants to augment its militia and gain 20 or to conduct free elections and end up with 30. Thus, the equilibrium is for *C* to allow for free elections and for *L* to conduct local elections in response. Such an equilibrium corresponds to the unbroken boldface path from the initial node to a terminus.

This simple example demonstrates how an extensive-form representation captures dynamic competitive interactions among players. Such representations can be embellished to allow for more players, strategies, and decision points, as well as for a more interesting information structure. In the latter case, players may not know what decisions have preceded their own decision node, so they may not know where they are among a number of possible nodes. When matching pennies, for example, a player does not know whether a choice of heads or tails by an opponent preceded his or her decision node. For some games, learning can occur; earlier choices may signal or reveal useful information, thus allowing a player to better estimate the likelihood of being at a particular place on the tree.

A distinguishing feature of game theory during the last two decades has been this greater reliance on extensive-form games. Even though games can be expressed in either strategic or extensive forms, it is easier to keep track of the temporal information when a game is displayed in its extensive forms. To capture a complex sequence of moves, a game in strategic form may become very complicated. Another virtue of using extensive form is that it allows for the identification and elimination of equilibria based on incredible threats or promises.

Thus far, this chapter has focused on noncooperative games. With concerns over global warming, ozone shield depletion, and other instances requiring transnational collective action, a renewed interest is being shown in cooperative games. Consider a Prisoners' Dilemma where players employ their dominant strategies and end up with poor payoffs that could be improved if they could agree to cooperate. The promise of cooperative game theory is to improve on low payoffs associated with some noncooperative outcomes by allowing two or more players to coordinate their efforts. Any cooperative outcome is judged against the status quo payoffs that individuals receive in the absence of an agreement. Acceptable proposals must improve all participants' well-being, or else they will not participate. Moreover, the grand coalition of everyone must be able to match the aggregate payoff of any agreement involving the entire population. A *core solution* satisfies a set of conditions that ensures that no feasible coalition can be formed and do better for itself than its core payoff.[25] That is, a core solution involves a coalition whose members cannot form an alternative group and thereby improve their payoffs over those in the core. Quite simply, when a core exists, there is no blocking coalition that represents a better deal for participants. In international relations, the sharing of the cost of an electric power system among countries can constitute a core solution (Sandler and Tschirhart 1980).

Unfortunately, a core solution may not exist, so that no agreement may be found that can satisfy the required conditions. One obvious means for circumventing this difficulty is to refine the notion of the core to permit less stringent requirements. When the core does exist, there may be many such solutions with no obvious means of distinguishing which would follow. Another drawback of the core is its static nature,

---

[25] Cooperative games and the core are analyzed in Eichberger (1993), Gardner (1995), and Luce and Raiffa (1957).

which lacks the temporal structure characteristic of modern thinking about noncooperative games. I am frequently struck by how cooperative game-theoretic analysis does not capture much of the physical aspects associated with a host of global issues (for example, wind direction in a core representation of a pollution pact). When I raise this issue to authors, they typically respond with the need for tractability and solvability. Although I am sympathetic to the need for tractability, it is essential that the model capture the essential features of the problem under investigation. These aspects appear to be more demanding when working with cooperative rather than noncooperative games. The profession seems to be quite sensible in concentrating its efforts on noncooperative games. Having said this, I should also point out that the difference between cooperative and noncooperative games is becoming blurred, as recent analyses examine coalition formation and communication in a noncooperative framework.

MAJOR CHALLENGES TO GAME THEORY

Game theory has taken economics by storm, but will it continue to be such a dominating methodology in the decades to come? Certainly it has many of the ingredients identified in Chapter 1 as those required for staying power. There is no question that it is applicable to important economic phenomenon. For example, game-theoretic principles were in large part behind the design and implementation of the Federal Communication Commission's (FCC) auction of select frequencies along the electromagnetic spectrum to private interests. In fact, one would be hard-pressed to find a field of economics not touched by game theory and its representation of strategic interactions. Unless the economic situation includes just a single agent or else so many that each agent's actions are imperceptible, game theory is relevant. We may act independently as economic players, but actions of others typically impinge on our choices, and our choices influence their actions. If they were to ignore these strategic interactions, economists would leave out a crucial aspect of the situation and, in so doing, would derive incorrect answers.

Noncooperative game theory possesses a simple elegance that allows researchers to distill the essence of a problem, which should also bolster its staying power as a tool of analysis. Simple strategic-form representations can capture much of the underlying strategic interaction, while the temporal character can be taken into account with an elementary extensive-form representation. Another feature that lends staying power is the novelty of many game results. This is particularly true when game-theoretic results are compared to traditional economic analysis of strategic interactions involving a small number of agents, in which agents are not always examined in a consistent and symmetric fashion. For example, game-theoretic thinking about entry deterrence in an oligopoly is at odds with earlier representations and findings, where the encumbent firms make no adjustment as entry occurs.

The sole aspect of game theory that could jeopardize its enduring influence is its empirical testability. Economics has a strong empirical component, where theories are tested and either predict reasonably well or are discarded and replaced by better theoretical representations. From the origins of game theory, experiments have been used to ascertain whether or not subjects respond according to game-theoretic predictions. As mentioned earlier, these experimental results are mixed. There must also be empirical tests using real-world data. If game theory is to maintain its dominance as a theoretical method, more energy and attention needs to be allocated to devising appropriate statistical tests of game theory. This is not an easy task, because the strategic nature of game-theoretic models means that appropriate empirical tests must account for the interdependencies of the underlying equations.[26] Of course, there have been many tests of game-theoretic models,[27] but these are relatively few in number compared to the number of theoretical papers. A better balance is required. These tests must involve single-stage and multi-stage games and must encompass noncooperative and cooperative game theories. Surely, the core notion of cooperative games would be a difficult concept to identify and then test empirically. I would guess that noncooperative game theory will have a greater staying power than cooperative game theory, because the former is probably easier to test and possesses a greater range of applications, such as the FCC auction mentioned earlier.

Interesting challenges remain for game theory that will provide a fascinating agenda for future research, which should keep the next generation of economists occupied. Included in this agenda will be the formulation of an alternative equilibrium notion that is Nash in many standard scenarios but assumes an alternative form when risks or other considerations lessen the compelling nature of a Nash equilibrium. A better dynamic representation is required, one in which repeated games do not require that the same game be played from period to period. Progress in this area is already being made by researchers who use computers to examine equilibria when the set of players and their strategies can change from period to period. This dynamic development will also concern building a more interesting learning structure into game theory,

---

[26] In technical terms, this means using simultaneous-equation estimation procedures to address the identification problem implied by this strategic interdependency.

[27] Examples include McGuire and Groth (1985) and Sandler and Murdoch (1990).

a chore that is also addressed by evolutionary game theory. Economists need to consider psychological aspects of agents and how they process information.[28] A better interface between cooperative and noncooperative game theory must also be devised. Advances in cooperative game theory need to involve developing better theories for the endogenous formation of coalitions. To date, there is still no convincing explanation of the formation of treaties and other coalitions. If there were such an explanation, then surely there would be greater progress on the issue of global warming.

As economists continue to rely on game-theoretic methods, it is essential that there be a better awareness about the boundaries at which game theory loses its relevancy. There is good reason why Adam Smith, who was primarily concerned with competitive economies where each agent exerts an imperceptible influence on others, had little to say about strategic interactions.

---

[28] This point is a basic message of Kreps (1990a).

4   It Takes Two or More: Public Economics and Collective Action

For a moment, imagine yourself in a truly anarchic society with no rules or laws, no protection of property rights, no defense, no publicly provided goods or services, and no taxes. Would this society be paradise or a nightmare? Each morning, if you have not been murdered the night before, you would have a daunting decision: how to divide your time that day among providing for your needs, guarding the fruits of your past labors, and stealing from others. The greater the amount of time devoted to either guarding your "pile" or robbing others, the less would remain for productive activities that augment your overall wealth and that of society. Stealing or watching over your assets uses up scarce resources in an unproductive activity that reduces society's overall well-being. Under the best of circumstances, theft is a zero-sum game.

In this natural anarchic state, there would evolve a collective of individuals – perhaps thugs – who would specialize in providing protection in return for a share of the wealth of those being protected. These guardians would amass weapons to counter threats both within and beyond their society. Some of the additional goods, produced because you now have time released from having to watch over your assets, could pay the protectors. If the value of this tribute were less than the value of these additional goods, then both the protected and the protectors would gain from the arrangement.[1] As defenders of lives and property, the protectors essentially assume the role of a government, whose services are then financed through a tax or tribute. Anarchy is a disequilibrium state in which incentives exist for the creation of a government that secures the society's people and property. Governments that perform this activity well gain legitimacy and, with this legitimacy, may take on additional functions by providing a justice system, education, roads, and other

---

[1] This version of the genesis of government is in keeping with the analysis presented in Bush and Mayer (1974).

infrastructure.[2] In many ways, feudal lords represented the first governments. As these lords formed networks to control larger territories, the dynastic state evolved, becoming the main governmental unit in 1648 with the Treaty of Westphalia. The modern nation-state with its collective identity and democratic ideals followed with the birth of the United States and later France.

So, try as we might, it is difficult to imagine a society existing for long without some form of government. During the twentieth century, there has been an unprecedented growth of the public or governmental sector in every industrial country.[3] Within the United States, there are now over 86,000 governments, including 50 state governments and thousands of county governments (there are 99 in Iowa alone). There are also thousands of city and district governments. The most rapid growth in government expenditures (*G*) in the United States as a percent of gross domestic product (GDP) came during the period 1935–45. After a temporary decline, the *G*/GDP *ratio* remained constant for the years 1955–65, before it again grew over the period 1965–75. From 1975 to 1995, *G*/GDP has remained constant in the United States at about 32% to 34%. Over the last five years, this percentage has, however, fallen to about 29%, with most of the decline coming at the federal level. Most of the earlier growth in the public sector has been at the federal level, where expenditures grew from 3% of GDP in 1929 to nearly 24% in recent years (Mueller 1989, p. 321). The US experience is mirrored by other industrial countries, with the US share on the low side. The *average percent* of GDP devoted to the public sector was 43.5% in 1999 for the United States, Canada, the United Kingdom, Germany, France, Italy, and Japan (Bruce 2001, p. 6).

What does the public sector do? Although the government does many things, its activities can be broadly characterized in two categories: correcting market failures and redistributing income among its constituency. The former involves providing public goods and correcting externalities. Recall from Chapter 1 that a pure public good possesses benefits that are nonexcludable and nonrival among users. Nonexcludability means that there is no ability to keep nonpayers from experiencing the public good's benefits, while benefit nonrivalry indicates that there is no cost in

---

[2] Olson (1993) makes a fascinating distinction between roving and stationary bandits in terms of the origin of governments. Stationary bandits had a greater interest in the prosperity of their subjects (prey), and would therefore provide public goods so as to enhance their tax base. Roving bandits would have little concern about their prey's well-being, because they would move on to pillage a new community.

[3] This public sector growth is documented in Bruce (2001, Chapter 1) and Mueller (1989, Chapter 17). The facts in this paragraph are from Bruce (2001) unless otherwise indicated.

allowing additional people to consume the good. Externalities arise when the economic activities of one agent create costs or benefits for other agents, and these costs or benefits are not reflected in the activities' prices. Firms that discharge their wastes into the environment impose costs on others, not party to the firms' productive activities, and, when they do so, an externality is created.

With pure public goods, private provision is anticipated to result in an undersupply or no supply at all, so that there may be a role for government provision of these goods.[4] Generally speaking, positive or beneficial externalities (for example, an attractive garden) are expected to be in short supply, while negative externalities (for example, car emissions) are expected to be too plentiful. Once again, government actions to regulate externality-generating activities through taxes or subsidies, rules, and other means may lead to a more optimal allocation of resources. These actions to provide public goods, eliminate public bads, and control externalities show up as government-provided goods and services.

When not correcting market failures, the government is engineering an "ideal income distribution," which attempts to incorporate the ethics of society as to how income should be distributed among individuals. For instance, a society with an egalitarian ethic will use progressive taxes to collect a greater proportion of income from the rich than from the poor. In stark contrast, a parasitic dictator will tax everyone except his own inner circle so as to redistribute as much income as possible to himself.[5] Only the potential for a revolt or reduced productivity limits such thievery. Of government's two basic activities, it is perhaps surprising to discover that 39% of government spending in the United States in 1999 went to providing goods and services associated with correcting market failures, with most of the rest focused on redistributing income – for example, social security payments, aid to needy families, medical assistance, disaster relief (Bruce 2001, pp. 5–6). This pattern is in keeping with other countries and time periods during peacetime.

During the twentieth century, economists directed a great deal of attention to *public economics* or the study of government spending and taxing activities with allocative and distributional goals. Some government actions are also aimed at promoting growth and stabilizing the economy (for example, limiting inflation), but these actions if properly performed also constitute public goods. Many recent Nobel Prizes in economics reflect the importance of discoveries in public economics – for example, Ronald Coase's study of externalities, James Buchanan's

---

[4] On externalities and public goods, see Cornes and Sandler (1996), Arrow (1970), Heller and Starrett (1976), Johansen (1977), Mishan (1971), and Samuelson (1954, 1955).
[5] See, for example, Grossman (1991, 1995).

contributions to public choice, James Mirrlees's and William Vickrey's writings on asymmetric information, and Jan Tinbergen's insights on policy instruments.

The task of this chapter is to indicate how findings in public economics have enriched not only economics but also the social sciences in general. Public economics is arguably the most encompassing field of economics and includes myriad activities. I could easily write volumes (and have already done so) if I wanted to do the field justice, but that is not my goal here. Instead, I provide the reader with a small appreciation of what public economics has to offer and why it will remain a pivotal area of research for the foreseeable future. I shall be selective, again without apology, as to what I stress and ignore. My proclivity is to force my reader to think and recognize the many unanswered questions and the clever insights used on those that are answered.

When undergraduates and graduates come to me for advice and ask me to suggest classes to take outside of the required theory and tools courses, I always respond with public economics and international economics. Given government's intrusion in modern-day market economies, an economics major must be knowledgeable about the public sector. Furthermore, trade and international finance are becoming increasingly crucial determinants of global resource allocation and income distribution. The internet will augment trade's importance still further.

MYTHS AND REALITIES OF PUBLIC ECONOMICS

In the last half-century, economic research has dispelled numerous myths in public economics, among which is the perception that public goods must be provided publicly. When Paul Samuelson (1954, 1955) made the concept of a public good widely recognized, the only policy recommendation that he put forward to escape the free-rider problem was public provision. As researchers delved closer into public goods and their properties, a rich array of these goods emerged based on the extent to which their benefits are either nonexcludable or nonrival.[6] Consider highways, where an exclusion mechanism can be employed to monitor and charge tolls for trips; drivers, whose demand is greater, use the road more frequently and are charged accordingly. Toll roads can be provided publicly or privately. A host of public goods – golf courses, parks, recreation facilities, courts, extension services, schools, and security – are provided both

---

[6] Important papers on these properties include Buchanan (1965), Davis and Whinston (1967a), Margolis (1955), Mishan (1971), Oakland (1972, 1974), Olson and Zeckhauser (1966), Pauly (1967, 1970), Sandler (1977), Sandler and Tschirhart (1980), and Vickrey (1969).

publicly and privately. If exclusion can be practiced, there is no necessity for public provision.

Even in the absence of exclusion, public goods that also yield contributor-specific benefits – for example, a good feeling from giving to a charity, recognition from providing a public good, political concessions granted to an ally for bankrolling defense – motivate private provision even when a share of the benefits are purely public to the group. These jointly produced contributor-specific benefits can motivate action when great value is placed on them.[7] Suppose, for example, that a country receives significant benefits from controlling its sulfur emissions insofar as the lion's share of these emissions falls on the emitter's own soil.[8] Obviously, the country is motivated to limit these emissions greatly even though doing so helps downwind neighboring countries. No wonder curbing sulfur emissions has been a success story in Europe, where in many cases more than 60% of emissions land on the emitter's own soil (Sandnes 1993).

Another myth is that government provision of public goods necessarily improves society's welfare. Markets fail because of lack of information, improper incentives, monopoly distortions, and externalities, but government provision is subject to these same concerns. For example, government officials would have difficulty in ascertaining their constituents' true tastes for a pure public good. How does the US president really know how much national defense is desired by the country's citizens? Even if these preferences could be known, the president's incentives to win reelection may require him or her to please special interests whose preferences are not consistent with those of the constituency as whole (see Chapter 5). Mancur Olson (1980) expressed this problem eloquently:

> The theories of economics and political economy then lead to the depressing but surely plausible conclusions that – in contrast to the beliefs of the nineteenth century advocates of laissez-faire – markets often fail, but that – in contrast to those who held high hopes about what massive government intervention would achieve – governments usually work badly too. In order to make sensible recommendations about what to do in each of the many cases of market failure, we must at least look closely at the specific circumstances of the market failure and the specific structure of the program and the collective decision procedures that would control any government intervention. (p. 6)

[7] On these joint products, see Andreoni (1990), Cornes and Sandler (1984, 1994), Murdoch and Sandler (1982, 1984), and Sandler (1977).

[8] The sulfur emission problem is addressed by Eliassen and Saltbones (1983), Mäler (1989), Murdoch, Sandler, and Sargent (1997), Sandler and Sargent (1995), and Sandnes (1993).

A third myth associated with public economics is that an optimal or desired level of a negative externality is zero. Suppose that a smoker and a nonsmoker share a dormitory room at the University of Wyoming, where in the dead of winter the outside temperature could be –40°F, with a windchill of –80°F or lower. Further suppose that the first cigarette smoked in an evening in the room gives the smoker $5 worth of satisfaction. Given the inclement conditions, smoking the cigarette outside of the dormitory is not really an option, even if it could be lighted! If the nonsmoker's dissatisfaction from the first cigarette is just $1, then a deal can be struck between roommates whereby the smoker bribes the nonsmoker into allowing the cigarette to be smoked. If, in addition, a second cigarette gives the smoker $3 worth of additional pleasure while inconveniencing the nonsmoker by $3, then the optimal number of "smokes" is two – the externality is best allowed to occur twice in an evening, with the smoker paying the nonsmoker $4 for the privilege of smoking two cigarettes.[9]

Next consider an optimal level of pollution, which sounds like an oxymoron. A common friction between economists and environmentalists, which I have experienced all too often, is over an "optimal pollution level." An environmentalist is ideologically predisposed to think that this optimum is zero, which assumes that eliminating the pollution has zero opportunity cost. Suppose that, after curbing car pollution, car exhausts add only one metric ton of carbon monoxide (CO) to the atmosphere each period. If eliminating this remaining CO costs $100 trillion but improves health and other considerations by just $1 billion, then the CO should not be curbed further. In economics, the optimum is achieved when the marginal gain from another unit of action equals the marginal or added costs of the action. This determination of an optimum by considering both the associated benefits and costs has much to offer to all branches of the social sciences.

Yet another myth concerns the concept of *piecemeal policy*, where correcting part of the problem is thought to be preferable to doing nothing.[10] To illustrate how this belief may be wrong at times, consider a monopoly that creates an externality in the form of pollution. Just breaking up the monopoly without addressing the pollution problem may not improve things. By its nature, a monopoly restricts output by charging

---

[9] This example is a demonstration of the so-called Coase Theorem (Coase 1960), which is one of Coase's two contributions for which he was awarded a Nobel Prize – see also the discussion in Chapter 2 about the ostrich rancher and the farmer, and the exhibitionist and the voyeur.

[10] The pitfalls of piecemeal policy are associated with the literature of "second best," where not all distortions are corrected. See Davis and Whinston (1965, 1967b), Dusansky and Walsh (1976), Lipsey and Lancaster (1956–7), and Sandler (1978a).

too high a price (that is, a price above marginal cost), and this restriction *limits* the externality. Breaking up the monopoly gives more output at a cheaper price, but at the expense of more pollution. The net gain from busting the monopoly depends on the relative size of two opposing effects and need not be positive.

As a second example of piecemeal policy, consider two neighboring African countries confronting the same animal poachers. In its efforts to eliminate poaching at home, each country is expected to spend too much on deterrence, as neither accounts for the negative externality that its enhanced surveillance causes – namely, transferring the poachers to the neighbor.[11] If there are two policy choices for a common response by the two countries, and they cooperate with respect to just one of these instruments, then both may be worse off. Suppose that one policy is to combine policing efforts and the other is to share intelligence about the preferences and resources of the poachers. If only the intelligence is shared, then each country may become more effective in its efforts to shift the poachers abroad, which will cause an even greater overspending on surveillance, to the detriment of both countries. In point of fact, countries are reluctant to coordinate internal policing efforts owing to a loss of autonomy, but do share intelligence on poachers. This example illustrates that criminal studies and political science may both profit from economic insights. There are, however, times when piecemeal policy can work: those times when the two policies' impacts are either supportive of one another or else unrelated. An understanding of such situations can make for more effective policy.

Although other myths exist with respect to public economics, just one additional one is considered, which concerns the ability to address allocative and distributional issues independently. For example, government provision of a public good is presented as though it is only a matter of choosing the level of the good, where the sum of its additional benefits to the recipients matches its additional provision cost.[12] The distributional implications of achieving this match are ignored, despite the fact that expenditures on the public good provide income to workers and input owners involved with the good's production. Moreover, to finance the public good, the government must raise revenues by means of taxes

---

[11] The underlying analysis of this paragraph is analogous to the terrorism example from Sandler and Lapan (1988) presented in Chapter 3.

[12] In economic texts, this shows up as the requirement to equate the sum of the marginal rates of substitution (MRS) of the public good for the private good to the relevant ratio of the marginal costs. MRS is the marginal benefit derived from the public good in terms of a private good's marginal benefit. The traditional analysis of vertically summing demand curves for public goods implicitly assumes that allocation and distribution are separable concerns.

that alter the distribution of income, since taxpayers who pay more will have less income to spend on other goods. By the same token, policy that influences income distribution can have a profound impact on allocative efficiency in terms of the level of externalities and the provision of public goods. If, for example, environmental quality is highly income responsive or elastic (that is, a 10% rise in income results in a greater than 10% increase in expenditure on preserving the environment), then an increase in the income of influential voters can lead to a greater demand for and supply of pollution abatement.

WHY HAS THE PUBLIC SECTOR GROWN?

The size of the public sector, accounting for a third to one-half of GDP, means that economists must continue to investigate public economics if the discipline is to remain relevant. This growth is still not fully understood.[13] Of course, it is not difficult to understand that public spending will peak during wartime because of defense spending, but this does not explain why public spending grew in an unprecedented fashion during the post–World War II years. If one looks to the provision of public goods and the correction of externalities for an explanation, then this growth could be partly explained if either the constituency's demand for public goods is highly income responsive, or its demand is price unresponsive (inelastic) and the relative price of such activities has risen. Empirical evidence does not support the income elasticity argument, except for the growth of expenditures regarding the preservation of the environment. There is more support for the second hypothesis, because voters' demands for government activities tend to be price unresponsive, and some rise in the relative price of such activities has occurred. But even here these factors are quite modest and cannot explain much of public sector growth.

Thus, one must either turn to some bureaucratic theory, whereby bureaucrats maximize their budgets and are ratcheting up these budgets over time by a constant rate of growth, or else attribute the growth to government's actions to alter the distribution of income. There is some evidence consistent with the bureaucratic hypothesis, but this evidence is inconsistent with the uneven growth of the public sector and its leveling off during the last couple of decades. If income redistribution is considered as the underpinning for the growth of the public sector, then the growth of suffrage, which has extended the vote to poorer segments of

[13] This paragraph draws from Mueller (1989, Chapter 17). For specific empirical studies, see the citations given there. The price elasticity measures the percentage change in the quantity demanded resulting from a 1% change in price. Demand is price inelastic if a 10% fall in price results in a less than 10% rise in quantity demanded.

society over time, means that voters have on average become poorer over time and may be won over by officeholders who redistribute income to them.[14] Yet another explanation of public sector growth hinges on the increased number of special interest lobbies, which support the campaigns of candidates who in return further these lobbies' goals with special legislation. In the political arena today, virtually every interest is represented, or so it seems; there are lobbies for retired people, farmers, insurance companies, teachers, the handicapped, veterans, food safety, chemical companies, doctors, patients, HMOs, and so on. As these lobbies have multiplied, legislative programs catering to their interests have also grown. To date, the empirical support for either the suffrage theory or the growth of lobbies theory is not convincing.

What I would find convincing is a theory, combined with empirical support, that explains the growth of G/GDP during the third quarter of the twentieth century, its subsequent leveling off, and its recent decline in the latter 1990s in the United States. Another disturbing feature of the debate over the causes of public sector growth is the absence of an analysis that aggregates these diverse causes. Only partial theories have been put forward thus far. The recent stability of the share of GDP devoted to the public sector is as interesting as its earlier growth, because it is important to know why this ratio has hit some kind of ceiling and then fallen in the United States. My own guess is that there is a natural ceiling on the size of the public sector for each society, which differs among societies. Those that seek higher minimal standards of health, welfare, education, and social security will have a higher ceiling on their G/GDP ratio – for example, the Scandinavian countries, where the income distribution is "flatter," with greater overall equality. Increases and decreases in this ratio's natural rate take place as either the country's political philosophy changes or the ability of special interests to orchestrate policy changes.

SOME LESSONS FROM PUBLIC SECTOR ECONOMICS

Public sector economics has yielded many useful insights over the last half-century, making it difficult to focus on just a few lessons. Nevertheless, I shall do so. One important lesson derives from the recognition that policy has its own costs and unintended consequences. These costs can be classified as transaction costs from implementing the policy. By slowing traffic, toll booths on bridges create a transaction cost associated with user financing. This particular transaction cost can be almost halved by collecting twice the toll in just one direction. Additional transaction

---

[14] This is the argument put forward by Meltzer and Richard (1981, 1983); but also see Peltzman (1980), who viewed increased equality, not inequality, as behind this growth of the public sector.

costs are associated with staffing and maintaining the booths. For tolls, the associated transaction costs are typically modest compared to the gains in efficiency from charging the users and not financing through some general-fund taxes, collected from both users and nonusers of the bridge.

Next, consider taxes used to finance a public good. In particular, suppose that an income tax surcharge is used to help support local schools, as is the case in the college town of Ames, Iowa. This tax distorts the choice between labor and leisure by lowering the effective wage, thereby making work less attractive. Virtually every tax instrument except a lump-sum tax or a poll tax (which is a tax per head) distorts prices and adversely impacts an individual's choices. In so doing, most taxes introduce an inefficiency that is known as an excess burden.[15] The lump-sum tax circumvents this problem by being unrelated to any conscious choice, but this also makes such taxes a rare species.

There are means to limit this excess burden. In the simplest of terms, the tax must not affect one's decision if the excess burden is to disappear. If the government taxes something that one buys in the same quantity no matter what the price, then the tax will have no influence on one's purchasing behavior or choices. If, therefore, the good's demand is price unresponsive or inelastic, then the excise tax will not distort choices. Cigarettes, liquor, and gasoline are goods with price inelastic demands; not surprisingly, these goods all carry excise taxes. Given this price unresponsive demand, one must seriously question whether the large tax per pack of cigarettes is *really* intended to keep us from smoking. A more plausible rationalization for cigarette taxes is that they are a great revenue source with little distortionary influence. The excise tax not only fails to cure a smoker of the habit, but also reduces her discretionary income so that she is less able to afford medical treatment from smoking-related diseases. The excess burden of taxation reminds us that well-intended policies may result in unintended consequences. Just because the policy goal is admirable, there is no assurance, without proper thought being given to the design of the policy, that the final outcome will improve the status quo. To this excess burden must also be added the institutional costs associated with implementing the policy. These latter costs may be lower for a less desirable policy, making it preferable to a more efficient, but more costly, policy. The real world of policy choices is seldom an economist's ideal.

Another important lesson, already mentioned in Chapter 2, concerns whether market failures must necessarily be corrected. Consider an

---

[15] On excess burden, consult any undergraduate public finance text – for example, Bruce (2001, pp. 354–6). On distortionary tax, see Atkinson and Stern (1974).

externality associated with an apiarist who locates beehives in a meadow adjoining an apple orchard owned by someone else. Each day the industrious bees fly next door, collect the apple pollen on their thighs, and return to the hive. If the apiarist compensated the apple orchard owner for the pollen, surely the latter would plant more trees, and both individuals would be better off. Suppose that the necessary technology is developed to fit each bee with a little jacket that can measure the pollen collected. Further suppose that infrared transmitters on these jackets can send information concerning the quantity of pollen on each bee to an infrared receiver located in the orchard. With this ingenious device, the externality could be monitored and compensated completely. Just two concerns remain. First, there is the problem that the gain in efficiency is unlikely to offset the expense of implementing this transaction, because outfitting each bee is a costly proposition, while the value of the additional honey produced is apt to be small. Hence, there may be no net gain from "fixing" the externality with this scheme. Second, there is the very tricky task of getting the jackets with their transmitters onto the irritable bees! Although this example is admittedly extreme, its message is applicable to a wide range of circumstances: the existence of a market failure does not in itself imply that something must be done about it.

The bee example again highlights the transaction costs associated with engaging in an exchange. In the beekeeping case, the transaction costs to account for the externality through monitoring are prohibitively high, but this does not mean that other, cheaper institutional designs are not available. The bees also confer an external benefit on the apple orchard owner by pollinating the apple trees. Each player can gain from bargaining to an arrangement where the two activities are increased so as to account for the reciprocal spillovers of benefits. Even if the bargained solution does not adjust for every tree pollinated or every particle of pollen transported back to the hive, the bargaining outcome will improve both individuals' well-being and is cheap to implement. This solution may not be perfect, but it may be good enough. The choice of institutions when addressing market failures matters greatly. In fact, institutional design is a recurring theme throughout this book, one that is addressed in detail in Chapter 6.

Related to the institutional choice question, there is the lesson that a nongovernmental alternative may be preferable. Bargaining has already been mentioned. Another nongovernmental alternative is a club, where members voluntarily share a public good financed through tolls or a membership fee.[16] If exclusion of a public good is feasible at a reason-

---

[16] Clubs were introduced by Tiebout (1956), Wiseman (1957), and Buchanan (1965). See Cornes and Sandler (1996, Chapters 11–14) and Sandler and Tschirhart (1980, 1997).

able cost, so that utilization rates can be monitored, then the users can form a club and provide the shared good. Club goods – communication networks, the electromagnetic spectrum, parks, highways, transportation systems, the internet, universities, cities – come in many forms. Benefits of club goods are not only excludable but also partially rival in terms of crowding from increased use that detracts from the benefits received. In a communication system, crowding takes the form of interference and/or signal delays. Crowding on highways results in longer trips and a greater risk of accidents. Ideally, members can finance the club good through tolls that charge for the crowding costs that a visit or use of the shared good imposes on the other members. Unlike pure public goods, club goods can be allocated efficiently by the members, since the tolls collect payments that account for the crowding consequences. Resources for providing the club good are thereby directed to their most valued use. Even taste differences among members can be taken into account: members with a stronger preference for the club good will visit more frequently and end up paying more in tolls than those with weaker preferences. If exclusion cannot be practiced or is prohibitively expensive, then the club alternative is not an option.

Clubs can be used for allocating resources to some interesting goods. For instance, a commando squad, used to control terrorist incidents involving hostages, can be shared based on a deployment fee when needed to manage an incident. These fees can be geared both to the duration of deployment and the size of the commando squad dispatched, so that the charges can be tailored to the logistical difficulty of the crisis being managed. Another example is INTELSAT, a private consortium of nations and firms that operates as a club to share a communication satellite network that carries most international phone calls and television signals.[17] Similarly, LANDSAT is a private firm that operates as a club and provides remote surveillance images from space to those who pay a fee. Bands of the electromagnetic spectrum can also be shared in a club arrangement. If exclusion is practiced and tolls reflect the value of congestion, then the resulting club provides a useful alternative to public provision. Other clubs include cemeteries, learned societies, and churches. As technology advances, novel exclusion and monitoring mechanisms will greatly expand the range of club goods. The internet is also a club good, in which the access provider (for example, America Online) can exclude nonsubscribers and charge a toll based on utilization rates, such as time spent online. As the server's capacity of the provider is neared, subscribers either experience congestion when logging on or delays when surfing the net. Clubs are particularly

---

[17] On INTELSAT, see Edelson (1977), INTELSAT (1995), and Sandler and Schulze (1985).

attractive institutional alternatives to governments because transaction costs tend to be small.[18]

Modern public economics emphasizes that the economic impact of a policy may have nothing to do with who is in charge of implementing the policy. I shall illustrate this wisdom based on the study of tax incidence, or who pays the true burden of a tax. Consider a per-unit excise tax, such as a gasoline tax, collected by the seller and paid to the government. In economic principles, one learns that the tax typically impacts both sellers and buyers. The more price-unresponsive of these two groups bears more of the tax burden. Thus, a tax on insulin to a diabetic is fully carried by the buyer, who cannot cut back on the medication because of the price rise, while a tax on a product in fixed supply is borne by the seller, who cannot adjust supply to the tax-induced reduction in revenues. This is all very standard. But now suppose that the tax is paid directly to the government by the buyer and not by the seller. Instead of the supply curve shifting up in a parallel fashion by the amount of the per-unit tax, the demand curve shifts down and to the left by the same amount. The end result is that the distribution of the tax burden is the same; *the statutory responsibility has nothing to do with how the tax impacts buyers and sellers.*[19] One needs to remember this lesson the next time the US Congress agonizes and debates for days over who will collect a new tax. It simply does not matter in terms of the economic effects of the tax.

Although many other lessons derive from modern public economics, I shall conclude with only a few additional ones. First, public economics now recognizes that strategic competition may occur between regions to attract a greater tax base. It is, therefore, commonplace that jurisdictions offer substantial tax incentives to attract new firms or to keep existing ones from leaving. The downside of this action is an erosion of the tax base with no apparent gain if all competitor states engage in the same practice. It is analogous to a wasteful arms race that leaves security unchanged as weapon systems are matched. The consequence of the arms race is that the economies grow weaker and discontent festers from within. An increased awareness of strategic policy and its consequences is an insight that also applies to Europe's subsidization of Air Bus. Game theory has many relevant applications in public economics owing to the opposing interests of the agents in the public sector who seek strategic advantage.

Another essential lesson is the recognition that, in some situations, a partial-equilibrium analysis dealing with a single market cannot truly

---

[18] Clubs can themselves have alternative institutional forms and can be owned by members or provided by a firm (Cornes and Sandler 1996, Chapter 13).

[19] See Bruce (2001, Chapter 10) on statutory versus economic burdens of a tax.

indicate the impact of a policy that impinges on many markets. In these instances, a general-equilibrium analysis that examines spillover effects from one market onto another is needed. Moreover, feedback influences from these other markets back on the market in question require study. Everything ties together, and this needs to be analyzed. For example, a tax on cars will, by reducing the number of cars sold, have negative consequences on the input used intensively (in greater proportion to other inputs) in the car industry, as this input's wage drops and the input seeks employment elsewhere.

A final lesson involves an understanding of which goods should be publicly or privately provided. In cases where incentives either can be made "right" through institutional redesign, or are already right to motivate public good provision, private efforts can succeed.[20] Resources to address public goods can be limited greatly if they are solely directed at those cases where proper incentives are nonexistent. There is no reason to bother with a problem where action is imminent.

COLLECTIVE ACTION

The term *collective action* refers to activities that require the coordination of efforts by two or more individuals. Activities that involve the furtherance of the interests or well-being of a group are examples of collective action. The need for collective action permeates many aspects of our lives. Consider the common activity of driving a car on a two-lane highway with oncoming traffic. A coordination problem requiring collective action arises each time two cars traveling in opposite directions approach one another. Conventions exist in every country whereby each driver stays to the right or left. If two people share a rowboat, their rowing must be in unison or the boat will go in circles. Collective action problems are typically characterized by interdependence among the participants, so that the contributions or efforts of one individual influence those of other individuals. Because of this interdependence, game theory can be used to understand many failures and successes of collective action.[21] Applications of collective action include the provision of public goods and the correction of externalities. In recent years, global challenges from disease, global warming, transnational terrorism, tropical deforestation, acid rain, and other concerns have rekindled interest in the study of collective action.

The path-breaking work is Mancur Olson's (1965) *Logic of Collective Action*, which underscores that individual rationality is not sufficient for

---

[20] This is a message of Sandler (1998).

[21] On collective action, see Hardin (1982), Olson (1965), and Sandler (1992). Sandler (1992) examines the game theory aspects.

collective rationality. This is aptly illustrated by the following scenario involving a pure public good and ten potential contributors. Suppose that *each unit of the good* provides $10 in benefits to the contributor and all others owing to benefit nonrivalry and nonexcludability. Further suppose that each person must decide whether or not to contribute one unit. If each unit costs the contributor $15, then an individual's net gain from contributing alone is −$5 ($10 − $15), which confers a free-riding gain of $10 to each of the nine noncontributors. No matter how many people contribute, a noncontributor is $5 better off by free riding and thus would refrain from contributing. If all ten people are in similar situations, then no one contributes and society gains nothing. If, however, all ten were to contribute, then each would gain $85, which consists of the $100 of public good benefits from the ten units (each of which gives a $10 benefit) minus the individual's $15 cost of contributing one unit. Collective rationality requires everyone to contribute, while individual rationality requires everyone to take a free ride. The under-lying game is the Prisoners' Dilemma with a dominant strategy not to contribute. Even slight alterations to the institutional rules may lead to everyone's contributing. Suppose that the ten individuals agree to share costs no matter who contributes. Again consider the calculus of a lone contributor, who now pays only $1.50 ($15/10) owing to cost sharing with the other nine people. Based on the agreement, the net gain from contributing a unit is $8.50 ($10 − $1.50), so that everyone is motivated to contribute and collective rationality is achieved. Because everyone has agreed to share costs, there is no longer a gain from free riding; each individual's interests are now consistent with those of the collective.

Olson (1965) put forward three general principles or maxims of collective action, which he presented as universal truths:

1. The larger the collective, the more inefficient the outcome and the less likely that any collective action will be accomplished.
2. The more diverse the collective members' endowments, the greater the likelihood that the large, rich members will shoulder the burdens for the collective good of the smaller members. Moreover, a greater diversity of membership promotes the achievement of some collective action.
3. Collective action can be fostered by changes in the institu-tional rules and the presence of selective incentives or private inducements.

Although each of these statements is true for many important scenarios, they are not universally true unless qualified by some restrictive implicit assumptions.[22] The group size statement is true for Prisoners' Dilemma situations such as the one cited earlier: if there are ten people, the loss in efficiency is $85 per person; if, however, there are twenty people, the loss is $185. The proposition that the possibility of collective action may decline with group size holds if there are organizational costs. According to Olson (1965, p. 48), the share of the group's benefits going to a contributor is also important for collective action: "the larger the group, the smaller the share of the total benefit going to any individual, or to any (absolutely) small subset of members of the group, the less the likelihood that any small subset . . . will gain enough from getting the collective good to bear the burden . . ." This statement is true for our case where a unit costs $15 and provides a benefit of $10, and costs are not shared. But it is not true if costs are shared as just illustrated, since group size then brings down the opportunity costs of collective action.

The first part of the second statement is known as the exploitation hypothesis, whereby the rich underwrite the costs of the collective action for the poor. This hypothesis and suboptimality can be illustrated by the following example in which four fishing firms – denoted *A*, *B*, *C*, and *D* – with various fleet sizes are lobbying the government to defeat legislation that adds $100 in operating costs per vessel.[23] Assume that each firm can start only a single lobby to defeat the legislation. Further suppose that the likelihood of defeating the legislation increases with the number of lobbies. This chance of success is 30% with one lobby, 50% with two, 65% with three, and 70% with four. Finally, assume that the fleet sizes are: firm *A*, 100 vessels; firm *B*, 50 vessels; firm *C*, 30 vessels; and firm *D*, 20 vessels. If a lobby costs $1,000, then which firms will gain sufficiently from establishing a lobby? Firm *A* stands to gain $3,000, or the probability of success added by one lobby of 30% *times* the saving in operating costs on 100 vessels or $10,000. Since firm *A* stands to gain $3,000 in expected benefits at a cost of $1,000, it will form the first lobby, thereby conferring an expected benefit on the three smaller firms. A second lobby, financed by firm *B*, improves success by an added 20%, thus giving firm *B* an expected gain of $1,000, or 20% of 50 vessels × $100 from supporting a second lobby. This expected gain means that a second lobby is just feasible. No further lobbies can form under this scenario of independent firm behavior. Exploitation results because the two large firms do the lobbying for the two small firms, which free ride. Inefficiency is present insofar as four lobbies are justifiable from a collective viewpoint. For a fourth lobby, the expected savings to *all four firms* is

---

[22] See Sandler (1992, pp. 193–200) and Ostrom (1999).
[23] This example extends a somewhat similar analysis in Mueller (1989, Chapter 16).

$1,000 = .05 \times 200 \times \$100$, in which the marginal probability of success from a fourth lobby (.05) is multiplied by the savings in operating costs of the collective's entire 200 vessels. Thus, a fourth lobby adds as much in collective benefits as its cost of $1,000, and a third would add even more benefits than its cost.

The exploitation hypothesis is even clearer if each firm can open multiple lobbying offices. Given its large fleet size, firm A is the likely candidate to open multiple lobbies. Clearly, this firm can gain from opening a single lobby, as already shown, but can it gain from starting a second lobbying office? The answer is yes, since a second lobby yields firm A additional expected gains of $2,000 (.20 \times \$10,000) by raising the success probability to 50%, which more than offsets the additional $1,000 in lobbying costs. Even a third office is profitable, as its expected gain of $1,500 more than covers the added cost of $1,000. Firm A, however, will not gain from underwriting a fourth office, insofar as its expected gain of $500 (.05 \times \$10,000) does not cover its costs. When a firm can provide multiple offices, the possibility of exploitation grows worse. In this example, the large firm provides three offices for the three small firms, which do not support the lobbying – they could not have it better than this!

Exploitation shows up in the real world in many situations. For example, the large rich allies – the United States, the United Kingdom, and France – shouldered much of the defense burden for the small, poorer allies during the period that NATO relied on nuclear deterrence in the 1950s and 1960s.[24] Efforts in Bosnia and Kosovo were primarily supported by a few rich NATO nations. This exploitation is so prevalent today between rich and poor countries in providing collective action that I have characterized it as "free-riding aid" (Sandler 1998, p. 183). If the reader considers his or her own collectives in the community, instances of exploitation of the large are not difficult to spot. But there are notable exceptions, which rob Olson's proposition of maxim status. Consider the US-Israeli alliance, where Israel allocates a much greater percentage of its GDP to defense than does the United States. This aberration hinges on country-specific risks that Israel faces given its location surrounded by hostile countries. If, therefore, the small has a greater preference for the collective action than its larger counterparts, then preferences and not income may drive burden sharing and, in so doing, offset or reverse exploitation.

Olson's third maxim about institutional design also has much validity and provides significant policy direction. Selective incentives or side payments to participants may induce individuals to overcome free-rider

---

[24] This is established in Murdoch and Sandler (1982, 1984), Olson and Zeckhauser (1966), and Sandler and Hartley (1999).

tendencies. Revolutionaries may act despite the horrible retribution for failure if driven by the vast wealth and power that they will control if successful. Free riders in revolutions are unlikely to get this control. Analogously, the United States assumed a disproportionate burden in NATO because it obtained political concessions as its allies supported US positions.[25] The US Centers for Disease Control (CDC) coordinates efforts worldwide to monitor and address new diseases and outbreaks, because of increased paranoia in the United States that these diseases may arrive there. Thus, efforts to control tropical diseases, which may pose little initial threat to the United States, are closely followed. In this case, a selective incentive for the United States is its ability to decide the priorities in terms of which diseases get attention.

There are many design tricks that foster collective action, as high-lighted by the earlier cost-sharing example. For example, some collectives at the national level employ a federal structure, so that much of the action is initiated at the local level, where small groups are present and individuals' support of the collective action is very much noticed.[26] Labor unions use this organizing principle, as does the United Way charity. Other collectives bolster cooperation through selective incentives; thus, local stations of the Public Broadcasting Service (PBS) give out program guides and other donor-specific benefits to induce contributions through selective incentives. PBS organizes its campaign drives at the local level, like the United Way. Some organizations try to tie down a big contribution before starting a campaign drive involving smaller contributors and a designated target or threshold of support. The large contribution encourages smaller contributors to believe that the arbitrarily imposed threshold is now feasible and often induces others to add their support. The specific institutional innovations that promote collective action are not as important as the realization that institutional engineering can circumvent free riding and related impediments.

Olson's maxims are important because they are excellent rules of thumb. Had Olson been more circumspect, there is a real possibility that his legacy might not have been as great – this is a lesson that many social sciences need to learn. His *provocative* and easy-to-understand state-ments have meant that the general principles of collective action have influenced literally all branches of the social sciences and all fields of eco-nomics. In sociology, his maxims have changed the way that group behav-ior is viewed, because groups are no longer viewed as necessarily furthering the collective's well-being. The theory of collective action has much to offer for political science regarding the behavior of political

[25] This point was made by Morrow (1991).
[26] This is an organizing principle favored by Olson (1965).

parties, interest groups, and international organizations. In environmental studies, collective action is behind how treaties are framed to address transboundary pollutants and whether such treaties accomplish real gains. For example, pollutants involving mostly individual actions, such as driving vehicles, are harder to control than pollutants involving more concentrated actions, such as power plant emissions.[27] Thus, sulfur-induced acid rain stemming from power plants has been easier to correct than nitrogen-induced acid rain from vehicles. An understanding of why the Montreal Protocol curbing ozone-depleting substances was easier to achieve than a treaty limiting greenhouse gas emissions depends on a knowledge of collective action. For example, the Montreal Protocol had an easier time because only a small number of key polluting countries were needed to control ozone depleters, unlike the global-warming problem, which involves many more key players. There was also a greater overall asymmetry in the ozone-depletion problem, with production of CFCs concentrated in a small number of nations. When these nations discovered that there was a net gain from reducing their production and use of CFCs, even if acting alone, the collective action was well on its way to being achieved.[28]

Regional problems – for example, river pollution and acid rain – often involve few participants with more country-specific incentives and are easier to address than global problems. In the case of acid rain, selective incentives include the self-pollution avoided and recognition in the region as being a leader. As a general rule, the more localized the problem, the better the prognosis.

The study of collective action has many remaining puzzles. An important unanswered question concerns collective action among generations in maintaining economic sustainability. I am always amazed when I walk around the magnificent churches of Europe, such as York Minster, how multiple generations carried on the dreams and aspirations of previous generations until the church was finished. What makes generations work collectively in an effective manner for some goals and not for others? If this question can be answered, then humanity can achieve more farsighted collective action (see Chapter 10). Further study is also required on institutional design that promotes more effective collection action. The influence of participant heterogeneity also needs additional analysis. How, for instance, should tastes and incomes be distributed within a collective to foster more effective collective outcomes? Surely, the desired distribution varies among alternative collective action

---

[27] Thus, Murdoch, Sandler, and Sargent (1997) show that sulfur emissions from power plants are easier to control than nitrogen oxide emissions from vehicles.

[28] See the discussion in Benedick (1991) and Sandler (1997, pp. 106–15).

difficulties. Another question that is just being analyzed concerns the efficacy of partial cooperation, in which the collective includes only a subset of those affected by the action.[29] The real issue is how effective the noncooperators are in undoing the accomplishments achieved by the cooperators.

PROGNOSIS FOR PUBLIC ECONOMICS AND COLLECTIVE ACTION

Public economics will continue to blossom as a field in the new century. As economics regains its relevancy and preoccupation with political economy, public economics will increase in importance. From its origin, public economics has had a significant empirical component to test its theoretical advances. By their very nature, the topics of public economics have real-world relevancy, because this entire field is grounded in public policy concerns. Recent theories of public goods provision have a minimalist simplicity and elegance that allows for much future development and embellishment.[30] In addition, recent findings – for example, the idea that income redistribution may not influence the undersupply of public goods – have a surprising, novel character. In short, public economics possesses the four essential ingredients for staying power.

In the next decade, public economics will undergo a number of transformations. First, it will consider larger governmental units, such as supranational structures. Recent developments in the European Union are foreshadowing this need. Loose structures in the form of treaties will gain importance as transboundary externalities and transnational public goods are addressed in a world of growing interdependency. Second, there will be further work on understanding the linkage between allocation and distribution issues. Third, there will be an improved integration between the revenue side of taxation and the expenditure side. How public goods are financed has much to say about allocative efficiency, and vice versa.

In Chapter 1, I have ready made the case that collective action theory has staying power owing to it simplicity, which makes it widely accessible to so many disciplines. The applicability of collective action is ubiquitous and concerns all levels of human society and its governance. The theory is testable both in the laboratory (Ostrom 1999) and from empirical data. As the theory has developed, novel insights about institutional design and other issues have emerged.

---

[29] An initial analysis is contained in Buchholz, Haslbeck, and Sandler (1998).

[30] See, especially, the private provision of public goods model in Cornes and Sandler (1985, 1996) and Warr (1983).

5 Government for the Politician? Public and Social Choice

Have you ever wondered why discount stores all locate in the same parts of the city, and are typically right next to one another? This is also true of car dealers, bookshops, furniture stores, antique dealers, and fast-food restaurants. Travel to other countries and you observe the same phenomenon. What does this clustering of similar stores have to do with candidates in two-party elections espousing almost identical positions? Among the major candidates who ran for US president in the 2000 primary campaign, it was virtually impossible from listening to their positions – if they bothered to reveal one – to know their party affiliations. Is John McCain a Republican or a Democrat? The same question could be asked about Bill Bradley. Party labels have become less descriptive of candidates' positions. This is not only true in the United States; for example, is Britain's Tony Blair a Tory or a Labour Party member? The field of public choice, which applies economic methods to the study of political science, addresses the convergence of candidates' platforms as well as myriad other questions. These questions include the following. Does a multiparty system provide more choice than its two-party counterpart? Does logrolling serve a useful purpose, or does it lead inevitably to too much government as vote trading allows for the passage of more spending programs? Can majority rule lead to the efficient provision of public goods? And then there is the ultimate question: are governments run in the interests of the people or of the elected politicians?

In the last chapter governments were seen as a necessary evil, needed to provide an infrastructure that allows markets to flourish. Governments also supply public goods, correct externalities, and engineer ideal income distributions. Essentially, public choice focuses on how governments perform when controlled by self-interested, rational actors. By contrast, social choice takes a more ideal or normative view of how individuals' preferences should be reflected in social decisions.[1] Both public choice and social choice have had a profound influence on economic policy during the last fifty years by lowering expectations of policy effectiveness and indicating alternative nongovernmental remedies. Thanks to these two areas of study, economists and political scientists distinguish between the intentions of a policy prescription and its actual accomplishments. Governments are no longer viewed as necessarily benevolent institutions that always further the interests of their constituencies. Since there is no escaping some level of government, an evaluation of its performance and how this performance can be improved are of considerable interest. Modern economies, with anywhere from a quarter to 60% of GDP devoted to the public sector, can ill-afford to ignore such concerns.

Many novel insights of public and social choice are nothing short of revolutionary and, in some instances, rather depressing. From the study of public choice, the supply of public goods is understood to be as vital as their demand. In addition, public choice teaches us that democracy may lead to a tyranny of the majority and, in still other cases, may result in a tyranny of the minority. The former may occur when the majority institutes taxes that burden those who do not benefit from the publicly provided good, while the latter may occur when a small plurality decides tax and spending programs that adversely impact most citizens. Another disturbing finding indicates that, with sufficient disagreement among voters' tastes, any outcome may follow depending on who controls the sequence of votes and/or the voting rules.[2] I once told this to some disbelieving department members when I was on the faculty at the University of Wyoming and was challenged to prove it. When, a week later, I was elected to the university's promotion and tenure committee as the college representative after having been given control of the election procedures by the dean, I was never challenged by these colleagues again, nor was I ever again given this responsibility!

Social choice indicates that the consistency of choice displayed by individual decision makers may not be inherited by social decisions, even when they are based on these consistent individual preferences. In fact, Arrow's (1963) impossibility theorem tells us that there is no social choice procedure that passes some minimal set of ethical criteria, which includes a consistency criterion. Welfare economics, which evaluates the consequences of economic policy on the well-being of individuals, is

---

[1] Some of the seminal books in public choice include Black (1958), Buchanan and Tullock (1962), Downs (1957), Niskanen (1971), and Riker (1962). Unquestionably, the two most important books in social choice are Arrow (1963) and Sen (1970).

[2] This has been referred to as voting "chaos" (Kelly 1988, Chapters 3–4). Also see Craven (1992), Mueller (1989), Plott and Levine (1978), Riker (1986), and Sen (1970).

based on achieving a higher level of welfare as measured by some aggregate social welfare function (SWF).[3] A social planner's SWF aggregates over individuals' utilities (that is, the satisfaction that they derive) and indicates some overall well-being of society for various states of the world. In going from individual to social well-being, the SWF places different weights on the utilities of the constituency, and these weights reflect some ethical norm. If higher weights were placed on those individuals with lower satisfaction levels, then this SWF would reflect some kind of egalitarian norm. Social choice cautions that, if tastes differ greatly, it is exceedingly difficult to go from individual utility levels to the social welfare level when constructing the SWF. If there is no means to judge social welfare and its improvement, then economic policy cannot be evaluated. The doubts cast on the SWF by social choice brought a pessimism that shook the very foundations of economic analysis. Thus, social choice findings were indeed revolutionary and quite sobering.

WHAT IS PUBLIC CHOICE?

Public choice applies economic methods to study topics drawn from political science. In particular, public choice is concerned with nonmarket decision making involving public goods, externalities, and income redistribution. Other topics involve campaign strategies, platform formulation, voters' behavior, lobbying, constitutional choice, and bureaucratic decision making. Political agents – for example, voters, bureaucrats, elected officials, constituents, political parties, and revolutionaries – are viewed by public choice as maximizing some objective, subject to one or more constraints on behavior. Relevant constraints may reflect resource scarcity or institutional influences. Institutional constraints can stem from reelection criteria or campaign fund-raising rules. If, for example, these financing rules inhibit the candidate's ability to maximize his or her objective, whatever this may be, then he or she is expected to discover ways of circumventing these rules, even if this circumvention is not in the public interest. Leave open a loophole, and the candidate will exploit it fully. Thus, one has a picture of American politics today, with all of the candidates complaining about the need for campaign reform, and no one doing anything but becoming better at minimizing the impact of these constraints. In contrast to traditional political science, public choice does not characterize political agents as always pursuing the public interest in carrying out the responsibilities entrusted to them.

Public choice increasingly incorporates strategic behavior in terms of game theory, so that political agents are viewed as operating in an inter-

---

[3] On welfare economics, see Boadway and Bruce (1984) and Johansson (1991).

active fashion. For example, a candidate's choices depend on what he or she thinks that the opponent will do, and so it goes for the opponent. Consider a candidate's choice of a platform, in which each of two candidates (myself and an opponent) must take positions on alternative issues to achieve a winning majority. Suppose that the candidates must decide which of three spending issues to support, where each issue is favored by just one of the *three-voter* constituency. Further suppose that each voter favors passage of one issue more than he or she dislikes the other two issues combined, so that *passage of all three issues* makes each voter better off in a net sense than the defeat of all three issues. If my opponent announces nonsupport of all three issues because each only benefits one person, then I can gain a unanimous victory by announcing my support for all three issues, since each issue is intensely favored by its supporter. In fact, any platform in this example that is announced *second* can muster a winning majority.[4] For example, once I reveal my support for all three spending initiatives, the other candidate can now defeat me by supporting any two and opposing the third. My opponent's platform to support two initiatives improves the well-being of two of the voters, a bare majority, who get their favored proposal and do not have to be taxed for one of the two projects that they oppose. If, however, I first announced my support for two of the three initiatives, I can still be defeated by a candidate who then supports just one of those two initiatives. This follows because the voter in favor of the initiative supported will vote for this other candidate, since this voter is not then taxed for the other initiatives. Moreover, the other voter who is not in favor of the initiatives that I support does better with this other candidate too, since his or her taxes are also reduced. Two of three voters – a bare majority – can again be expected to support the second-announced platform, and so defeat me. This example illustrates a crucial public choice insight: announcing a platform first usually leads to a strategic *disadvantage*. Thus, it is no wonder that candidates talk circuitously and leave the voters in the dark about their stands on so many issues.

Public choice yields numerous novel insights. First, it explains why candidates assume similar platforms in a two-party system, as shown in the next section. Second, public choice demonstrates that individuals may rationally choose not to vote if they view their expected gain from voting to be less than the hassle associated with voting. If one's vote has a small likelihood of determining the outcome, then this expected gain from voting, which equals the probability of making a difference times

---

[4] See Downs (1957) and Mueller (1989, pp. 183–4). Examples such as this one, with just three voters and three issues, are sufficient to make the point while keeping the analysis simple. Many public choice analyses have just a few voters and issues.

the net gain from one's favored position, is small and may consequently justify staying home. Even a little rainfall may be enough to limit voter turnout. There will still be those who vote if they value civic duty. Third, public choice establishes that, for proportional representation where seats are allocated to a party based on the proportion of votes won in the election, multiple parties exist with distinct positions. If no party gains a majority of seats, then the coalition government that is formed often involves a *minimal winning coalition* or just enough seats to govern, because larger coalitions are not required to rule and would have to share the gains from power with a larger set of interests when making policies.[5] Fourth, public choice teaches us that, for issues involving redistribution, virtually any position can win depending on the order that positions are taken up in the sequence of vote comparisons. This means that the person who controls the agenda or voting sequence can strongly influence the outcome. Fifth, public choice shows that lobbying may, but need not, result in too much government. Sixth, public choice findings indicate that majority rule is unlikely to achieve efficient outcomes – another disappointing realization. Seventh, actions taken by interest groups are judged to create, at times, tremendous wastes for society as these groups focus on their own gain and ignore the inefficient consequences of their actions. Eighth, candidates are characterized as adopting platforms with simple right-left distinctions to simplify choice in the complicated reality of multidimensional platforms (Downs 1957). Thus, candidates appeal to labels like Democrat and Republican, or tax-and-spend liberal and fiscal conservative, to focus voters on a single-dimensional choice. Ninth, public choice also warns that the competition to influence legislative outcomes can lead to wasteful competitive behavior known as rent seeking.[6] This list is by no means exhaustive.

SOME BASIC PARADIGMS

I shall now return to answer the location question posed at the outset. In a classic paper, Harold Hotelling (1929) introduced the notion of spatial competition, where competitive firms selling identical products gravitate to the center of their market to be near as many customers as possible. If customers are evenly distributed along an eleven-mile-long road, the firm positioned at the six-mile post will be nearer to more customers than a firm at the eight-mile or two-mile post. In fact, the center

---

[5] This is based on Riker's (1962) theory of a minimal winning coalition, which assumes simple majority-rule decision making and zero-sum games of redistribution.

[6] The first article on rent seeking is Tullock (1967). Other influential articles include Bhagwati and Srinivasan (1980) and Krueger (1974). Also see Buchanan, Tollison, and Tullock (1980).

location outdoes any other for minimizing the distance to the most customers. With identical products, a firm's competitive advantage hinges
on being close to the most customers, so that their effective price, which
includes commuting costs, is kept low. The customer will buy from the
nearest merchant. To maximize their profits, firms selling identical wares
move to the center of their market, and clustering is observed. A stark
example of this tendency is the strategic placement of pay toilets (or
phones) by competitors in a park where activities are evenly spread over
the grounds. A toilet in the exact geographical center of the park will
outdo any alternative location for customers, leading all entrepreneurs
to site their toilets together.

Next consider the level of spending in a referendum where there are
five voters labeled *A–E*. The voters' ideal spending levels are as follows:
$200, voter *A*; $350, voter *B*; $800, voter *C*; $1,000, voter *D*; and $1,400,
voter *E*. Further suppose that each voter becomes more dissatisfied as
the spending level is further from his or her ideal. Thus, voter *A* prefers
a spending bill of $800 more than one for $1,000, and still more than one
for $1,400; while voter *D* prefers a spending bill of $800 more than one
for $350, and still more than one for $200. If this five-person committee
must support by majority rule one of these five positions, only the middle
or *median* position of $800, the position of voter *C*, can defeat all the
others by majority rule. That is, both voters *A* and *B* will support *C*'s
spending position over those of voters *D* and *E* to spend more. Similarly,
voters *D* and *E* will support *C*'s spending position over those of voters
A and *B* to spend less. A majority supports *C*'s median position over the
four alternatives.

Next suppose that a spending issue is being decided by a large group
of *n* voters with ideal or most preferred spending levels normally distributed over some range of spending alternatives. The normal or bell-
shaped distribution of voters' ideal spending levels is symmetric about
its median position, with at least *n*/2 voters' ideal levels either equal to
or to the right (left) of the median. The median position can defeat any
smaller or larger spending level, because a majority of voters prefer the
median level of spending to these other levels.

Finally, assume that a candidate is running for election and must
assume a single position along a left-right political spectrum, along which
right (left) has the standard designation of conservative (liberal). For a
normal distribution of voters' ideal political identifications, the median
position is unbeatable. To illustrate, consider Figure 5.1, where candidates' positions are indicated along the horizontal axis, and the *number
of voters* whose ideal (or most preferred) left-right identification corresponds to each political position is measured on the vertical axis. A candidate who assumes a position *L* in Figure 5.1 to the left of the median

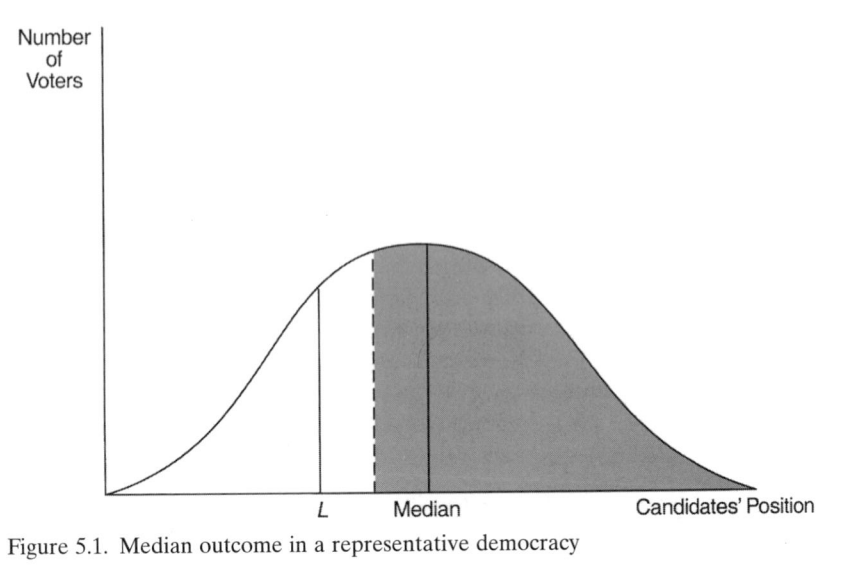

Figure 5.1. Median outcome in a representative democracy

loses to a candidate taking the median position. This follows because the candidate at L loses all voters whose ideal identifications are to the right of the median as well as those whose ideal identifications are to the right of the halfway position between position L and the median, denoted by the dashed line. This outcome is based on voters' supporting the candidate whose position is closest to their ideal identification. Because this loss of voters constitutes well over half of the voters, as denoted by the shaded region, the candidate espousing the median identification beats the one at L. Similarly, the median position defeats any position to the left or right of the median. Candidates are best off adopting positions as close to the median as possible and, consequently, as close to one another's platforms as feasible.

As is true with any theoretical development, things can become more complicated if, say, the distribution of voters' most desired positions is not symmetric, or if preferences are not so well-behaved – that is, always decreasing as one moves away from a person's ideal position. Even with these assumptions relaxed, the center position may still have the same attraction, except when the voter becomes alienated and does not vote if his or her position is too far from those of the candidates.[7] This median voter result is quite illustrative of public choice methods and results. For example, public choice borrows from other areas of economics to enlighten us about political processes and outcomes. In this case, the median voter analysis derives directly from Hotelling's spatial competi-

---

[7] For more details, the reader should consult Hinich and Munger (1997) or Mueller (1989).

tion. Thus, firms cluster at the same locations for *precisely* the same reasons that candidates take on identical positions in a two-party system – that is, clustering maximizes one's "market." This analysis also highlights how public choice is adept at simplifying a question by reducing it to its most elementary parts. It is common in public choice to consider three or four voters (as I did above) and/or a handful of issues, since these representations capture the essentials of a problem. The median voter analysis has a powerful empirical implication: when the median voter can be identified, his or her demand for a public good will be that of society. If, for example, the median voter is the person with the median income, then focusing on this person will tell us what the majority of society demands in schooling or other public goods. In practice, this identification is difficult.[8]

Another important public choice analysis involves the constitutional choice of the voting rule to decide various kinds of issues. The constitutional stage is determined prior to voting and legislating, and involves establishing procedures for choosing among different positions. Buchanan and Tullock (1962) conceptualized this choice as minimizing the costs associated with alternative sizes of the required majority to win. There are two relevant costs associated with this majority: political externality costs and decision-making costs. Political externality costs represent the burdens imposed on those in the loser group when a vote decides a policy. If the required majority is unanimity, then these political externality costs are zero, because each person would only support positions that made him or her better off. If, instead, a simple majority is required, then those in the minority may prefer the status quo to the winning outcome and, thus, endure a loss of well-being as the policy is implemented. The smaller the required majority, the larger the political externality costs as the decision is imposed on a greater number of losers. A required majority of one-half plus one results in more external costs than one of two-thirds. A dictatorship has the greatest political externality costs. As the required majority increases, the political externality costs fall, reaching zero at unanimity. For any required majority less than unanimity, there is a tyranny over the minority in the form of these external costs.

Decision-making costs refer to resources, including time, spent to redefine issues to achieve the required majority. These costs are virtually zero for a dictator who knows his or her own mind. As the number of votes needed to win increases, decision-making costs also increase, since an issue must be redefined to please a greater number of required

---

[8] Median income is not necessarily associated with the identification of the median voter – see Bergstrom and Goodman (1973) and Borcherding and Deacon (1972).

supporters. These costs are greatest when the required majority is unanimity. Contemplate for a moment how long it would take for the US House of Representatives to decide issues by unanimity voting. By the time the issue had been sufficiently reworded to pass, it would be unlikely to bear much resemblance to the original motion. Thus, there is a clear trade-off associated with increasing the required majority, as decision-making costs rise but political externality costs fall. At the point at which the fall in political externality costs matches the rise in decision-making costs from including another voter in the required majority, *an optimal majority is reached*. Issues that are associated with greater externality costs, other things constant, will justify a greater majority. This may explain why a two-thirds majority is needed to ratify treaties in the US Senate or to overturn a presidential veto. Similarly, high political externality costs may have resulted in unanimity as the decision rule for UN Security Council actions or decisions taken by the Joint Chiefs of Staff in the United States. The NATO alliance requires unanimity when approving military actions or an enlargement of membership.

By choosing the voting procedures, the constitutional stage helps define the bounds of the tyranny over those on the losing side. Another implication of this constitutional analysis is that society is apt to have winners and losers when policies are implemented. Unanimity voting eliminates losers but at the price to everyone of large resource outlays needed to obtain universal support of decisions, which may not achieve much owing to the compromises engineered to please everyone. Invariably, democracies require trade-offs, and we thus observe majority rule far more frequently than unanimity. Some tyranny over losers characterizes every democracy.

I cannot resist relating the choice of voting rule for president at the constitutional stage to the 2000 US presidential election, where winning the popular vote did not assure Al Gore the victory. Making the presidential election hinge on who wins the majority of the votes in the electoral college was engineered by the founding fathers to appease the smaller states, which feared that a minority of more-populated states could otherwise control the election outcome. This compromise served to muster the required unanimity among the states at the constitutional stage. Since an amendment doing away with the electoral college requires ratification by three-quarters of the states, the electoral college is here to stay, despite the chaos following the 2000 election. Amendments were considered by the founding fathers to have serious political externality costs, hence the large required majority. It was impossible for the framers of the Constitution to have foreseen voting machines that did not always work. Had they foreseen the result of the 2000 election, they might merely have excluded Florida from the electoral college!

Consider next the implications of logrolling, where issues that would not pass by simple majority rule can be made to pass if voters feel strongly enough about an issue to support another issue that they oppose in order to gain a majority through vote trading. Logrolling is a simple case of "you scratch my back, I'll scratch yours." To illustrate the analysis in its simplest form, consider just three voters – A, B, and C – who must vote on two different spending bills, X and Y. Suppose that each spending bill costs 9, and the expense is evenly shared among the voters, so that they pay 3 apiece for each bill that passes. Further suppose that voter A gains nothing from the passage of either spending bill, so that her net gain is –3 from either bill's passage. Voter B is assumed to realize a net gain of 7 from the passage of bill X after his assigned cost of 3 is deducted from an assumed gross gain of 10. Insofar as he has no interest in bill Y, his net gain from its passage is –3, or just his cost obligation. In contrast, voter C is assumed to realize a net gain of 11 from the passage of bill Y after her cost share is deducted from her gross gain of 14. These net payoffs are displayed in the left-hand matrix in Figure 5.2.

If bill X is considered in isolation, then it fails because a majority – voters A and C – opposes it. If bill Y is considered in isolation, it too fails, as voters A and B opposes its passage. Without vote trading, neither bill passes. When, however, voters consider their net position from the passage of *both* X and Y through logrolling, both bills pass. By trading his vote on bill Y for C's support of bill X, voter B makes a net gain of 4 (7 – 3). Similarly, voter C achieves a net gain of 8 (11 – 3) if her support of bill X garners her B's support on bill Y. Thus, the left-hand matrix is a case where issues that cannot pass on their own can muster a majority through vote trading. With this vote trade, society achieves a net gain of 6 (8 + 4 – 6) from the passage of the two bills when the three voters' net

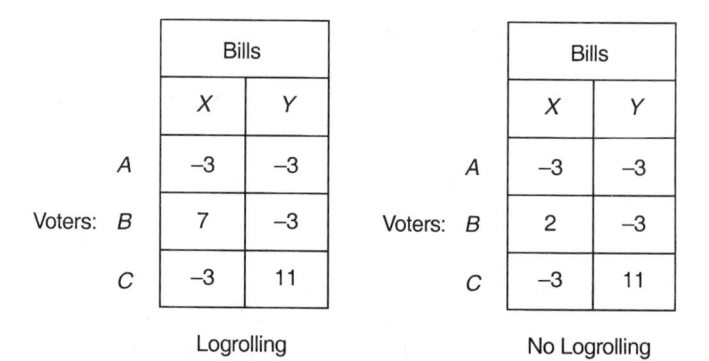

Figure 5.2. Voters' payoffs and logrolling

gains are summed. Thus, logrolling can potentially improve total social welfare if we allow for these interpersonal comparisons of well-being. If the vote traders realize a sufficient gain, they can potentially compensate the loser(s) – just voter A in the example – and remain gainers, allowing for a conclusion that *logrolling does not necessarily lead to too much government*.

Unfortunately, other, less optimistic logrolling scenarios are possible. For instance, suppose that we change just voter C's gross payoff from bill Y's passage from 14 to 7, so that the bottom right-hand cell in the left-hand matrix of Figure 5.2 would contain a net payoff of 4 (all other payoffs are unchanged). Now the net gain to society is −1, and logrolling is causing too much spending. Such a scenario can result in a tyranny of a minority in which the overall losses to society exceed the resulting gains from the vote trade. Surely, one can find many instances of pork-barrel politics with this kind of outcome. It is even grimmer in a representative democracy, for which the payoffs in Figure 5.2 are those of the representative and not necessarily those of his or her constituency. Thus, passage of bill X may make B better off because he receives support from a lobby interest that gains disproportionately from its passage. The net gain to B does not necessarily mean that his entire constituency realizes a net gain. When this constituency does not get a net gain in B's district, logrolling can be viewed as excessive. No wonder that a heavily lobbied defense project like the Osprey, which can be both a helicopter and a plane, remains funded even though the military has its doubts about the feasibility and mission of the Osprey and significant cost overruns have plagued its development. The Osprey concept seems worthy of the pages of a Kurt Vonnegut novel!

In the right-hand matrix of Figure 5.2, voter B's gross benefit from bill X has been reduced to 5, so that his net benefit is now 2. The other payoffs are unchanged from the first example. Logrolling is not possible for this second example, because voter B no longer realizes a net gain from the trade insofar as his interest in X does not offset his disinterest in Y. This highlights the importance of intense support for some issues if a logrolling situation is to result.

Public choice also provides insights about alternative voting procedures and rules for committee choices. Suppose that an academic department has invited five candidates for a job interview, and a vote must be taken to choose one. With enough diversity of preferences among the department members, it is unlikely that any candidate can command a majority of votes. Plurality rule could result in a winning candidate who is intensely favored by a few department members and ranked the lowest by all others. Under these circumstances, the plurality winner would be a poor choice, since some other candidate may be more acceptable to

V_1	V_2	V_3	V_4	V_5	V_6	V_7
W	W	W	X	X	Y	Y
X	X	X	Y	Y	Z	Z
Y	Y	Y	Z	Z	W	W
Z	Z	Z	W	W	X	X

Figure 5.3. A preference profile for seven voters

almost everyone. If a candidate defeats all other candidates in pairwise majority rule comparisons, then this candidate has much to offer. Such a candidate is said to pass the *Condorcet criterion* of pairwise comparisons. Another voting rule is a Borda count, according to which each committee member ranks the candidates from highest to lowest. If there are m candidates, the voter assigns 1 to his or her first choice, 2 to the second choice, and so on. The candidate whose rank total is the lowest is declared the winner. Yet another voting rule is approval voting, where each committee member votes for any number of acceptable candidates and the candidate with the most votes wins. Many other alternatives to majority rule exist, including runoff elections and elimination schemes involving either the most last-place votes or the fewest first-place votes.[9]

To demonstrate briefly a few of these voting rules, consider Figure 5.3, which displays the preference profile for a seven-person committee over four candidates. The persons or voters are denoted by V_1 to V_7, while the candidates or choices are indicated by W, X, Y, and Z. Each voter's preferences are read in a downward fashion, so that V_1 prefers W the most, X the second most, Y the next to last, and Z the least. For the preferences listed in Figure 5.3, there is no simple majority-rule winner, since no candidate receives four first-place votes, but there is a plurality winner, W, with three first-place votes. Moreover, there is no Condorcet winner, since X beats Y and Z, but not W, whereas W beats X but no one else. No alternative defeats all three of the others. If the alternatives are ranked from 1 to 4 by each voter, then Y is the Borda count winner, since her total of 15 is the lowest. X is second with a total of 16; W is third with a total of 17; and Z is last with a total of 22. This example is particularly fascinating, because if we eliminate the loser, Z, and then take a Borda count over the remaining three alternatives, the preference ordering of society is now reversed![10] That is, the rank totals are 13 for W, 14 for X, and 15 for Y, so that W is first, followed by X, and Y is last.

---

[9] Mueller (1989, Chapter 7) has a discussion of these alternative voting rules. Also see Ordeshook (1986).

[10] This "preference for winner-turns-loser" paradox is taken from Ordeshook (1986, p. 69).

The preference ordering over X, Y, and W has been reversed when a seemingly inconsequential choice is eliminated. Thus, the ordering of the subset of alternatives, which has not changed with the removal of Z, is not the sole determinant of the winner of the Borda count. Seemingly unimportant alternatives matter for a Borda count.

The importance of the voting rule, which is part of the agenda setter's choice, is important insofar as different voting rules can result in drastically different outcomes. In Figure 5.3, an approval vote where each voter casts his or her vote for the two candidates of whom he or she most approve makes X the winner, while Y is the winner with a Borda count. But with plurality rule, W wins. If there is sufficient diversity of preferences, an astute agenda setter can get almost any outcome, as I demonstrated to my colleagues in Wyoming when I was elected to the promotion and tenure committee.

Each voting rule has its strengths and weaknesses. Roughly speaking, desirable properties of a voting rule include being decisive, demonstrating ease of implementation, choosing broadly acceptable candidates, picking Condorcet winners, and promoting honest voting. Decisiveness simply means that some outcome is reached by the rule, while ease of implementation refers, among other things, to a decision's being reached in a single polling. For example, runoff elections may require multiple elections. Although a candidate is favored intensely by a minority, the voting procedure should not choose this candidate if he or she is anathema to most voters. If a Condorcet winner exists, it makes sense that acceptable rules should pick this alternative, since a candidate who beats all others in head-to-head contests has much to recommend him. A procedure like the Borda count does well on this score even when the number of candidates is large.[11] Strategic voting occurs when voters can alter the election outcome in their favor by misrepresenting their preferences. Again consider the preference profile in Figure 5.3. Suppose that both V_4 and V_5 switch their rankings of Z and Y, so that they represent Z as their next-best choice and Y as their third choice. The Borda count winner is now these two voters' top choice, X. Being immune to this kind of dissembling is known as being *strategy-proof*, which is not possessed by the Borda count.

No voting rule scores high on all reasonable criteria; however, approval voting and the Borda count do well on most criteria. As my department's resident "expert," these are the two that I recommend. If a Borda count is used, then *all* candidates must be ranked; a Borda count that calls for the ranking of only a subset can give widely

---

[11] See, for example, Mueller (1989, p. 115).

different election outcomes depending on how many candidates are ranked.

The study of alternative voting rules has highlighted the power of the agenda setter and the trade-offs involved when a committee chooses among three or more choices. I must emphasize "three or more," because all voting rules give the same outcome in a two-candidate election. This study also underscores that the choice of voting rule has a smaller influence as preference profiles display less diversity of tastes. It is no wonder that business boards, chairman's advisory committees, and student associations' executive councils often include members with similar views, insofar as decisions thereby become easy to reach and do not typically vary with alternative decision rules. Of course, the downside is that diverse tastes and interests – minority or majority – are not reflected in decisions, and there is no one to tell the chairman or executive decision maker that he or she is "naked" when a particularly stupid decision is about to be implemented. Many of my readers have surely observed this phenomenon at their own institutions!

AN EVALUATION OF PUBLIC CHOICE

Public choice possesses many of the ingredients needed for staying power. Its basic principles rest on simple concepts and analysis, as some of the examples in the last section so aptly illustrate. Moreover, public choice analysis is novel, testable, and applicable. Nevertheless, there are some disturbing trends in public choice that can limit its appeal and long-run influence. Much of its analysis is extremely pessimistic. I recall writing a review of a public choice book on government welfare programs some years back that did not identify a single success for such programs.[12] Because income distribution will never be ideal from a social viewpoint, and some public goods will have to be provided, a government sector is inevitable. The pitfalls of government must, of course, be identified, but the analysis is not complete unless better institutional arrangements are recommended. I often wonder whether this negativism, in the case of public choice, comes from the researchers' ideological antigovernment attitudes. My concern is not directed at the founding fathers of the field, who have been constructive, but rather to some of their disciples. A second worrying trend is the field's rush to formalism, which is frequently poorly motivated by the author. A prime example of this is an article that I once read, whose author shall remain nameless, that used advanced mathematics to demonstrate that an

---

[12] The book was Silver (1980), *Affluence, Altruism, and Atrophy: The Decline of Welfare States.*

incumbent has an advantage in an election. Could anyone have doubted this finding before struggling through thirty pages of mathematics? If I had any doubts about an incumbent's advantage it was after I read the article and reflected upon all of the assumptions needed for the demonstration! This example also represents a third disturbing trend in public choice, which is that many of its insights are not novel. One must wonder how many models are really needed to show the wastes associated with rent seeking. Some new insights, rivaling those of the early classics, are needed in the field.

Perhaps the recent decline in the share of US GDP devoted to government expenditure is due in part to the realization brought about by public choice studies that governmental policies may fail owing to the self-interest or incomplete information of elected officials. Much of the government bashing by economists comes with hindsight (Nowell and Tschirhart 1993). If public choice analysis were more constructive and focused on the design of better policies and institutions, then government's performance could be improved. Too often, economists are not present when policies are being formulated, but surface quickly to criticize a failed action.

SOCIAL CHOICE AND ANYTHING GOES?

Consider the following preference profile for three diverse voters:

$$V_1: xyz$$
$$V_2: yzx$$
$$V_3: zxy$$

where V_i again denotes the ith voter. For voter 1, the ordering xyz indicates that this voter likes x best, then y, and finally z. The other voters' preferences are interpreted similarly. This preference profile is known as the *voting paradox*.[13] Clearly, these three voters do not agree on anything, holding different views for first, second, and third place. Plurality rule cannot come up with a single winner, because each of the three options – x, y, and z – gets a single first-best vote, making all three plurality winners. Even a Borda count is stymied to identify a single winner. Furthermore, there is no Condorcet winner, because each option can beat just one other in a direct comparison. This example is particularly interesting because the order of pairwise comparisons allows any option to win, thus giving the agenda setter who determines the sequence of votes complete power over the outcome. This is shown as follows.[14] If x

[13] For extended analyses of the voting paradox, see Arrow (1963), Craven (1992), Hinich and Munger (1997), Kelly (1988), Mueller (1989), Ordeshook (1986), and Sen (1979).
[14] Remember, if two voters prefer x to y, then x wins, as is true in the example.

and y are paired first and then the winner (x) paired against z, z wins; if, alternatively, y and z are paired first and then the winner (y) is paired against x, x wins. The final sequence with x and z paired first permits y to win. With this diversity of views, anything can happen, as claimed under paired majority comparisons. Of course, one might object that this preference profile is rather extreme, but this is not at all true. Any set of policy options that involves a redistribution of income among the voters can have such a preference profile.[15] This voters' profile illustrates beautifully that, with a mere three voters and three choices, things can get pretty weird.

BASIC MESSAGE OF SOCIAL CHOICE

An essential message of social choice theory is *that well-behaved individual preferences are not sufficient for well-behaved social preferences.* Individual preferences are well-behaved if a choice can always be made and if an individual's ranking of alternative choices is consistent or transitive.[16] A person prefers x over y, denoted by xPy, if his or her well-being is greater with x than y. If given a chance to have either, a person chooses x when xPy. Preferences are transitive when someone who prefers x to y, and y to z, also prefers x to z.

To give an inkling of the difficulties in moving from individual preferences to those of society, I again consider the voting paradox profile of the previous section. Suppose that social preference (P_s) is defined over simple majority rule – that is, if a majority of voters prefer x to y, then x is preferred by society to y, or xP_sy. Since both V_1 and V_3 prefer x to y, we have xP_sy. Similarly, V_1 and V_2 prefer y to z, so that yP_sz. When x and z are compared by majority rule, V_2 and V_3 prefer z to x, so that zP_sx, which completes a cycle – $xP_syP_szP_sx$. This cycle implies an intransitivity or inconsistency because society cannot prefer x to itself.

Kenneth Arrow won the Nobel Prize in 1972 in part for the Arrow paradox, for which no social choice process exists that can satisfy five "reasonable" and minimal assumptions.[17] The first assumption, *the unanimity principle*, requires that a social ordering preserve any set of individuals' orderings between two alternatives that is unopposed by any

---

[15] See Kelly (1988, Chapter 3) and Mueller (1989, Chapter 5).

[16] Strictly speaking, if an individual's indifference relationship is transitive, then one can show that the individual's preference ordering is also transitive. Preferences are also assumed to be complete and monotone. Preferences are complete when some ordering, even indifference, is held by each person, while preferences are monotone if more of a good is preferred to less. See Kelly (1988) for details.

[17] This is shown in Arrow (1963), originally published in 1951. The theorem is discussed in Kelly (1988) and Sen (1979).

other person's preference over these alternatives. If, for example, everyone ranks x higher than y and no one ranks them opposite, then society should prefer x to y. A second assumption of *nondictatorship* mandates that no individual's preference ordering over two alternatives be decisive for society when opposed by all others; thus, no one has dictatorial powers over two or more alternatives. A third assumption is that social preference or indifference is *transitive*. *Universal* or *unrestricted domain*, whereby all possible orderings for individual preferences are allowed, is the fourth assumption. Quite simply, all voting profiles, even that of the voting paradox, are admissible; there is no culling of dissent. The most difficult, and controversial, assumption is the independence of the irrelevant alternative, in which the social choice between two or more alternatives depends only on the ordering over these alternatives. The earlier "winner-turn-loser" example for a Borda count violates this fifth assumption, because the "irrelevant" loser alternative was not irrelevant at all and could reverse the outcome of the choice over the other three alternatives.

Arrow's logic is impeccable (Plott and Levine 1978). If one accepts the "reasonableness" of his five minimal requirements, there is no escaping the disappointment that one cannot necessarily go from any set of individual preferences to a social choice unless consistency or dictatorship is compromised. Neither compromise appears acceptable. So-called "escapes" hinge on relaxing one or more of the five assumptions and do not constitute true escapes. The seminal work on devising "escapes" or "possibility theorems" is by Amartya Sen, whose work received the Nobel Prize in 1998.

An alert reader should now be wondering how a median voter could be decisive for society, as shown in Chapter 4, or how committees manage to decide anything in the real world. The median voter result avoids the Arrow paradox by relaxing unrestricted domain. In particular, only those voters' profiles are permitted in which every voter has a best alternative and his or her ranking of all other alternatives declines as their distance from the voter's ideal increases. The voting paradox profile can be shown not to share this property.[18] In real-life committees and social situations, choices are often reached by limiting membership so that tastes are sufficiently similar, thus eliminating the taste diversity that leads to cycles. After thirty years on faculty committees, I have observed that decisions often fall into three classes: those that result from adept agenda manipulation; those imposed by a dictatorial minority; and those that are inconsistent. In the third case, a vote on the same issue taken, say, a year later

---

[18] See Kelly (1988, Chapter 3).

(or even tomorrow) can give the opposite outcome even when membership is unchanged. I have witnessed this depressing inconsistency innumerable times in votes on graduate curriculum matters. Living this Kafkaesque reality in two academic departments at my last university has convinced me that the study of social choice is applicable to understanding reality.

Social choice remains an active area of research, with articles appearing in theory and general journals. There is even a field journal, *Social Choice and Welfare*. Possibility theorems often involve either relaxing universal domain, as in the case of the median voter outcome, or relaxing transitivity. In the latter case, a certain amount of inconsistency of social choice must then be tolerated. If I had to choose between which of these two to relax, I would favor relaxing universal domain, thus limiting the diversity of tastes. Even a little taste inconsistency I find objectionable. But limiting universal domain also has negative implications, because certain interests may be excluded, and this is undemocratic. Additionally, income redistribution issues cannot then be adequately analyzed, which is worrying when we recall that governments typically spend much of their budgets on achieving a "more desirable" income distribution. What is desirable may be of dubious value if there is no way to go from individual preferences to social preference without allowing for dictatorial powers or inconsistent choice. There is little sympathy for relaxing the unanimity assumption or nondictatorship. When the independence of the irrelevant alternative is relaxed, strategic misrepresentation of preferences become a problem, as demonstrated previously by the Borda count example.

PROGNOSIS FOR SOCIAL CHOICE

My prognosis for the influence of social choice on the future of economic thought is going to be a bitter pill for some to swallow. Although social choice has been of tremendous value to economics, political science, and sociology in demonstrating the difficulties involved in displaying a group consciousness that adequately reflects individual preferences, it has reached the point of diminishing returns. The creation of new possibility theorems through some arcane relaxation of an assumption seems to serve the researcher's needs for tenure and intellectual gratification more than that of providing new economic insights. The zombielike reception of its analysis from the students in my public choice class is probably mild compared to what one would receive when explaining his or her latest findings to policy makers. From my class, I usually get the preference-revealing question: "Do we have to know this for the exam?" I view social choice analysis as having lost much of its novelty. It is no longer necessarily based on elementary concepts and, as such, is not widely accessible. More important, social choice has not led to testable hypotheses. I am not surprised that a great economist and thinker like Amartya Sen has turned much of his attention in recent years to the study of poverty and development.

6 Institutions Matter:
The New Institutional Economics

Until the twentieth century, economics treated the internal workings of its three primary agents – the consumer (or household), the firm, and the government – as given, nondescript, and beyond analysis. The standard assumptions in economics have been that: consumers' tastes are given; firms exist to maximize profits; and governments act in the interests of their constituencies. Perhaps the greatest mystery of economic thought is that the discipline chose to ignore for so long how firms and governments come into existence and what determines their true behavior. By not bothering to justify the presence or actions of any of its three essential components, economics rested on a tenuous foundation, open to much criticism. In many ways, it is a wonder that the discipline, sufficiently arrogant to have seen no need to explain the motivation or genesis of its key agents, would have been taken seriously by anyone but other economists! Yet the sheer number of economists and their pivotal positions throughout industry, governments, and other institutions bear testimony to the fact that society has put its faith in economics. Are economists the ultimate con artists to have pulled off this acceptance? No answer will be offered.

This neglect of its three component players has since been addressed by economists, especially during the latter half of the twentieth century. In recent studies, consumers' tastes are allowed to be influenced by the consumption process itself, as in the case of habit formation and addiction.[1] Thus, tastes are no longer necessarily taken as given and may actually change in the act of consuming. The *new institutional economics* (NIE), the subject of this chapter, addresses why firms exist and the forms that they should take based on the costs of doing

---

[1] On habit formation and other issues of endogeneous tastes, see the recent survey by Messinis (1999) and the paper by Becker and Mulligan (1997). I shall return to the issue of habit formation in Chapter 10.

business, known as *transaction costs*. Finally, public choice examines the origin and performance of alternative government structures, as shown in Chapter 5.

Economists woke up one day and had a brilliant insight: institutions and their internal structure matter and are a legitimate part of economics. Pioneers who have made one or more seminal contributions to the NIE include Kenneth Arrow, Ronald Coase, Friedrich von Hayek, Gunnar Myrdal, Douglass North, Herbert Simon, and George Stigler.[2] Essentially, the NIE studies why firms and other institutions exist and what forms they should take based on a *transaction costs approach*. Classical economics assumed that the cost of exchange within the market, firm, or institution is nil. As such, classical economics could not explain the boundary between firms and markets; that is, it could not indicate when a firm should rely on the market for an exchange (say, the purchase of a specialized labor input) and when the firm should make the exchange internally (that is, produce its own specialized input). This boundary question affects institutions in all fields of economics – for example, should a city government provide its own waste treatment facility or should it contract with a private firm; should the military train its own pilots or pay a private firm to train its pilots? An example of this boundary in the twenty-first century is whether private firms or governments should incarcerate criminals.

With its concern for the appropriate institutional structure in alternative economic and social scenarios, the NIE addresses the importance and influence of property rights, incentives, information, strategic behavior, and transaction costs on economic behavior and the design of organizations. Modern economic studies of institutions touch on as many other social sciences – anthropology, sociology, political science, sociology, and law – as any single advance in economic analysis during the last century.[3] For example, the analysis of property rights and their influence on the choice of institutional form has legal implications, as reflected in Coase's prescription for assigning liability, a type of property rights, for externalities (see Chapters 2 and 4).

This new study of institutional economics originated with Coase's (1937) landmark paper, "The Nature of the Firm," which raised and addressed the boundary question as to which activities should be transacted within the firm rather than across markets. His article is particu-

---

[2] Many of these Nobel Prize winners won for a number of contributions in addition to their work on the NIE. For this reason some economists, such as Arrow, are mentioned in this book in connection with several different innovations in economic thought.

[3] This was pointed out by Coase (1998). Also see papers by Williamson (1998, 2000), Grief (1998), and Nee (1998) in this same symposium.

larly noteworthy for introducing transaction costs or *expenses associated with alternative modes of allocation.*[4] For example, transaction costs in a market involve learning the prices, identifying the suppliers, and consummating a contract. If there is a good deal of uncertainty about a product's quantity or quality, then transaction costs to resolve this uncertainty prior to contracting will be high. Coase distinguished production costs, associated with the actual creation of an item, from the transaction costs of exchange between its maker and the ultimate user. Classical economics was concerned only with production costs, while the new institutionalists are focused on transaction costs.[5] When uncertainty and other factors complicate an exchange in a market and result in high transaction costs, a firm that economizes on these costs is better suited to doing the transaction internally. Quite simply, activities within firms are justified when their transaction costs are smaller when compared to the transaction costs of a market exchange.

Since the late 1960s, economists have shown an interest in the study of institutional forms, with the greatest activity on this topic coming in the last two decades following the publication of *Limits to Organization*, by Kenneth Arrow (1974b), *Markets and Hierarchies*, by Oliver Williamson (1975), and "Production, Information Costs, and Economic Organization," by Alchian and Demsetz (1972).[6] The NIE differs greatly from the old institutional economics of John Commons (1934), who focused on institutional details and viewed an organization as correcting the collective action problem by imbuing members with a collective identity and common goals. Obviously, Commons did not have the benefit of Olson's (1965) writings on collective action. The work of Commons, a forerunner to the NIE, is noteworthy for its exploratory efforts to show that institutions are important. Unlike the new institutionalists, the old institutionalists were antitheoretical and unconcerned with the architecture of ideal institutional arrangements. Furthermore, these early institutionalists never identified transaction costs as a crucial determinant for comparing among alternative institutional arrangements. Thorstein Veblen, another famous early institutionalist, was interested in social norms embodied in institutions. In fact, there is little commonality among the old institutionalists, nor is

---

[4] Even Coase (1992) identified the introduction of transaction costs as this article's greatest contribution. Also see Alchian and Demsetz (1972), Williamson (1975, 1998), and Yang (1993). Williamson (2000) provided an evaluation of the NIE.

[5] Uncertainty and incentive problems also characterize production costs, so that the choice of institutions may also have an impact on these costs, a point raised by Langlois and Foss (1999).

[6] Other important pioneering works include Demsetz (1967, 1968), Hurwicz (1973), March and Simon (1958), and Stigler (1968).

there much commonality between their work and that of the new institutionalists (Blaug 1997, pp. 700–3).

THE NATURE OF THE NEW INSTITUTIONAL ECONOMICS

In the simplest of terms, the NIE views institutional choice as an economic decision, determined along with other allocative choices. As such, institutional form is "endogenous" or germane to the economic problem and is no longer given and outside of (exogenous to) economic decision making. If alternative institutional structures have the same production costs and provide the same outputs, then the best institutional arrangement is that which minimizes transaction costs. Suppose, for example, a club good (for example, a park) can be provided either by the national government through taxes and user fees or by a private firm solely through user fees. If the quantity and quality of the club good is the same under the alternative arrangements, but the private firm has lower transaction costs, then it is the preferred institution. Thus, the choice among institutional forms is fairly simple, provided that transaction costs can be computed for the alternative forms and that the forms themselves do not affect the output. But, in fact, this output may itself depend on the institutional form, and this complicates matters considerably.

To illustrate how institutional form may alter the outcome, I shall consider two alternative sharing arrangements in a labor-managed firm or a commons where the output must be shared in some fashion.[7] Suppose that the worker-owners institute an egalitarian sharing arrangement whereby each receives $1/n$ of the output or revenue (if the price is fixed), where n is the number of owners. Under this institutional arrangement, each worker-owner has an incentive to shirk and rely on the others to do the work, because his or her reward is independent of effort. The end result is that too little effort is expended as compared to some efficient standard, and thus output and revenue suffer.[8] There is a tradeoff between individual benefit from reduced effort and shared costs from reduced output. If, instead, worker-owners institute rewards based upon their share of the total effort expended, then the incentive to work hard is bolstered. A person who expends a quarter of the total effort is rewarded with a quarter of the output, and so forth. Each worker-owner is now pitted against all others in a contest that results in too much effort

---

[7] On commons, see Cornes and Sandler (1983, 1996), Ostrom (1990), and Chapter 11 of this volume. There is a large literature on common property.

[8] The efficient standard is that of Pareto efficiency, where each worker equates her marginal disutility of effort to her marginal product or the increase in output from another unit of effort. See Cornes and Sandler (1996, pp. 283–9) and Cauley, Cornes, and Sandler (1999).

as compared to some efficient standard.[9] For equal sharing, the worker-owners ignore the positive benefits that their effort confers on others through the sharing arrangements, while for proportional effort sharing, the worker-owners ignore the costs that their effort implies for others. In the latter case, costs result because one's effort not only increases the size of the pot, but also reduces the share going to everyone else. Economic systems based on egalitarian principles or seeing to everyone's needs, such as Marxism, are doomed to rampant free riding.

Even slight changes in sharing rules can cause significant changes in the way people behave. The *institutional environment* denotes "the rules of the game" and includes the incentive structure, laws, contracts, and property rights assignments, while *institutions of governance* refers to the "play of the game" or the use of a market, firm, or government bureau.[10] Change these rules that identify alternative institutional arrangements and rational players will respond rapidly and predictably. Several years ago, the administration at my former university devised a scheme intended to get more outside funding from its faculty. In particular, the administration announced that departmental operating budgets would be allocated partly by how many grant proposals were submitted; neither the amount of the proposal nor the success in obtaining funding mattered. This scheme rewarded the writing of lots of small, unsuccessful proposals that could be submitted repeatedly. I recall someone remarking to me when my sizable National Science Foundation grant was funded that "I didn't know how to play the game and was not really helping my department." This senseless incentive structure was quickly modified to stress funding amounts awarded, once its predictable outcome was experienced and understood by the myopic administration.

The new institutionalists are concerned with two decisions: the choice of the best institutional structure from a set of alternatives, and the design of an ideal structure. Both choices must be based on some objective, such as minimizing transaction costs. If this is the objective, then the first decision is not too difficult, provided that there are a small number

---

[9] With equal sharing, each worker-owner works short of equating his marginal disutility of effort to his marginal product, whereas with proportional effort sharing, each worker-owner works past the point of equating his marginal disutility of effort to his marginal product. This analysis assumes that everyone is identical in terms of taste and productivity. Analogous findings hold if worker-owners differ in their productivity. Schemes can, however, be devised that choose rewards judiciously, so that efficiency results (Cauley, Cornes, and Sandler, 1999).

[10] The expression "rules of the game" as applied to institutions and organization is due to Douglass C. North (1994), who won the Nobel Prize in 1993 for his work on institutions and economic history.

of alternatives and the transaction costs associated with each are known. The identification of these transaction costs is, however, not so simple, insofar as information is a precious commodity in institutions. As explored in the next chapter, well-informed participants may have little incentive to reveal what they know – that is, information may be impacted. Rules can be devised to make telling the truth a dominant strategy or always in your interest, but only at the expense of additional transaction costs stemming from an incentive mechanism. Truth telling may be a costly process, especially when people are essentially spying on themselves.

The optimal design of an institution requires that one or more of its parameters be varied to optimize some institutional objective. Who is in charge can, however, make a big difference, since this person's objective may be at odds with that of the owners of the institution. If, for example, the decision maker is remunerated based on his or her level of responsibilities, then this person's attempt to maximize these responsibilities may diminish the owners' well-being and result in too large an institution. Readjusting incentives so that the decision maker's rewards more closely coincide with those of the owners can promote better outcomes. For example, profit-sharing schemes and stock options in firms are a means of aligning the interests of managers and owners, while deductibles in insurance policies serve this same purpose for the insured and the insurer. When institutions are properly designed, choices must be made not only over incentive schemes, but also over the actual structure of the organization. The latter involves how many levels of decision making there should be, and how many agents there should be at each level. Nonhierarchical alternatives must also be considered.[11]

The NIE teaches us that profit maximization – the economist's mantra – should not be accepted blindly. Moreover, the choice and design of institutions are legitimate economic decisions. Economic behavior and organizations are integrally tied together; ignore one and there is not much meaningful left to say about the other. In addition, the study of institutions reminds us that exchange is costly even in markets. Which institutions to rely upon depends, in part, upon these transaction costs. Moreover, the NIE indicates that noneconomic factors – social norms, networks, and laws – also have a role to play in economic interactions.[12] The new institutionalists have shown that the firm is no longer an immutable or nondescript entity on the economic landscape.

---

[11] The hierarchical choice was considered by Williamson (1967, 1975), while Sah and Stiglitz (1986) analyzed the choice between hierarchical and nonhierarchical forms. Also see Sandler and Cauley (1980) for a hierarchical theory of the firm.

[12] On the roles of norms and social cultures in the study of institutional economics, see Grief (1998) and Nee (1998).

FIRMS VERSUS MARKETS: A CLOSER LOOK

Coase's explanation of the firm rested on the realization that market exchanges are not costless and that organizing some transactions within a firm through contractual arrangements may be advantageous. The use of contracts within the firm could fix prices for certain inputs and thereby limit haggling over the duration of the contract. Although the ideas of Coase's 1937 paper do not appear innovative today, they were revolutionary – even heretical – for their day because they indicated that markets could be outdone by an alternative institutional arrangement through a recognition of the costs of market transactions. But Coase did not go far enough in explaining the firm's existence, since he did not identify the comparative advantage of firms over markets.

To identify this advantage of firms, Alchian and Demsetz (1972) focused on firms' serving a monitoring role, which is necessary to reward team members more in line with their individual productivity. When two or more inputs are combined, it is often difficult to discern the inputs' individual contributions. Suppose that two workers must design a computer program together. Each worker has an incentive to shirk and rely on the other. The role of a monitor is to curtail this shirking by assigning rewards based on individual contributions to the team effort. In larger teams, the shirking problem becomes even worse and the need for effective monitoring and subsequent rewards even greater. Team production can often yield a larger output than that produced when each member works alone. It is this surplus that can defray the firm's monitoring costs and still leave a net gain from organizing the activity within a firm where team synergism occurs. Successful firms acquire expertise in their monitoring activity, which creates a larger surplus for the team by matching rewards to productivity. Team synergism is absent in markets where each producer works independently and then sells the resulting output. Alchian and Demsetz's explanation of the firm's existence certainly underscores why rewards to the monitor must be tied to the surplus that the monitor's vigilance produces. If the monitor is remunerated based on profit sharing, then the monitor's incentives are aligned with those of the firm. Any net surplus in nonprofit organizations is not distributed to team members or monitors; consequently, these organizations are apt to be plagued by shirking among team members.[13]

My thirty years in nonprofit institutions – namely, universities – have given me a great appreciation of this last insight. In academia, the ultimate example of team effort is the multiple-authored article or book,

---

[13] On these alternative forms and the consequences of monitoring, see Alchian and Demsetz (1972, pp. 785–90). On nonprofit organizations, see Weisbrod (1988).

where shirking is rampant but difficult to gauge as a monitor. If the authors admire each other, then their estimates of the others' efforts, when solicited, are apt to add up to over 100%. When, however, their mutual admiration has waned, each may claim a personal contribution of more than 100%, because the paper had to be produced and coauthors' erroneous efforts corrected.[14] For joint teaching assignments, individual effectiveness is readily revealed by student evaluations, so that monitoring this particular team effort is not such a problem in US universities. When I taught in Australia and England, however, I noticed a disturbing tendency among students to interpret a teacher's inability to communicate coherent thoughts as a sign of supreme intelligence. When students came to me for help, they would point out that the other instructor was too brilliant to explain things. For the first time in my career, I realized that my clarity was a sign to some of my inferior intellect.

Alchian and Demsetz's explanation still does not tell us enough about the key issues surrounding the existence of firms and their various forms. Surely, there are more gains from the contribution of firms than monitoring team production. Although these two authors indicate the failings of some types of firms in light of team production, they do not really explain the presence of so many alternative organizational forms or describe which are best under various scenarios. The work of Oliver Williamson (1967, 1975) and others address these issues. According to Williamson, internal organization minimizes transaction costs compared to market transactions owing to more effective auditing, improved dispute-settling procedures, and a reduced ability of individuals to extract team gains. Only the last benefit was recognized by Alchian and Demsetz. For Williamson, firms minimize transaction costs if they can limit input owners' opportunistic behavior, which is especially worrisome for small-numbers exchanges.[15] If, for example, only two people are party to a trade, then a struggle ensues in which each tries to extract the greatest gain. This follows as the seller tries to get the highest price possible, and the buyer seeks the lowest price. In large-numbers exchanges, competitive forces restrict traders' abilities to influence price, letting markets present both sellers and buyers with the same price. Institutional factors, such as uncertainty and bounded rationality (that is, humans' inability to account for all relevant considerations) promote opportunistic gains, thereby emphasizing the role that internal organizations have in aligning incentives, but always at a cost. Alternative institutional structures for firms must then hinge on the bottom line – the lowest transaction cost.

---

[14] Nevertheless, one would hope that authors who repeatedly write with the same coauthors do not do so because they free ride.

[15] See, especially, Williamson's (1975, pp. 8–9) summary of his approach.

TRANSACTION BENEFITS, NOT TO BE IGNORED

I have always found that the transaction costs approach lacked an important element: alternative institutional structures for firms, governments, and other organizations may also entail institution-induced benefits. *Transaction benefits* are solely attributable to the institutional arrangement and are not part of the output being produced for exchange. If institutional design makes a difference for transaction costs, then it can surely also affect transaction benefits. Suppose that aid to the poor can either be given through a nonprofit organization financed by voluntary donations, or provided by a government program supported by taxes. Even if the associated transaction costs and the relief provided to the indigent are the same with either allocative mechanism, charity based on voluntary donations may also result in a warm glow to the donor. This nice feeling is a transaction benefit derived from the nonprofit institutional arrangement that is not associated with tax-mandated giving. You can hardly feel good about helping the needy when the government has to reach into your pocket to facilitate the assistance. Another instance of transaction benefits involves treaties addressing environmental problems such as the depletion of the stratospheric ozone layer. In addition to cooperation-based efficiency gains over independent national actions to control ozone depleters, these treaties also establish communication networks that provide information and related benefits that vary among alternative institutional arrangements, such as nonvoluntary control by an international agency. Such institution-induced gains represent examples of transaction benefits.

Once transaction benefits are admitted, minimizing transactions costs may not have the same sway or give the best institutional arrangement. If one institutional alternative has transaction costs of, say, $1.5 billion, and a second has transaction costs of $2 billion, then the second may still be more desirable if it comes with $3 billion of transaction benefits while the first alternative only comes with $1 billion of such benefits. What really matters is identifying the institutional structure that maximizes the *net transaction benefits* or the difference between transaction benefits and transaction costs, whenever benefits or outcomes are not invariant among alternative institutions.[16] Institutional design can involve at least three distinct steps. First, institutional forms must be identified that make every participant better off while accounting for transaction benefits. If each party to the institution is better off, then an overall positive collective gain is also achieved. Second, the institutional arrangement with the

---

[16] This line of thinking has been developed by Cauley, Sandler, and Cornes (1986), Sandler (1997), Sandler and Cauley (1977), and Sandler, Cauley, and Tschirhart (1983).

greatest anticipated net transaction benefit over some set time interval should be chosen. Third, the structure must be reviewed periodically and restructured or eliminated as warranted.

"NEW" NEW INSTITUTIONAL ECONOMICS

In recent years, there has been a marriage between game theory and the new institutional economics, whereby social institutions are interpreted as representing the rules of the game.[17] In game-theoretic parlance, the rules of the game indicate how actions or strategies get translated into payoffs and indicate the order of play when a sequence of actions is relevant. From a game-theoretical perspective, institutions need to be designed so that members take actions that further their well-being and *that of the institution*. Suppose that a Prisoners' Dilemma plagues a particular interaction within an organization, where doing the wrong thing from the institution's vantage point is a dominant strategy from an individual's perspective. In particular, assume that the individual views his or her action as yielding personal benefits of 6 but at a personal cost of 8. If, however, this action also confers 6 in benefits to all other members in the institution, then it is clearly in the interest of the institution as a whole to encourage the member to take the action. This may be accomplished by altering the institutional rules so that the individual views it to be in his or her interest to act – that is, payoffs are changed to make action a dominant strategy. Suppose, for example, that all individual costs are shared collectively by the institution's members. With, say, eight members, the individual's costs are now just 1 (8/8), and he or she will act, motivated by the net gain of 5 (6 – 1). This cost-sharing innovation has already been introduced in Chapter 4 with regard to promoting collective action. Well-designed institutions must encourage collective action through incentives.

An alternative means of encouraging individual actions in this situation would be to reward by more than 2 any individual taking the desired action. If, say, the reward is 3, then the individual now realizes a net gain of 1 (6 – 8 + 3) from acting and will do so. Acting in the institution's interest is now "self-enforcing" or individually rational. Alternatively, penalties can be imposed for inaction, so that the –2 from acting is made better than the consequences of inaction. Any penalty greater than 2 will do the trick. Surely, the Mafia dishes out horrible punishments to ensure that borrowers do not renege on loans, since loans otherwise imply a

---

[17] See, in particular, Eggertsson (1990), Gardner and Ostrom (1991), Ostrom, Gardner, and Walker (1995), and Schotter (1994a). A number of journals, such as the *Journal of Economic Behavior and Organization* and the *European Journal of Political Economy*, have devoted many pages to such articles.

Prisoners' Dilemma scenario – the dominant strategy is to take out a loan and never pay it back. Drug cartels employ similar Draconian measures to eliminate informants among associates.

Another institutional device to circumvent the Prisoners' Dilemma is the development of institutional norms of "good behavior," where individuals learn that if everyone adheres to some accepted rules of conduct then everyone can expect reciprocity from others. To remind participants of these practices, exemplary behavior leads to recognition (for example, employee of the month or best teacher awards). I am always surprised that universities do not recognize more of their faculty members, since academics respond so fully to any ego-gratifying event, and it is so inexpensive to provide such recognition. Certainly, the repeated nature of the interactions within an institution means that tit-for-tat type strategies, where noncooperative behavior is punished, can lead to cooperative outcomes.[18] In fact, a major purpose of institutions is to provide an air of permanency to interactions among a set of individuals. This interest in norms of institutional identity and their influence on the behavior of agents within institutions suggests that concepts in the NIE have implications for organization theory, sociology, and evolutionary psychology.

Douglass North (1994) would go even further and argue that the rules of institutions provide structure to the economic landscape and determine the strategic plays of the component organizations and individuals. Economies with rules that promote property rights and anonymous exchange will prosper over time. According to North, a successful economy is one with supportive institutions that develop over time through a trial-and-error process. Evolutionary games, which study the population dynamics of repeated games or social interactions, have been applied by the new institutionalists to investigate how economic interactions are determined over time.[19] Behavior that results in high payoffs is imitated and eventually adopted as the norm by society and its institutions. The transition of the economy and its norms of behavior depends on whether new strategies outperform those associated with current institutional arrangements. The prognosis for transition depends on how well strategies resist novel "invader" strategies. Without a change of the rules governing institutions, transition may be stalled at those strategies that work best for established economic institutions. Although evolutionary game theory sounds very abstract, it

---

[18] On tit-for-tat strategy, see Axelrod (1984), McMillan (1986), and Sandler (1986).

[19] Vega-Redondo (1996) and Weibull (1995) have examined the theory of evolutionary games. The former work is a more accessible source. An important early work on evolutionary games is by Maynard Smith (1982). The *Journal of Economic Behavior and Organization* has published many relevant papers on evolutionary games and the study of institutions.

represents an interesting approach for understanding transition and change.

The marriage of game theory and the NIE sometimes takes the form of designing "incentive-compatible" contracts between a principal and an agent.[20] The principal may be the owner or manager of an enterprise, while the agent is a worker. Principal-agent analysis involves not only the presence of an authority structure but also some form of asymmetric information, where one party is informed and the other is not. In particular, the agent knows how hard he or she is working, but the principal may not be able to observe this effort. The principal can monitor the final output, but a random event may also affect this output, so that a disappointing output may be due to some outside influence and not the result of a lack of diligence. Suppose that you hire someone on an hourly wage to cut your lawn, and when you return an hour later you find that only half of the lawn has been mowed in the time that it normally takes for the whole job. When quizzed about her lack of progress, she tells you that there were three garter snakes that had to be coaxed out of the way, and that this was time-consuming. If this is true, the random event is the number of snakes on the lawn. Your dilemma is to devise a reward scheme that makes the mower expend good effort even though slowness is, on occasion, justifiable. A reward scheme is incentive-compatible if it makes working hard a dominant strategy for the agent despite the inherent randomness that can justify some excuses. Since asymmetric information is the topic of Chapter 7, I shall defer further discussion until then.

THE PROSPECTS FOR THE NEW
INSTITUTIONAL ECONOMICS

One of the easiest predictions for this book to make is that the study of institutional economics is here to stay. I find it incomprehensible that economists could for so long have taken institutions as given and beyond economic scrutiny. The study of these institutions is applicable not only to every branch of economics, but also to virtually every social science. For example, Douglass North has taught us that to fathom economic history, and history in general, the rules and play of the game as embodied in institutions must be studied. Economic institutions cannot be taken as immutable and passive to the transactions that they facilitate.

The architecture of institutions is pivotal to a host of problems of great importance today and tomorrow. First, there is the need to design treaties for addressing transnational contingencies that include curbing global warming, protecting biodiversity, and thwarting transnational terrorism.

---

[20] On principal-agent analysis, consult Ross (1973) and Stiglitz (1974).

Second, disappointing results with respect to foreign assistance over the last half-century necessitate a restructuring of the institutions whereby donor and recipient countries interact.[21] Third, the European Union (EU) with its emerging integrated monetary system requires the design of novel institutions, whose complexity will increase as the EU continues to enlarge its membership. The design of supranational structures is about to enter a new era in which nations may be prepared, for a few specific activities, to sacrifice some autonomy. Fourth, peacekeeping activities need a better institutional arrangement; the United Nations was ill-prepared to direct the greatly augmented demands for peacekeeping in the 1990s. NATO has stepped in to assist the United Nations in Bosnia and Kosovo, but NATO's growing diversity and its unanimity decision rule may limit its future effectiveness.[22] Fifth, increased resource scarcity signals the need for improved institutional arrangements regarding the management of common-property resources, particularly those involving water, whose scarcity will become more acute over the coming decades. Sixth, the transformation of China and the ex-communist European countries into market economies requires a better understanding of state-owned enterprises and other types of institutional structures for firms (see Chapter 13). Seventh, the continued growth of the nonprofit sector of most advanced economies means that institutional economics can enlighten us on how alternative nonprofit institutions are apt to perform. There is no shortage of worthwhile applications of the NIE in the social sciences. The identification of more effective institutions for firms and governments in the transitional economies and the LDCs may do more for self-sustained growth than any amount of foreign assistance. Such institutions must encourage high effort and low corruption.

Institutional economics has, thus far, developed numerous accessible paradigms that foster its appeal to a broad audience. When an economic concept is generally understood, it becomes widely applied, and that gives it lasting power. Many of the analyses of the NIE possess an elegant simplicity that draws on a vast number of methods from economics, game theory, sociology, and law. Such diversity of thought also bolsters its long-term influence, because as some forms of analyses lose their appeal, others remain in vogue to encourage further research in the NIE. The underlying methods of the NIE rely on both logical reasoning (without mathematics) and mathematics. Although the NIE rests on a sound theoretical foundation, which can be rather abstract at times, its

---

[21] See Kanbur, Sandler, and Morrison (1999) and World Bank (1998) for evidence of these disappointing results and suggested institutional innovations.

[22] UN problems regarding peacekeeping are addressed by Sandler and Hartley (1999, Chapter 4).

theoretical predictions have been tested both empirically and in the laboratory.[23] Consider the performance of alternative institutional firms for Chinese enterprises in the 1990s and beyond. China is in the throes of a bold experiment that allows various kinds of enterprises to coexist, including state-owned enterprises (SOEs), private firms, township and village enterprises (TVE), and collectively owned enterprises (COEs). Each has its own internal structure and incentive mechanism. Theoretical hypotheses about which are best under alternative scenarios can be tested with recent data on key input and output measures of these alternative firms. If, for example, China's current policy of promoting some of the SOEs and making them even larger is not as efficient as supporting smaller COEs, then this needs to be uncovered and used for enlightened policy making.[24]

Another factor that should maintain the continued presence of institutional economics concerns its novelty. For example, the whole issue of what is maximized in firms is called into question when institutional structures, property rights, incentive arrangements, and information are integral to the analysis. Things once taken for granted may no longer be valid because of the insights of the new institutionalists. Take the case of common-property resources and the so-called "tragedy of the commons," whereby overexploitation is the outcome (Hardin 1968). Analyses in the NIE indicate that common-property institutions exist that provide the proper incentives to use the resource efficiently, provided that access to the resource is restricted. Thus, indigenous people on a tract of the Amazon jungle may well punish wastefulness and reward conservation within their clan, so that a sustained resource is passed down through the generations. Once access to the commons is, however, open, exploiters from the outside have little incentive to account for the consequences that their actions imply for the level of the resource available to others today and tomorrow. In some cases, the fate of trespassers is used by tribes to ward off others so as to limit access; a trespasser's corpse may be displayed at the territorial boundary as a warning to others. Open access, and not common ownership, is now understood to be the root of the tragedy.[25]

UNANSWERED QUESTIONS

Yet another reason why institutional economics has a promising future is that there are many unanswered questions. There is still much to be

---

[23] Ostrom, Gardner, and Walker (1995) have reviewed laboratory tests.

[24] See Cauley, Cornes, and Sandler (1999) and the citations therein. Also see Hay et al. (1994) and Lee (1991).

[25] See Ostrom (1990), Ostrom, Gardner, and Walker (1995), and Cornes and Sandler (1996, Chapter 8).

learned about institutional design. Choosing among two or three alternatives is not as complex as devising design principles that result in more efficacious institutional configurations. A better understanding of the steps and procedures of institutional design is required, especially when participants may differ at each stage. As an illustration, again consider treaty formation. At the framing stage, negotiations are often conducted by the executive branch of government, but, at the subsequent ratification stage, the legislators must vote for approval. Still later, the enforcement of ratified treaties reverts to the executive branch. Because all of the various participants may have different agendas, framed treaties may be ratified only years later, if ever. The recent experience of the United States with respect to the Kyoto Protocol on curbing carbon emissions is an apt example of this difficulty, in which the US Congress refused to ratify a treaty negotiated by the Clinton administration. A more forward-looking framing decision that anticipates legislators' wishes can better address such problems.

Another issue concerns institutional design when a network of institutions with overlapping jurisdictions and agendas exists. In Europe, there are a host of different institutions with overlapping memberships concerned with regional security – examples include NATO, the Western European Union, the Partnership for Peace, and the Organization for Security and Cooperation in Europe.[26] Such overlapping institutions lead to wasteful duplication that fails to utilize these institutions' comparative advantage. Within organizations, functional overlap also exists. For instance, the US State Department, Department of Defense, and Central Intelligence Agency all investigate problems associated with transnational terrorism.

Another unanswered question involves the design of institutions to address issues with long-range consequences that affect current and future generations of members. Can such organizations be designed to be farsighted in their actions? To date, the application of evolutionary game theory represents the initial attempt to study this and related questions where membership changes over time.

---

[26] This is not a complete list; see Sandler and Hartley (1999, p. 203).

7   Knowledge Is Power: Asymmetric Information

I once had a friend who owned a house beside a stream. Unlike his neighbors' houses, plagued by mice and rats, his house had been rodent-free during his ten-year occupancy. His neighbors thought him dishonest when he would reply to their incessant complaints about rats that he had never seen a single rodent in his house. On the day before he was to sell his house, he was awakened in the middle of the night by a weird sound coming from the attic. Thinking that he would come face to face with his first rat, he went with a flashlight to inspect the attic. When he opened the trap door and stuck in his head, he let out a scream and dropped the light. The ten-year-old mystery had been solved – a large beady-eyed snake stared at him with a rat in its coils. My friend faced a real dilemma: should he tell the prospective buyer about the snake, or try to rid the house of the reptile, or just be quiet about it? He chose silence, as the other options could either jinx the sale or be very costly. He reasoned that the snake was harmless and served a very useful purpose. So he said nothing, and the house and the snake were sold together. This rather bizarre, but true, story represents an instance of asymmetric information, where one party to a transaction is more informed than the other party. Additionally, it is not necessarily in the informed party's interests to reveal the information. In some cases, a truthful response may not be believed, because the informed party is expected to give that answer whether or not it is true. Who would believe a statement by the seller that the snake was well-behaved and, except for the absence of rodents, would be unnoticed?

Classical economists assumed that all parties to a transaction are equally well informed. The study of informational economics and asymmetric information, in particular, began in the latter half of the twentieth century. At first, decision making in the face of uncertain outcomes was addressed, but later the analysis was extended to transactions between differentially informed agents. In 1996, the Nobel Prize in economics was awarded to William Vickrey and James Mirrlees for their innovative work on asymmetric information.

My intention in this chapter is to give the reader a sense of and an appreciation for this fascinating area of study by considering some instances of asymmetric information. Even though I must be selective in what I present, the cases discussed will provide a sufficient flavor of the importance of studies involving asymmetric information. Whenever one side to a transaction is better informed than the other, a market failure results, as some costs and benefits are inevitably left out of the market price. In the snake example, a buyer fearful of snakes is going to pay more than she would have had she known of the occupant of the rafters, while a buyer who dotes on snakes is going to pay less. An understanding of asymmetric information can provide insights into the following practices: why insurance companies have deductibles, why warranties are given, and why there is no privately provided unemployment insurance. Asymmetric information is behind the study of contracts, incentive-compatible mechanisms, principal-agent analysis, and labor screening.

There is little question that an understanding of asymmetric information and its implications can yield numerous insights about effective economic policy. For instance, regulations can be justified to protect uninformed customers and buyers. Disclosure laws can limit the extent of strategic trading associated with one-sided information, so that known problems, say with a house, become a matter of public record after inspections. Much of the recent literature in regulatory economics has been preoccupied with the implications of asymmetric information,[1] but it also has much to tell us about policy making in other areas of economics. In the study of transition economies, it can inform us about the appropriate design of component institutions: if, for example, state-owned enterprises in China can be designed so that workers have the proper incentives to expend high effort, then the Chinese economy will be more efficient. In environmental economics, a knowledge of asymmetric information makes for more sophisticated policy making when the pollution can derive from any of a number of sources, known to the polluter but not to the policy makers. The study of defense procurement and the design of contracts, when the producer is more informed than the government and costs cannot be known in advance, can also benefit from knowledge about asymmetric information.[2]

---

[1] For studies on the usefulness of asymmetric information for regulatory policy, see Laffont and Tirole (1990, 1993).

[2] The following studies concern defense procurement contracts under asymmetric information: Cummins (1977), McAfee and McMillan (1986a, 1986b), Rogerson (1990, 1991), and Tirole (1986). Also see Sandler and Hartley (1995, pp. 127–49). Lewis (1996) is a good example of environmental policy and asymmetric information.

Over the last decade, there has been an explosion in the literature on asymmetric information. As useful as this study is, one must also wonder whether it is reaching the point of sharply diminished or even negative returns. Is all of this focused effort providing sufficiently novel insights? Will there come a time, to paraphrase Yogi Berra, when "nobody goes there anymore because it's too crowded"? I shall also address this issue.

A SECOND-PRICE AUCTION: A CLEVER DEVICE

Suppose that an auctioneer is selling John Lennon's glasses and would like to induce the bidders to reveal their true valuation for these spectacles. In the standard ascending-price auction, the winner need only outbid the person with the second-highest valuation to obtain the item, which may result in a winning bid well below the winner's true valuation. If, say, the object is worth $100,000 to you, and there are no further bids after you call out $50,000, then you purchase the glasses for just half of their true value to you. In a standard auction it is in your strategic interest to reveal the smallest amount of information about your true valuation until the auction price just passes this valuation, at which point your silence reveals everything. Even in a sealed-bid auction, there are incentives to underreport an item's true worth if you surmise that the other bidders' valuations are below yours. In such a case, you would submit a bid just above your guess of the top valuation of the other bidders. Thus, there is still a strategic value to bidding less than the item's worth.

A clever way to devise an auction whereby bidders reveal what the item is really worth to them is to *sever the link between the bid price and the price paid by the highest bidder.*[3] This eliminates the rationale for potential buyers to hide their true valuations. William Vickrey (1961) engineered a *second-price auction* in which each bidder secretly submits his or her bid to the auctioneer, who then sells the object to the highest bidder, but at the second-highest bid. Revealing your true valuation is now a dominant strategy regardless of the actions of the other bidders, whose bids are unknown to you. Suppose you try to get the glasses, which you value at $100,000, cheaply by bidding just $80,000. If someone else bids $90,000, then you lose the glasses, which if you had bid their true worth would have cost you just $90,000 or the second-highest bid. Any strategic attempt to bid below your valuation could result in your losing the glasses at a price at or below their true value to you. Next, suppose that you bid beyond your true valuation to enhance the likelihood of

---

[3] Relevant studies on second-price auctions include Cornes and Sandler (1996, pp. 114–15, 221–2) and Vickrey (1961).

acquiring Lennon's glasses, but at a second-highest bid that you hope will be no greater than \$100,000. A bid of \$102,000 could, for example, mean that you will have to pay \$101,500, if that is the second-highest bid, thus resulting in a loss of \$1,500 from paying more than your valuation. Even an overbid of just 50 cents could mean an overpayment of 49 cents. The smaller the overbid, the smaller the possible overpayment, but also the less likely that this overbid will affect the outcome as compared to bidding your true valuation. To avoid such losses, you should never overbid. Bidding your true valuation can never make you worse off, and it will make you better off whenever the second-highest bid is less than your valuation. Thus, truthful revelation is, indeed, the dominant strategy in such an auction.

This "preference-revelation" mechanism indicates three important lessons to remember when inducing individuals to tell the truth about information that only they possess, and whose revelation is not usually in their interest. First, making the actual price paid different from the one revealed allows the mechanism to limit the scope for being dishonest. Second, telling the truth must be made a dominant strategy through an implied cost from dishonesty. Third, making people tell the truth is typically a costly affair. In the glasses example, the cost to the seller is the difference between the highest valuation and the second-highest bid, because this difference represents potential gains not captured by the seller. The item still sells below the highest-held value, so that the relevant marginal benefits and marginal costs are not equated.

CLEANSING A STREAM

Owing to their nonrival and nonexcludable benefits, pure public goods pose a real problem when a policy maker is trying to ascertain each person's increased well-being from a proposed public good. Ideally, if these increases in well-being (or marginal benefits) are known for all individuals, then the public good should be provided to the point where the sum of marginal benefits matches the good's marginal costs.

Suppose that a local government is considering cleaning the pollutants from a stream that runs through its jurisdiction. Cleansing the stream is the pure public good, whose benefits are nonrival and nonexcludable to those along its banks. For simplicity, I shall assume that there is only a single level of cleansing available, which costs \$1,000. This assumption means that the relevant choice is whether to provide the cleanup or not. Assume that the government asks each of its citizens how much the proposed cleanup is worth to him. If the sum of these reported values exceed or equal \$1,000, then the cleanup is undertaken, and each citizen is subsequently charged in proportion to his stated value. If, therefore, a person reports a value that is half of the total reported, then she covers $500 of the costs. This scheme is not incentive-compatible, since it is not in the respondents' interest to be honest. Each citizen who perceives a positive gain from the cleanup has an incentive to free ride and to claim no benefits, in the hope that others will be more forthright and that the cleanup will thereby occur at no expense to them. When someone perceives a negative value from the cleanup, it is in this person's interest to exaggerate this cost to keep the action from taking place. By connecting a person's payment to her reported value, this first scheme fails to provide incentives to be truthful. As a consequence, it is unlikely that the sum of reported benefits will cover the requisite costs, so the cleanup will probably not be undertaken.

It is tempting to generalize from Vickrey's second-price auction and reason that the trick for truthful revelation is to sever the link between a person's reported value and his assigned costs, but this is not enough when a public good is involved, owing to the added strategic concerns of free riding. For a private-good auction, the buyer receives the entire benefits of the item purchased, but for a pure public good, everyone receives gains from the good provided. Not only must the link between one's assigned costs and one's reported value be severed, a cost for being dishonest must also be imposed that makes each respondent face the social consequences of his reported values.

To see why cutting the link is not enough, suppose that each individual's cost, c_i, for the cleanup, if it goes ahead, is preassigned. Each citizen is again asked to state his or her value, v_i, for the cleanup. When the sum of the net values ($v_i - c_i$) *reported* is positive or zero, the cleanup is undertaken. Incentives for truthful reporting are still not achieved. If your net value is positive, then you have an incentive to state a very high value to ensure the cleanup, since such dishonesty will not affect your payment, which is predetermined and independent of your response. If, however, your net value is negative, you then have an incentive to say that it has no value ($v_i = 0$) or even a negative value to keep the cleanup from taking place.[4]

To provide the right incentives, I shall now turn to a scheme that not only uses preassigned costs when the cleanup is instituted, but also charges respondents for the social consequences that result from their responses.[5] These charges are intended to impose a cost for dishonesty. Again suppose that individual costs are preassigned and that the cleanup

---

[4] The problems with such schemes are discussed in many places in the literature. See, for example, Varian (1993, pp. 595–600).
[5] The scheme described is a variant of the Clarke (1971) or Groves-Clarke tax (see Groves and Ledyard, 1977). Also see Schotter (1994b) and Tideman and Tullock (1976). The discussion in the text follows from Varian (1993, pp. 596–8).

is undertaken when the sum of reported net values (deducting c_i) is greater than or equal to zero.[6] In the public-good scenario, the respondent has an influence on the well-being of others only when her response is "pivotal" or alters the outcome. There are two relevant pivotal cases. In the first case, the other persons do not want the public good, so that their sum of reported net values, R_{-i}, is negative, but the respondent's stated net value causes the public good to be provided. This pivotal respondent is charged $c_i - R_{-i}$, or her preassigned costs plus the alleged harm to others resulting from the public good being provided. Clearly, this person is made to confront the social decision, where the cleanup is provided only when the sum of reported net values (those of others and that of the person) is greater than or equal to zero. In the second pivotal case, the other persons want the public good, because their sum of reported net values is positive, but the respondent's stated value causes the good *not* to be provided. The pivotal respondent is now charged $c_i + R_{-i}$ to impose the social consequences of his influence on the outcome. The "social-consequence" tax is paid to the government and not to the other persons, so that their responses are not influenced by the tax payment. More than one respondent can be pivotal, in which case each such respondent would pay the tax.

Respondents are not aware ahead of time of whether or not they will be pivotal, and this makes truth telling the best strategy for all persons. A numerical example can add clarity to this seemingly abstract scheme. Suppose that a person exaggerates his *net value* from the cleanup as 100 when it is really only 50. Further suppose that the reported net values of everyone else for the cleanup sum to −80. In this case, the sum of reported net values is 20 (100 − 80), and the cleanup is provided. The person who exaggerates is then pivotal and has to pay an additional tax of 80, resulting in a personal net loss of 30 (50 − 80) from being dishonest. Exaggeration is no longer smart; honesty pays despite the tax. Suppose, instead, that the respondent understates her true net value as 50 when it is really 100. If everyone else reports an aggregate net value of −60, then the cleanup is not provided, since the sum of reported net values is −10. This dishonesty again results in a personal loss, because had the respondent been honest and reported a net value of 100 the cleanup would have been undertaken, and she would have been better off by 40 despite the tax of 60. Dishonest underreporting can lose the respondent this net benefit of 40, because it can cause the good not to be provided.

---

[6] The scheme described has a technical requirement that there are no income effects or that, no matter how income is distributed, the best level of the public good is unchanged. This assumption is shared by all preference-revelation mechanisms and limits their applicability.

Like the second-price auction, this tax scheme makes telling the truth a dominant strategy, but at a real cost. This waste comes from the taxes paid by pivotal persons, whose consumption of other goods is reduced. In fact, the tax cannot go to any of the respondents, pivotal or otherwise, or else their truth telling may be corrupted. The only way to keep the taxes from having a distorting effect on the outcome is to eliminate them – for example, to lock them away in a box. This sequestration of the taxes collected limits consumption options, and this is where the waste occurs. There is the added difficulty that the socially desired level of the public good is unaffected by these waste-induced income changes. I can certainly imagine transnational public goods (for example, reducing global warming) where income influences can be very large; in these instances, a truth-telling scheme may be largely irrelevant.

There is an interesting irony here. If the number of respondents is large, then the likelihood that someone is pivotal is small and, with fewer pivotal persons, there are less of these wasted payments to elicit truth telling. So one may think that such processes would work well with large numbers of people; but transaction costs of instituting the procedure, ignored thus far, will then be huge. With sufficiently high transactions costs, the procedure's efficiency gain may not warrant these costs. Transaction costs are not so much of a consideration when only a few respondents are involved, but then wastes from truth-telling taxes are greater. So there is no free lunch. People can be made to reveal their private knowledge, but only at a cost to society.

Despite these schemes' inherent problems, it is clever to try to realign incentives not only to make people reveal what they really think, but also to get them to act in the interests of the group. In my interactions with students, friends, and family, I have used notions such as decoupling costs and reported values, and side payments to provide the requisite incentives for truth telling. I know that the outcome is not fully efficient, but it is interesting to uncover what my associates really think.[7]

HOME ASSESSMENTS

For those readers who found the last example too difficult, I shall provide an easier one, not involving public goods. Property taxes on a house are based on its assessed value. Suppose that a local government wants to save on appraisal costs and desires to institute a scheme that encourages owners to honestly reveal what they think their house is truly worth. Ordinarily, if asked, owners have an incentive to undervalue their houses, because this falsehood limits their taxes. But suppose that the government gives the owner a choice: taxing the house at the declared value *or*

---

[7] For a real-word application of a public good truth-telling mechanism, see Bohm (1984).

buying the house at this declared value. Incentives between parties are now aligned, and truth telling is dominant. If an owner undervalues his house, then the government purchases it at a bargain. If, instead, the owner overvalues it, then he pays more property taxes than he would had he been truthful. This simple taxing scheme saves appraisal fees, and is an incentive-compatible preference-revelation mechanism.

HIDDEN ACTION OR MORAL HAZARD

Imagine a situation where your actions, which are not observable, can help determine an outcome. For example, an exercise regime combined with a healthy diet influences one's risk of heart disease. Reading the assignments and studying for an exam improve test performance. Additionally, locked doors and secure windows lessen the chance of robbery, while maintenance of furnaces and the installation of detection devices reduce the likelihood of carbon monoxide poisoning. In our daily lives, we are confronted with opportunities where taking care can lower the risks of bad outcomes and raise the likelihood of favorable ones.

Suppose that you purchase insurance that protects you against theft. When this purchase *alters* your incentives to take care, and such care-taking actions are unobservable to the insurer, a situation of *moral hazard* occurs. One may reason: why lock my doors, I am insured. When this attitude is adopted by some of the insured, the resulting increased losses from theft raise everyone's insurance rates, even those of people who continue to take care. In choosing not to exercise care once insured, such individuals do not account for the costs, in terms of higher premiums, that their irresponsible actions impose on others. An externality is present. Moral hazard stems from the unobservability of an individual's actions, because had these actions been observed, insurance could have been suitably tailored to the risks. Safe-driving records and the absence of claims can, in part, indicate that care is being exercised, or that the person is extremely lucky. In either case, a lower premium can be justified. As long as actions remain unobservable, moral hazard remains even if there is circumstantial evidence of a good risk. When an insurance company requires a physical prior to writing a life insurance policy, the insurer is trying to ascertain not only the current risk but also something about the person's lifestyle and genetic makeup. Once the policy is written, there is nothing stopping the insured from taking up skydiving, snowboarding, or changing to a fat-rich diet.

There is a partial fix to the moral-hazard problem with respect to insurance. If a person has no insurance coverage whatsoever, then he or she will take the appropriate precautions, because the resulting consequences fall only upon him or her. With full insurance, the least care will be exercised. As the percentage of insurance coverage decreases, more of the risk is shared between the insured and the insurance company, so that the incentive for the insured to take care increases. The use of *deductibles* is a means to address the moral-hazard problem by making the insured partly responsible for their unobservable actions. Insurance premiums can be duly reduced as deductibles increase. This is probably a better solution to moral hazard than an "Ed TV" solution, where television cameras record our every action – every time you succumb to a cream puff or to unprotected sex, a higher insurance premium is deducted from your debit card.

The use of deductibles indicates that private actions can be devised to ameliorate the associated market failure without necessitating public intervention. There are many interesting ways to align incentives when there are hidden actions. A case in point is the practice of keeping servers' wages low and encouraging tipping.[8] This practice attracts and rewards good waiters, who can serve a sufficient volume to more than make up for the lower wages through tips. Bad waiters are better off finding a different line of work. Tipping allows the server and owner to share in the business's risk, and eliminates the server's incentives to shirk. This example strikes a chord with me. To pay for my college education, I worked at a country club where much of what I earned was in tips. This is where I learned to work hard and to use my wits. Of course, the deadbeats only got my attention once. The same principle as that of tipping applies to the practice of giving stock options instead of a raises to managers or commissions to salespeople, employees whose actions are not always observable.

Moral hazard involves many facets of daily life. For instance, when a surgeon suggests that you need an operation, you must wonder whether the diagnosis is based on medical expertise or greed, insofar as the surgeon profits from performing the surgery. The practice of seeking second and third opinions is an attempt to limit moral hazard. Actions by mechanics, television repairpersons, investment consultants, lawyers, and day-care providers are, in part, hidden and, thus, subject to moral hazard. The use of internet monitoring of day-care centers is a technology-driven "solution" to the associated moral-hazard problem. But even here the first best is not achieved, because the monitoring is costly for the day-care centers to set up and for the parents to watch. Some of the day-care internet costs are passed on to the parents. The more important monitoring is to the parents, the more of its costs can be passed on.

---

[8] This interesting example is due to Schotter (1994b, pp. 494–5).

HIDDEN INFORMATION AND ADVERSE SELECTION

Hidden information involves the presence of two or more types or qualities of goods offered for sale, where the true type is known to one side of the market but not to the other. An example is the so-called lemons market for used cars, briefly mentioned in Chapter 6.[9] Suppose that half of the used cars in a market are lemons with chronic problems, while the other half are reliable vehicles. Further assume that the lemons are worth $1,000 apiece, while the reliable cars are worth $5,000 each. In this market, the average car is worth $3,000 (0.5 × $1,000 + 0.5 × $5,000). If the market price is just $3,000, then most owners of reliable cars will either hold onto them or sell them to friends or family, who trust their word, at a higher price. At $3,000, only the lemons are worth selling and, as buyers realize that the proportion of lemons is increasing, the market-clearing price approaches $1,000. Saying that your vehicle is reliable does not mean much, since everyone says the same thing. The process whereby the bad risks drive the good risks from the market, leaving just the former, is known as *adverse selection*.

Adverse selection plagues health insurance markets, where genetics determines, in part, the insured's susceptibility to diseases. Insurance premiums must cover payments to both good and bad risks. If your health and that of your family is good, you might decide to self-insure and not purchase health insurance, since its costs exceed your expected gains. As in the lemons market, there are forces driving the good risks from the market, leaving more bad risks and still higher premiums.

Unemployment insurance is also troubled by an adverse-selection problem that limits the ability of private firms to provide such insurance. There are people who work hard and are sufficiently productive that they remain employed even during recessions, and then there are those who are slackers and/or less productive who are the first to be laid off during recessions. Unemployment insurance is most attractive to the slackers, who are quick to insure. Premiums must thus be sufficiently high to insure them, and this drives away the desirable workers from the insurance market. In fact, the self-selection process is so complete with this kind of insurance that private markets have not appeared. Governments, therefore, step in and lower the premiums charged employers by mandating that everyone be covered, so that good risks cannot take flight.[10] Government-provided universal health insurance

---

[9] The seminal paper is by Akerlof (1970).

[10] Ultimately, the cost of unemployment insurance is passed on to the employees in terms of lower wages.

and deposit insurance are also designed to eliminate the adverse-selection bias.

Like moral hazard, adverse selection involves a failure to account for external costs that an individual's action places on others. For example, the seller of an inferior product affects how buyers view the average quality on the market. This seller's action lowers the price and distorts the market for everyone. This kind of externality occurs whenever more than two qualities coexist and their differences are not apparent to one side of the market.

There are also private means to address adverse selection. Government-mandated universal coverage is not an efficient solution, because good risks are forced to remain in an undesirable trading situation. Private markets address adverse selection by providing signals or expert opinions, so that alternative types are better identified, but at a cost. Suppose that a used car dealer gives a five-year unlimited warranty on his cars. Such a warranty would only make sense for the guarantor if it reflected the true reliability of the product. The longer its term and the fewer limitations on the guarantee, the stronger are the signals that the product is of high quality. Signs indicating that cars are sold "as is" and that all purchases are final are not very reassuring. I am always amazed by the uncanny ability of producers to know the reliability of their products so well that they break down the day after the warranty is up. Warranties can also add to the price, so that addressing the adverse-selection problem in this way is not costless.

Another way to obtain information privately is to rely on an expert's advice, provided that the expert is independent of the seller. The payment to the expert eliminates a first-best outcome, but may improve the situation. Government's efforts to license doctors as well as professional organizations' certification processes are other efforts to reveal types and, in so doing, to limit adverse selection.

PRINCIPAL-AGENT ANALYSIS

I now return to a topic involving asymmetric information, mentioned in the last chapter, where a principal must design an optimal contractual arrangement with an agent.[11] The agent and principal must have different tastes, so that their goals are not already aligned. Participants at different levels of authority are differentially informed in virtually every institution. For example, a manager of a firm hires workers who know better than the manager how hard they are really working. In a govern-

---

[11] On principal-agent analysis, see Holmström (1982), MacDonald (1984), Ross (1973), and Stiglitz (1974). Cauley and Sandler (1992) have applied principal-agent analysis to examine economic reforms in Chinese enterprises.

ment, the principal is the electorate, while the agents are the elected officials; in a union, the principal is the union membership, while the agents are the union leaders. Neither the electorate nor the union membership can truly monitor the elected officials or the union leaders, but they can observe their final output. Other principal-agent relationships include club members (principals) and employees (agents); the Department of Defense (principal) and defense firms (agents); donors (principals) and a nonprofit charity (agent); the state governments (principals) and the federal government (agent); and countries (principals) and representatives of an international organization (agents).[12]

Asymmetric information is germane when a principal can view the final outcome (for example, an output level, an amount of the public good, the degree of tranquility, the level of poverty) but is unable to observe the agent's *actual* effort or action. This would apply when one or more random factors can intervene in the output or provision process so that the agent's effort is not uniquely tied to each outcome. Rather, a whole set or distribution of outcomes is associated with each effort level. If, for example, unpredictable outside influences can intervene to imply that a high effort level may, at times, still result in a bad outcome or that a low effort level may yield a good outcome, then the output level is not always indicative of the agent's effort. As a concrete example, suppose that I ask my graduate assistant to retrieve some data for me from the internet. Her effort may be high but the output low if, say, she experiences computer crashes, or encounters transmission problems where the internet connection fails repeatedly just before all of the data is downloaded. Similarly, she might expend low effort with good results due to fortuitous circumstances – for example, the downloaded data are already properly formatted, or low traffic on the internet site makes the transfer swift. Information is one-sided because the agent, and not the principal, knows of the intervening influences and knows her own true effort. This asymmetric information leads to a moral-hazard problem, insofar as the agent may take advantage of the principal's ignorance as an excuse to supply suboptimal levels of effort. Agent-principal difficulties can be minimized if the principal can design a contract or payment schedule for observable output that induces the agent to supply high effort.

In the simplest of terms, the principal wants to design an incentive scheme that makes expending high effort a dominant strategy. A sequential process is implied whereby the principal first chooses an output-to-payment schedule that maximizes the principal's objective (say, profit) subject to constraints based on how the agent(s) will respond to such

---

[12] Problems involving multiple principals but a single agent are known as common-agency problems (Dixit 1998).

incentive schemes in the subsequent period. The underlying two-stage game is solved backward by determining in the second round how the agent chooses effort to maximize some objective (for example, the difference between earnings and the disutility of effort), given an incentive arrangement. Two constraints from this round then bind the principal's choice of a contract or incentive scheme. First, the principal must satisfy an agent's *participation constraint*, where his or her net gain is at least as good as the best opportunity elsewhere. Second, the condition summarizing the agent's optimizing choice of effort must serve as an *incentive-compatible constraint*, restricting the principal's design of an incentive scheme. That is, the agent's own interests are welded together with those of the principal.

Because risks are associated with the random factors, an optimal arrangement calls for the agent to share some of this risk; that is, the agent must prosper from good outcomes that benefit the principal and also suffer from bad outcomes. The less accepting of risk is the agent, the more the agent must be rewarded for good outcomes to entice him to work hard even though a bad outcome may result by chance. *Agency costs* stem from the additional incentive payments required to make truth telling or expending high effort a dominant strategy.[13] These costs arise because the agent must be rewarded to work hard when factors turn out to be favorable and result in high output even without hard work. In addition, the agent is made to work hard when factors are unfavorable and a bad outcome nevertheless results. In neither case is high effort efficient. These agency costs keep a first-best outcome from occurring despite the incentive alignment. Again and again, we discover that there is always a cost from inducing people possessing hidden information not to exploit their advantage. It is this power that the well-informed individual has to extract additional payments that is referred to in this chapter's title, "Knowledge Is Power." It is human nature to exploit such knowledge for all that it is worth. For example, someone with "inside information" on the stock exchange can be expected first to buy the stock low (supposing the information is favorable about the company's prospects) and then to reveal the secret as widely as possible. This action will allow the person to realize the maximum appreciation in the stock's price as buyers bid up the price.

OTHER APPLICATIONS

An interesting application of principal-agent analysis and moral hazard involves the design of contracts for weapon procurement, where random

---

[13] On these agency costs, see Laffont and Tirole (1993) and Sandler and Tschirhart (1997, pp. 349–51).

factors can influence the ultimate costs of a new weapon system – for example, material needs may not fully be anticipated at the start of the project.[14] Uncertainty may also arise from the government's altering the weapon's required performance capabilities as time passes, because of changes in the combat environment and requirements. Depending on the contractual arrangements, risks are shared differently, and this sharing can impact behavior. For a *fixed-price contract*, where the defense firm submits a sealed bid and then must build the weapon at this price if the bid is accepted, risks are placed squarely on the defense contractor, which has incentives to limit costs after a successful bid. The firm may, however, stipulate that alterations by the government in the weapon's capabilities are not permitted unless the consequences of such changes are covered by negotiated price adjustments. If a successful bid is too high, it can do very well; if, however, a successful bid is too low, profits will suffer. The firm will, of course, tack on a risk premium to its sealed-bid price. Insofar as the firm is better informed about its cost environment than is the government, the latter must worry that it will get stuck by settling for too high a price. Fixed-price contracts are more attractive to the government when there is a single final supplier and limited uncertainty, so that the cost environment is observable by all parties.

At the other extreme, there is the *cost-plus contract*, in which the firm receives its costs and a fixed markup. Now the risks are fully assumed by the government, and the defense contractor has absolutely no incentive to keep down costs; thus costly hammers and toilet seats should come as no surprise. With a cost-plus contract, the government can change the weapon's specification as often as it wants but must cover any cost over-runs. Although such contracts are inefficient, they may be justified when the government is not completely clear about the weapon's specifications and is less risk-adverse than the defense firm, which can be expected to add a large premium to a fixed-price contract for sharing risks.

A hybrid contract that combines features of cost-plus and fixed-price contracts is the *incentive contract*. For such contracts, the defense firm is paid both a fixed price (which is a percentage of a fixed-price contract) and a fraction of the cost incurred. This contractual arrangement allows for risk sharing and is analogous to a principal-agent analysis if designed optimally. If competition is high and costs are transparent, then the incentive contract that places more weight on the fixed component may have much to offer. Quite simply, *the incentive contract trades off the*

---

[14] On procurement and the design of incentive-compatible contracts, see Cummins (1977), Kovacic (1991), Laffont (1986), Laffont and Tirole (1986), McAfee and McMillan (1986a), and Sandler and Hartley (1995).

strengths and weaknesses of the two extreme contractual arrangements and is best when conditions do not strictly favor either. A simple rule of thumb would be to choose the weights on the fixed component and the cost components depending on how initial conditions favor one or the other. Reliance on the fixed component rewards the firm with a risk premium, whereas reliance on the cost component limits incentives to reduce costs. The ability to engineer an optimum trade-off between the two components, as provided by a well-designed incentive contract, comes at a transaction cost, as the firm and the government must negotiate over a larger number of parameters. The architecture of more appropriate institutions comes at a cost that always puts the ideal out of reach.

The application to incentive contracts involves hidden action, while the next case addresses situations of hidden information. The new application concerns signaling, where one economic agent interacts with a second whose type is unknown to the first agent, who then tries to identify the second agent's type from his or her actions. We have already seen the usefulness of signals, such as warranties and expert opinions, in resolving uncertainty.

Suppose that a government is challenged by a terrorist group whose resources are unknown to the government. If, alternatively, the government knew that the terrorists possessed sufficient resources to force the government eventually to surrender, the optimal strategy for the government would be to concede at the outset, thereby avoiding the additional costs associated with attacks. If, on the other hand, the terrorists knew that they could never win, then it would make sense for them never to start the campaign. Full information does not make for a very interesting strategic environment or description of the real world. In fact, a government can only guess at a terrorist group's strength.

With asymmetric information, a resource-poor terrorist group with insufficient resources to force a government capitulation with complete information may try to appear to be stronger than it really is by a barrage of initial attacks, intended to make the government draw the wrong inference and concede to their demands. Similarly, a strong terrorist group, which the government would, if it knew its strength, concede to immediately, would also unleash a ferocious attack. Thus, it may be difficult for the government to distinguish the two types. Even if the government cannot distinguish the groups, the attacks provide a signal that the government processes to hypothesize its best course of actions – that is, to continue to resist or to capitulate. Regret may result if a government either capitulates to a terrorist group with insufficient resources, or does not capitulate to a group with sufficient resources to have resulted in capitulation under complete information.[15]

In order to trade off these two kinds of regret, the government may be best off settling on a signaling equilibrium, where a sufficiently high level of immediate attacks serves as a signal to concede even though a mistake may result. The Indian government's eventual capitulation to the demands of the six hijackers of an India Airline flight hijacked on 24 December 1999 represents a case where the hijackers demonstrated sufficient resolve and resources that the Indian government did not want to risk the consequences of not giving in. Hence, it gave in and released three Kashmiri prisoners from Indian jails in return for an end to the hijacking on 31 December 1999.

Signaling equilibria were first introduced by Michael Spence (1973) for a case of labor screening where a prospective employee may be a high-productivity or low-productivity type. In this interesting paper, Spence showed that finishing a degree program, while *not adding* to the workers' productivity, can still provide a signal that identifies or distinguishes the two types. This follows because the high-productivity type is smarter and can complete the degree program with less cost. A sufficient cost differential for the degree program for the two types can then indicate the tell-tale signal, insofar as it would not be in the low-productivity type's interest to complete the degree program.

KNOWLEDGE AND INFORMATION AS A PUBLIC GOOD

Knowledge is recognized by economists as a pure public good, whose benefits are nonrivalrous in consumption and nonexcludable.[16] For example, knowledge of the genetic codes of the human body when passed from one team of scientists to another does not diminish the benefits that the first team of scientists gains from understanding the codes. In fact, the transmission process may augment their understanding, much as teachers and authors gain additional insight as they pass along knowledge to others. Once the knowledge is revealed, it is difficult to exclude others unless the government protects the use of the knowledge through patents or copyrights. In the absence of this protection, there would be little incentive to spend large sums of money to discover a new drug if, after the discovery, others were free to exploit the discovery and produce their own drugs for sale.

Patents are a means for limiting asymmetric information with respect to discoveries in the *longer run* by providing seventeen years of

---

[15] Details of this analysis are contained in Lapan and Sandler (1993).

[16] The representation of knowledge as a global public good is presented by Stiglitz (1999).

exclusive rights in return for revealing the secret behind the discovery so that others may benefit from this knowledge in the future. Without the patent system, there would be greater expenditure on keeping findings secret, and this would inhibit future breakthroughs and, thus, limit the dynamic efficiency of knowledge generation. Moreover, there would be reduced incentives to generate knowledge, and this would also thwart the progress of knowledge. Patent protection of knowledge presents a trade-off in terms of limiting short-term publicness of knowledge so as to promote its longer-term publicness.[17] The choice of the number of years of patent protection is an attempt on the part of government to balance these two trade-offs. Given that every addition to knowledge has its own implications for this trade-off, the choice of a single time period for all such patents implies an acceptance of some inefficiency in return for economizing on the transaction costs associated with tailoring the number of years to each patent. The use of patents and, also, the realization that not everyone can understand a discovery indicate that the transmission process of knowledge may be partially rivalrous, unlike the inherent insight embodied in the knowledge. That is, teaching someone the formula to a new drug consumes resources and may restrict the teaching of it to others, but the benefits inherent in knowing the formula are not lessened as this knowledge is diffused.

We live at a time where monitoring technologies are curtailing the prevalence of asymmetric information and, by so doing, can augment market efficiency. When computers are networked, employers have the ability to ascertain workers' effort; that is, time spent surfing the internet and time spent word processing can be monitored. The electronic age can allow effort in a growing number of situations to be observed, thus limiting hidden actions. In some instances, scientific breakthroughs can address the problem of hidden types. Knowledge of the human genetic code can enable an insurance company to gauge from our DNA our susceptibility to diseases as well as our preexisting conditions. This information can curtail the adverse-selection process, but would leave millions with significant preexisting or pending diseases with either prohibitively expensive premiums or no coverage. If insurance companies are allowed access to this information, the frightening implication is that more uninsurable individuals would turn to the state for coverage. Ironically, the state can afford to provide this coverage only if it can include the good risks in the pool, and this need for universal coverage could end private health insurance coverage. By eliminating the adverse-selection problem, exploiting knowledge of the human genetic code can result in both winners (those with good genes) and losers (those with

---

[17] This trade-off was indicated by Stiglitz (1999, p. 311).

bad genes). Whether or not the sum of the marginal benefits from eliminating adverse selection in health insurance is positive or negative is anyone's guess. Moreover, one's net gain may be age-dependent if the insurance companies end coverage in later years, when the onset of many diseases is experienced. In fact, evolutionary biologists indicate that the self-selection process against aging is greatly inhibited because most age-enhancing diseases (e.g., Alzheimer's disease) take place only after humans have reached reproductive age, so that such diseases are passed on to the next generation and are not self-selected out.[18]

These bold horizons before humankind where asymmetric information is severely curtailed may require economists and other social scientists to rethink the whole trade-off associated with asymmetric information. The achievement of complete information on both sides of the market – the ideal of classical economics – may not turn out to be all that it was thought to be, especially when transaction costs and other consequences are considered.

AN EVALUATION OF THE STUDY OF ASYMMETRIC INFORMATION

There is no question that the original insights of Akerlof, Spence, and others about asymmetric information not only are germane to myriad real-world applications, but also are based on relatively simple notions. This elementary foundation has meant that the transmission of the knowledge embodied by their discoveries could be wide, thus leading to myriad follow-up contributions and extensions. The original insights of this analysis are so clear and uncomplicated that they can be made accessible to the broad readership of this book. Thus, the originators of asymmetric information theory ensured through its initial simplicity, varied application, and novelty that it would have a lasting legacy. This impact spilled over to the related social sciences. In political science, asymmetric information has been applied to the study of conflict where agents are differentially informed, and to numerous other issues. The study of environmental policy and even of law can profit from the application of asymmetric information concepts. For example, how should liabilities be assigned to a health problem that may or may not be caused by a pollution activity whose perpetrator cannot be known with certainty? Similarly, how should penalties be assigned when a firm's activities or a natural phenomenon may be behind an increase in an environmental pollutant, such as sulfur, and the courts cannot determine for sure which one is the cause? The answers to these two liability questions can be derived from a study of asymmetric information. In both cases, the firm

---

[18] See, for example, the discussion by Rose (1999).

possesses knowledge of its own actions that may resolve some of the uncertainty, but it may not be in the firm's interest to reveal this information. Even the study of history can prosper from an application of the principles of asymmetric information. In discerning why certain historical decisions were made, historians need to know how informed the relevant parties were at the time. If similar situations do not repeat themselves at a later time when other conditions are analogous, it may be due to the distribution of information – that is, the one-sidedness of information may have changed, leading history not to repeat itself.

Although there are still promising extensions for the study of asymmetric information, I am quite concerned that too much effort is being channeled into its study with ever-smaller insights being gleaned. An analogy to the wastes of monopolistic competition seems apropos, where too many entrepreneurs invest in the same industry with only a slightly differentiated product. As a consequence, many firms do not survive, and their investments are wasted. In the last five years, I have been struck by the percentage of job candidates who are pursuing similar asymmetric-information exercises. Their differentiation is rather thin – too thin for my taste – and the resulting insights not very novel, which, if I am correct, would limit their publication possibilities. The novelty often rests with the application and not with the conclusions. Of course, less competent analysis is more novel, but of dubious worth. I am also worried about the amount of detail required by recent analyses of asymmetric information – the simple elegance of earlier studies has been lost. There is a need to streamline the analysis and to translate it into a simple graphical presentation to foster intuition.[19]

If asymmetric information is to maintain its influence on economic thought, more real-world empirical studies and practical applications to institutions are needed. In some ways, the nature of the topic restricts empirical studies, because one side of the market is uninformed by definition, which affects data collection. Insurance markets can, nevertheless, afford an appropriate place for testing some hypotheses against data. Other tests can be conducted in a laboratory situation, where the experimenter can manipulate what the parties to a transaction know. To the best of my knowledge, there are relatively few instances where preference-revelation mechanisms have been instituted in real organizations. I surmise that this is because the actual implementation of these mechanisms is too complex. The instructions of the tax scheme and its step-by-step implementation are very involved – perhaps too involved for the average person to comprehend. There is also the problem that

---

[19] This is what we have tried, in a small way, to do in our book on public goods and externalities. See, especially, Cornes and Sandler (1996).

these mechanisms' desirable properties may not hold in light of significant income influences, which are likely to characterize many relevant public good applications.

While I am a big fan of the study of asymmetric information, I am not sanguine that it will maintain its huge presence in the near future unless some truly novel and simple paradigms are uncovered.

8   Everything Ties Together: General Equilibrium

> From the time of Adam Smith's *Wealth of Nations* in 1776, one
> recurrent theme of economic analysis has been the remarkable degree
> of coherence among vast numbers of individual and seemingly separate
> decisions about the buying and selling of commodities.
>
> Arrow 1974a, p. 253

When teaching economics, I always use examples from literature to
illustrate essential economic concepts and principles and to underscore
that economics permeates our lives and is a natural part of humankind.
From the Bible to great works of literature, economic thinking abounds.
I would not be surprised if the map of human DNA uncovers an
economic gene. Economics is so ingrained in our thought processes
that I sometimes wonder whether the standard Economics 101 with
its myriad graphs and equations does more to obfuscate than to
enlighten.

The piece of literature that I use when introducing the notion of
general equilibrium is "Harrison Bergeron," a short story by Kurt Vonnegut, Jr. (1970). The story begins, "The year was 2081, and everybody
was finally equal" (p. 7). As the tale goes, everyone is made equal not by
natural forces but by a "handicapper general," whose job is to devise
debilitating handicaps so that everyone is reduced to the level of the least
agile, dumbest, homeliest, and most inarticulate person. To accomplish
this bizarre task, the handicapper puts weights on the agile, implants
distracting transmitters in the brains of the gifted, covers the faces of
the attractive, and provides impediments to the orators. Although these
equalizers (minimalizers) work for a time, people slowly learn to cope
and overcome their impediments to some degree and begin to differentiate themselves from others. For instance, some dancers gain strength
and even become temporarily airborne despite the weights. The better
orators learn to use their handicap-imposed stutter with eloquence.

Gradually, the tendency for people to use their natural and acquired talents to advantage creates new inequalities, leaving the handicapper general the never-ending chore of imposing ever-greater impediments to keep everyone equivalent to society's most wretched individual. Of course, the story would be less ironic if the "handicaps" had been to raise everyone to the talents of the most gifted, but the tendency to return to inequality would be the same.

This story nicely illustrates the natural tendency for unequal distribution of endowments and income; any effort to inhibit this tendency requires large resource outlays and succeeds only temporarily. As in nature, economics deplores a disequilibrium and releases forces that rapidly return the system to an equilibrium where all opposing forces are in balance. In economics, this return is dependent on the interrelationship among markets as directed by signals in the form of prices, wages, and profits. No conscious direction or coordination of actions is required to allow for differences in talent to be rewarded.

It is fitting that my book's halfway chapter is devoted to elucidating the nature and contribution of the study of general equilibrium. Undoubtably, it represents the most important development in economics during the last century.[1] In many ways, the principles associated with general-equilibrium analysis provide the foundation for modern economic thought. This exalted status is partly defensible when taking stock of the early Nobel Prizes in economics given to Paul Samuelson in 1970, Kenneth Arrow and John Hicks in 1972, Wassily Leontief in 1973, Leonid Kantorovich and Tjalling Koopmans in 1975, and Gerard Debreu in 1983. All of these economists made pathbreaking contributions to the study of general equilibrium. Once the Nobel Prize for economics was created in 1969, the committee lost no time in recognizing living economists who have given a more formal underpinning to Adam Smith's "invisible hand," where markets achieve efficient results without explicit direction or control.

With their first exposure to economics, students are taught the workings of a market equilibrium where price equates the quantity demanded to the quantity supplied. If these two quantities are unequal, then one side of the market has unfulfilled plans. Either the resulting excess supply will create inventories that induce sellers to lower prices, or else the resulting excess demand will create a shortfall of stock that induces buyers to raise prices. In both cases, price adjusts until balance is

---

[1] Certainly, Arrow (1974a) and Starr (1997) would agree with this statement, but others might not. I make this statement owing to the status afforded to the pioneers of general-equilibrium theory and its dominance in the literature throughout much of the twentieth century.

restored. The equilibrium corresponds to the intersection of the demand and supply curves that relate the quantity demanded or supplied to the price, while holding other possible influences (e.g., income, prices of other goods) constant. The study of an isolated market is known as a *partial-equilibrium* analysis, where the market's own price is the focus of attention. For *general equilibrium*, the interrelationship of all markets is investigated and all commodities' prices are relevant.

My modest purpose is to provide a nontechnical explanation and evaluation of the general-equilibrium revolution that has guided much of economic thought during the last century. Why did Leon Walras's *Elements of Pure Economics* (henceforth called the *Elements*) hold such sway over economics? Another purpose is to present the essential issues in the study of general equilibrium. A third purpose is to relate its analysis to the notion of allocative efficiency, in order to address whether or not a general equilibrium is a desirable position for society. A final purpose is to expose general equilibrium's problems and prospects.

THE ELEMENTS OF GENERAL EQUILIBRIUM

An important concept for understanding market equilibrium – partial or general – is that of *excess demand*, which shows the *difference* between the quantity demanded and supplied at each price. If, at a given price, the quantity demanded by buyers exceeds the quantity supplied by sellers, there is a positive excess demand. If, instead, at a given price, the quantity supplied by sellers exceeds the quantity demanded by buyers, there is a positive excess supply or negative excess demand. With positive excess demand, buyers will increase the price they offer in order to obtain the quantity that is in short supply, while, with excess supply, sellers will reduce price to try to sell their wares to hard-to-find buyers. When excess demand is zero, the market is in equilibrium, with no unfulfilled wishes – at the given price, quantities demanded and supplied match one another and there is no pressure on price to adjust.

As a useful shorthand device for representing a market equilibrium, economists rely on the excess demand, E, relationship to indicate the difference between demand and supply. The right-hand side of Figure 8.1 depicts the downward-sloping demand curve, $D(p)$, and the upward-sloping supply curve, $S(p)$, as a function of price, p, indicated on the vertical axis.[2] Quantity is displayed on the horizontal axis.[3] The equilibrium price and quantity corresponds to F' at the intersection of the demand

[2] An equilibrium can also result if for a zero price the quantity supplied exceeds the quantity demanded. The zero-price case is ignored in the text.
[3] In Figure 8.1, economists wrongly place the dependent variable, quantity, rather than the independent variable, price, on the horizontal axis.

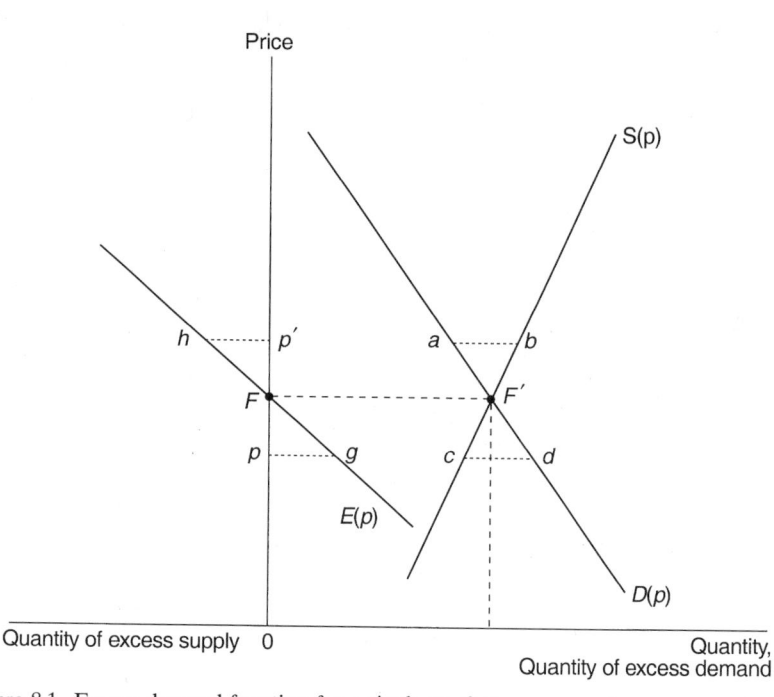

Figure 8.1. Excess demand function for a single market

and the quantity supply curves, or alternatively to F where excess demand, $E(p)$, is zero. The demand and supply curves are drawn linearly for convenience. In Figure 8.1, the excess demand curve is constructed from the difference between the quantity demanded and the quantity supplied at each price. For example, at a price p, excess demand equals pg (= cd), while, at a price p', excess supply equals hp' (= ab). Excess supply is equivalent to negative excess demand. In an isolated market, partial equilibrium corresponds to the point at which $E(p)$ intersects the vertical axis so that $E(p) = 0$.

With this background, it is easy to understand the notion of a general equilibrium, which occurs when a set of prices, one for each market, allows all markets to clear. That is, the *excess demand in every market is zero* for the market-clearing prices. In a general-equilibrium representation, each market's excess demand not only depends on its own price, but also on the prices of other goods. The price of gasoline can affect the supply and demand, and hence the excess demand, for cars. Similarly, the price of movies may influence the demand and supply of restaurant meals if people like to combine a night at the theater with a good meal. Even if goods are unrelated in consumption, price in one market may impact consumers' choices in other markets, because more money spent on one item leaves less for other goods. For sellers, input prices also influence the quantities that they can supply at each price. In short, everything is tied together through prices. Without any bureaucracy or bookkeeping, market prices perform sheer magic by directing resources to their most valued uses while balancing opposing forces from buyers and sellers. And once balance is attained in markets, there is no further pressure, for the time being, for change, because everyone's plans are satisfied relative to his or her means. This position of rest is not unlike a Nash equilibrium, encountered in the theory of games, where no individual wants unilaterally to alter his or her strategy.

A "yacht tax" passed in 1991 by the US Congress illustrates the essential insights provided by a general-equilibrium approach. This excise (or per-unit) tax on high-priced pleasure boats was intended to hit rich buyers and, in so doing, to help *redistribute income from the rich to the poor*. Unfortunately, the tax had just the opposite consequence by causing such a drop in the demand for new pleasure boats that their sales plummeted. Workers in this boat-building industry, who tended to be of modest income, lost wages or their jobs. Other input suppliers to this industry and other industries making complementary products were also damaged. Because of this damage to the relatively poor, the tax became so politically unpopular that it was rescinded in 1994.[4] Acknowledgment of the interrelationship among markets might have prevented such a costly mistake, in which the policy hurts those that it was intended to help.

A second illustrative example involves understanding how shocks or unexpected events in one industry can have far-reaching consequences in the economy. Cold weather in South America that destroys significant numbers of coffee trees results in a large price rise, which, in turn, increases sales of substitute drinks including tea, hot chocolate, and cola drinks. Cafés are also expected to be affected, along with bakeries, whose patrons enjoy pastries with their coffee.

The fourfold oil price hikes in the early 1970s by the Organization of Petroleum Exporting Countries (OPEC) brought home the fact that oil prices have a wide-ranging impact on both input and output markets. When the price of phonograph records rose during this period, I learned that oil is used in their manufacture. Such price hikes helped plunge the world into recession and eventually resulted in unprecedented discoveries of oil and conservation efforts. The dynamic general-equilibrium impacts, which were entirely unanticipated, led to a world temporarily awash in oil in the 1990s, when the real price, adjusted for

---

[4] See Bruce (1998, p. 421) and his analysis of the general-equilibrium effects of taxes (pp. 432–6).

general price inflation, fell significantly. More recently, the shift in market shares between passenger cars and sport utility vehicles (SUVs) has influenced not only the price of oil through increased gasoline demand, but also the price of tires. In addition, the price of insurance coverage on passenger cars has risen because collisions with these taller and more massive SUVs, or "urban assault vehicles," can be devastating.

From the analysis of tariffs and taxes to all kinds of policy decisions, the general-equilibrium revolution has taken hold in the last century. The study of isolated markets is of limited value in the complex, interrelated economy of the twenty-first century. With the rise of global markets and the internet, this interrelationship now involves markets at home and around the globe.

A BRIEF HISTORY OF GENERAL EQUILIBRIUM

Like finding the source of a great river, it is difficult to trace the precise origins of general-equilibrium analysis. Surely, Adam Smith's notion of an invisible hand guiding economic activities to a desirable outcome is a nontechnical recognition that everything ties together. Walras's (1874) *Elements* is unmistakably the most influential forerunner of the formal analysis of general equilibrium, which occupied many of the great minds in economic thought during the twentieth century. But Walras was influenced by the writings of Augustin Cournot (1838) and others.[5]

Walras represented a general equilibrium as an equality of demand and supply, where each depends on all market prices. To establish the existence of a general equilibrium, Walras merely counted equations and unknowns to make sure that they matched, a practice that is legitimate under some very restrictive conditions.[6] One of his major findings, derived from the satisfaction of everyone's budget constraints where income equals expenditures, is called Walras' Law, which indicates if all but one market is in equilibrium, then the remaining market must also be in equilibrium. In simple terms, this means that one price must be arbitrarily set and all other prices must be in terms of this set price. Then only relative prices, or the price ratio, of all goods in terms of some standard of value matters. In introductory classes, the notion that only relative prices matter can be illustrated by asking the students to imagine themselves awakening from a daydream in a strange new place with a

---

[5] On this history of general-equilibrium analysis, see Arrow (1974a), Blaug (1997, p. 550), and Starr (1997, pp. 7–9).

[6] Counting equations and unknowns would be sufficient if all excess-demand functions were linear and independent – that is, if each was mutually consistent and allowed for an intersection. Independencies rule out two excess-demand curves being parallel without intersecting.

pocket full of $100 bills – $100,000 in total. To exercise their imagined new spending power, they rush to a nearby CD store to buy a new release and place $100 on the counter, expecting change. Their elation turns to despair when the clerk informs them that CDs sell for $1 million apiece, ten times more than their imaginary endowment. In terms of CDs as a standard of value, these students' money is not going to buy much.

Another pioneer in the study of modern general-equilibrium theory was F. Y. Edgeworth, whose *Mathematical Psychics* (1881) presented the concept of bargaining among economic agents – the foundation of the modern theory of exchange and trade. Another pioneer, Vilfredo Pareto (1909), presented the efficiency criterion that figures prominently in evaluating economic equilibria of all kinds. In fact, his work set the normative standard by which economic efficiency is judged today.

In the modern era, economists have gone beyond counting equations and unknowns when establishing the existence of general equilibrium with formal analyses by Kenneth Arrow, Gerard Debreu, Lionel McKenzie, and others.[7] This work uses the optimizing decisions of consumers, input owners, and firms to derive the demand for goods, the supply of goods, and the demand and supply of inputs. Thus, their work relies on a behavioral framework for deriving the demand and supply relationship and, hence, the excess demand relationship that summarizes the buying and selling sides for each market. In proving the existence of a general equilibrium, these researchers rely on a fixed-point theorem, which identifies the equilibrium with a point (or points) which is (are) unchanged with some well-behaved transformation consisting of the excess demand functions. Fixed-point theorems are ubiquitous in mathematics and the sciences. In the study of plate tectonics or the movement of the Earth's crust, the identification of a fixed point or some global position that has remained stationary despite continental drift allows scientists to map the movement of the continents over time. In optics, the fixed point, where an image is not changed by a lens, is the focus of the lens. At a general equilibrium for an economy, the fixed point corresponds to a set of market prices that simultaneously make every excess demand zero. Once a general equilibrium has been established for an uncomplicated set of markets, researchers extend the analysis to allow for uncertainty, a money market, and multiple periods. Other technicalities have to be addressed – for example, when prices are zero or externalities are present.

---

[7] See, in particular, Arrow (1951), Arrow and Debreu (1954), Debreu (1959), and McKenzie (1954).

A ROBINSON CRUSOE ECONOMY

As a heuristic exercise, economists have constructed a one-person, general-equilibrium representation known as a Robinson Crusoe economy. This depiction is instructive because it clearly indicates that an economy contains both a production and a consumption side, each of which involves an optimization problem. Namely, the producer or firm wants to maximize profit subject to the available technology, resources, and market prices, while the consumer desires to maximize satisfaction subject to his or her budget constraints with given market prices. In a Robinson Crusoe economy, the producer and consumer is one and the same, so that his labor choice determines the alternative output levels that constrain his utility maximization.[8] If prices are given, then the equilibrium is characterized by the consumer equating his willingness to trade his labor for more output to the ratio of the wage to the price of output. In maximizing profit, Robinson equates his ability to transform labor into output to this selfsame ratio of prices. Since both the individual's willingness to trade in consumption and his production trade-off are equated to the same price ratio, these two trade-offs are equal to one another at equilibrium.

Although this setting is rather artificial, a couple of essential insights follow nevertheless. First, the given wage and price allow the consumer's wishes to match those of the producer, so that the coordination role of prices is clearly displayed. Second, the equilibrium is consistent with optimality. It can be shown either that optimization leads to an equilibrium, or that an equilibrium is consistent with both the consumer and the producer doing as well as possible. Thus, this simple exercise indicates that there is a close relationship between a general-equilibrium position and doing as well as possible.

The assumption of fixed prices is consistent with each person's being too small to have any perceivable influence on price, which implies competitive prices. It is this competitive price assumption of the Robinson Crusoe economy that is at odds with there being a single seller and buyer, each of whom is Robinson; thus, the assumption of fixed competitive prices is rather absurd. Nevertheless, this single-person representation yields many essential findings. If such prices exist, then the production and consumption decisions can be decentralized or decoupled yet still be coordinated in the final analysis. Prices perform magic without conscious coordination among market participants. If, however, prices are distorted by not including all costs or benefits, as in the case of

---

[8] This Robinson Crusoe characterization can be found in most books that discuss general equilibrium; see, in particular, Starr (1997, pp. 9–20).

externalities or public goods, then the magical coordination between buyers and sellers is lost.

In its pristine form, a Robinson Crusoe economy cannot address trade or interrelated markets except in terms of Robinson's output and labor markets. By introducing another person, say, Friday, exchange equilibrium can be addressed, along with an exchange-production equilibrium. As more people and activities are added to Crusoe's economy, the multimarket economy grows in sophistication and the general-equilibrium interrelationships become more complex. Nevertheless, the role of price in providing decision-makers' coordination within and among markets remains.

FOUR ISSUES OF GENERAL EQUILIBRIUM

First and foremost, there is the existence question: under what circumstances does there exist a set of prices capable of clearing all markets simultaneously? There must be no positive excess demand at an equilibrium. Moreover, each excess demand must account for any possible interactions by including *all market prices*. This existence hinges on some well-behaved function or relationship involving excess demands that contains a fixed point for which all excess demands are zero or negative. An axiomatic or minimalist approach is applied, so that existence is based on the absolute minimal assumptions regarding consumers' and producers' optimizing behavior. In particular, consumers' tastes must be well behaved, and the same is true of the production functions that relate inputs to outputs. For example, consumers' tastes must permit trade-offs or substitutions among goods, while production relationships must associate increases in inputs with an increase in output, but not at too fast a rate of increase.

Matters become complicated when a given set of prices is consistent with multiple equilibria. Another potential worry involves zero prices, where one or more goods are free. Yet another difficulty occurs if some of the excess demands are not well defined – that is, a set of prices may be associated with more than one value of excess demand or with none at all. In these and other cases, equilibrium can still be savaged if Walras' Law holds and some redefined excess demand relationship is "continuous," so that small variations in price result in small variations in excess demand. Much effort in the study of general equilibrium has been directed toward these aberrant cases.[9]

Once existence is established for a general equilibrium, a second issue concerns its stability. An equilibrium is stable if following a disturbance

---

[9] On the existence of general equilibrium see Henderson and Quandt (1980), Starr (1997), or any good microeconomics text with a section on general equilibrium.

that displaces it there is a natural tendency to return to the equilibrium position. Consider an isolated market equilibrium as displayed in Figure 8.1. This equilibrium is stable because a disturbance that reduces price and creates excess demand is met with actions by buyers to raise price to acquire the item in short supply and so restore equilibrium. Similarly, a disturbance that raises price and opens up excess supply induces suppliers to reduce price and rid themselves of unwanted inventory. If excess demand responds negatively to price, so that excess demand falls with a rise in price and increases with a fall in price, then the equilibrium is stable. In other words, if the slope of the excess demand curve is negative, as in Figure 8.1, then the isolated market equilibrium is stable.

John R. Hicks (1939) analyzed the stability of general equilibrium under various scenarios. In a general-equilibrium setting, a disturbance in any market can potentially upset the equilibrium in other markets, because each market's excess demand depends on prices in all markets. Thus, the stability of any market depends on the price and quantity adjustments and feedbacks from other markets. Traditionally, notions of static and dynamic stability are investigated with respect to general equilibrium (Henderson and Quandt 1980, pp. 267–74). For static stability, the overall change in a market's excess demand in response to the set of price changes, including its own price change, is the crucial consideration. If the excess demand in market j for a change in p_j is negative for all feasible combinations of price responses in other markets, and if, moreover, this is true of every market's excess demand, then the general equilibrium possesses static stability. Static stability for a general-equilibrium system implies isolated stability in the individual markets that comprise the economy.

Dynamic stability is more esoteric and involves the path taken over time for a multimarket system to return to equilibrium. Static stability is neither a necessary nor a sufficient condition for dynamic stability, which can involve two forms (Henderson and Quandt 1980, pp. 271–4). First, there is local dynamic stability, for which the system will return to equilibrium with time as long as the disturbance displacing the equilibrium is not too great. Second, there is global dynamic stability, for which the system will eventually return to equilibrium for any disturbance. Local stability is assured when all goods are gross substitutes for one another, so that a price rise in one market is met with an increase in excess demand in other markets. Global stability hinges on more involved conditions, which are left for the interested reader to pursue. For any analysis of equilibrium stability and convergence, an adjustment relationship must be specified for disequilibrium positions. That is, how price adjusts when it departs from the equilibrium must be indicated beforehand. This adjustment relationship introduces an ad hoc element into the exercise, since an alternative adjustment specification can result in a vastly different path of change. As there are an infinite variety of adjustment paths, stability analysis is viewed by some economists as rather arbitrary. Because the equilibrium must be identified prior to investigating its stability, existence must be established before stability.

A third issue involves uniqueness of equilibrium – that is, are there more than one set of prices that clear all markets? The easiest way to conceptualize the uniqueness question is to examine the excess demand curve, $E(p)$, of a single market in Figure 8.2. Every time excess demand crosses the vertical axis, $E(p) = 0$, an equilibrium is achieved so that points A, B, and C are all equilibria. Points A and C are locally stable, since excess demand responds negatively to a price change near these points, whereas point B is locally unstable, since excess demand responds positively to a price change in its vicinity. This figure suggests that stability is unlikely to characterize some equilibria when there are many.

With multiple equilibria, the distinction between local and global stability is essential. In Figure 8.1, the sole equilibrium can withstand any size displacement and still return to the original equilibrium, so that it is globally stable. In Figure 8.2, however, only displacements not too far

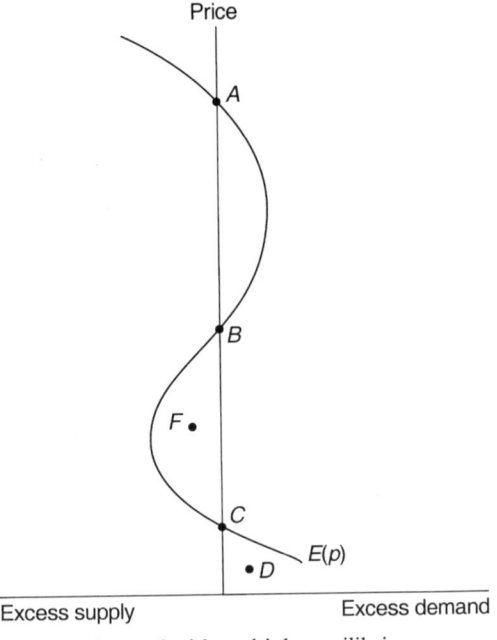

Figure 8.2. Excess demand with multiple equilibria

from a stable equilibrium A or C will return to the original equilibrium, indicating local stability. In devising procedures to identify an equilibrium in practice, nonuniqueness may mean that locating an equilibrium can be sensitive to the starting point of the search. For example, an initial price and quantity combination of points D and F in Figure 8.2 will lead the researcher to discover equilibrium C, while an initial disequilibrium point between points A and B will lead the researcher to identify equilibrium A. The practice of comparative statics, where the underlying demand or supply curves are shifted owing to a change in one or more of their parameters, may not result in a unique outcome if there are multiple equilibria. Uniqueness simplifies uncovering the influence on market behavior of policy changes and other shocks.

A fourth consideration of a general equilibrium concerns its allocative efficiency or desirability. In his description of a competitive equilibrium, Adam Smith characterized it as being a desirable position where everyone's interests are furthered. Once the notion of efficiency is raised, an ethical or normative standard is needed by which to evaluate a competitive equilibrium. The notion of efficiency must be distinguished from equity. An action that augments everyone's well-being may improve some people's welfare more than others. If those who benefit to a greater extent are the richest, then improved efficiency may be entirely consistent with increased inequality. Certainly, a person who cannot hear, see, or walk is unlikely to prosper in a competitive equilibrium that rewards people's productivity.

COMPETITIVE EQUILIBRIUM AND OPTIMALITY: FURTHER THOUGHTS

The notion of optimality used by economists is that of Pareto optimality. A position is said to be a *Pareto optimum* if it would be impossible to improve the well-being of one individual without harming at least one other individual. Under this normative criterion, a Pareto-improving action should be instituted if it makes at least one person better off and no one worse off. When I was a student and first learned of this criterion, I thought that economists must be really nice people to ascribe to this ethic. How could one doubt a criterion that tries to help someone, but not at the expense of someone else? And then I thought some more. Suppose that we lived in a world where I had great wealth and earnings and all others had only enough for the clothes on their backs and sufficient food to survive. If I were a selfish person who would suffer if I had to give up even a penny of my earnings, then this state of gross inequality would be a Pareto optimum. Taking anything away from me to give to others would make me worse off. In many ways, Pareto optimality is more a criterion of inactivity, since it tends to favor the status quo, as my example indicates. If, however, there are unemployed or inefficiently utilized resources, then there can easily be found Pareto-improving actions that make some better off and no one worse off.

So if Pareto optimality is consistent with states of gross inequality, then why does it reign supreme as the standard of social welfare for judging economic outcomes? The answer involves its close association with competitive equilibrium. There are two fundamental results or "theorems" of welfare economics, which examines the normative aspects of economic outcomes and systems.[10] The first theorem states that every competitive equilibrium results in a Pareto optimum, provided that there are no externalities or public goods. If, therefore, firms maximize their profits and consumers maximize their utility, the resulting competitive equilibrium is Pareto optimal. I like to think of this theorem as the *invisible-hand theorem*, which depends on competitive markets where no individual has any influence on prices. The second theorem indicates that any Pareto optimum could be supported as a competitive equilibrium if some tinkering with the income distribution is allowed.[11] This second theorem suggests that efficiency aspects can be separated from the problem of distribution.[12] Each Pareto optimum implies a distribution of well-being – that is, how well-off some people are relative to others. Both positions of relative equality and gross inequality can be consistent with a Pareto-optimal allocation of resources. The second theorem indicates that once one of these Pareto-optimal positions is chosen, there exists some competitive set of prices that can sustain it as a competitive equilibrium. If there were not this correspondence between competitive equilibrium and Pareto optimality, the latter would not play such a pivotal ethical role in modern economics.

Of course, some ethical judgment is required to decide which Pareto optimum to institute. It is easy to envision other normative criteria by which an allocative-efficient position could be chosen. For example, one could use a Rawlsian criterion, whereby the well-being of the least fortunate person is maximized, subject to this person's welfare not surpassing that of the next worse-off person.[13] Such a criterion would

---

[10] These theorems are discussed in the welfare economics chapter of any microeconomics or public finance textbook; see, for example, Bruce (2001), Henderson and Quandt (1980), and Varian (1993).

[11] Unlike the first theorem, the second has a technical requirement that production and utility functions be properly shaped; in particular, a condition of "convexity" must be met.

[12] For a good discussion of this separation and the implications of the second theorem, see Varian (1993, pp. 505–7).

[13] This Rawlsian rule is called the maximin criterion and appears in Rawls (1970).

promote equity and raise the welfare of the most unfortunate person. By contrast, a Nietzschean criterion places the entire weight on maximizing the welfare of the best-off person and, in so doing, augments inequality.[14] Myriad alternative criteria are possible, but have not captured the imagination of economists because other ethical criteria do not necessarily sustain a competitive equilibrium.

THE SECOND WELFARE THEOREM AND SOVIET-STYLE ECONOMIES

The second welfare theorem constitutes the theoretical justification for the implementation of a Soviet-style controlled economy. If an equal distribution of income is desired, then the second theorem indicates that a Pareto-optimal state could be supported if the *right* set of prices were found to *sustain* this state. Of course, the trick is to ascertain these prices, especially if market signals are eliminated and planners must guess the appropriate prices. Other problems have intervened in applying this second theorem in practice. First, there was a reliance on large-scale production units, so that competitive forces did not prevail and efficiency did not result. Second, mistakes in choosing prices created shortages and bottlenecks that resonated throughout the economy. Third, equality was either not achieved, or was transitory – remember the lesson from the Vonnegut tale. Fourth, administered prices and wages did not provide the proper producers' and workers' incentives.

FIRST BEST VERSUS SECOND BEST

Nothing is perfect, and this is certainly true of any economy that might be analyzed. There are always some distortions (for example, externalities and monopolies) that can inhibit the economy from satisfying one or more of the Pareto conditions for efficiency. When there are one or more distortions that cannot be removed, the theory of second best asks whether satisfying the remaining Pareto conditions is still desirable. At first the answer was given in a pessimistic form, claiming that, in general, it is neither necessary nor desirable to fulfill the residual Pareto conditions that can still be met.[15] This pessimism went too far and failed to take into account that in a general-equilibrium system some markets may, for all intents and purposes, be separate from others. Surely, a distortion in a candy bar market is unlikely to affect the trade-offs in consumption or production between plane and train tickets, so that the

---

[14] The Nietzschean criterion is a maximax rule and is found in Brookshire, Schulze, and Sandler (1981).

[15] The original paper on second best is by Lipsey and Lancaster (1956–7). This paper generated a sizable literature.

Pareto condition for these two goods is still worth satisfying. Goods that are related in consumption, either as complements or substitutes, are more apt to be affected by irremovable distortions in the market for one of the goods. For example, consumers' demand for car rentals would surely be influenced by a distortion that raised the price of plane tickets, because many air travelers rent cars at their destinations. Plane travel and car rental are complementary goods and, thus, highly related in consumption.

Today, the accepted practice with second best is to use the distortionary behavior as an additional constraint when optimizing. For example, the anticipated behavior of the agent is used to constrain the principal's choice of an incentive scheme in a principal-agent analysis, which is an example of second best. The agent's inefficient behavior is not, however, used to avoid making recommendations, even though some Pareto conditions are not satisfied. The theory of second best permits policy recommendations when an economy contains distortions and the interrelationship among markets is not ignored. A good example of why Pareto conditions should not be applied mindlessly in the face of distortions is illustrated by the presence of a monopoly in an industry that pollutes the environment. The pollution implies that production is too great, because external costs are not taken into account. If this pollution *cannot be corrected*, then increased competitiveness may be undesirable. That is, the monopoly restricts output that, in light of the pollution externality, is a useful market imperfection. In a general-equilibrium setting, two wrongs may make a right.

GENERAL EQUILIBRIUM: AN EVALUATION

Although general-equilibrium analysis has been the most important driving force in economics in the twentieth century, it has lost center stage over the last thirty years. This is due in part to the recent interest in game theory, which lends itself to a more focused study of a few opposing agents. Additionally, issues such as asymmetric information would be extremely difficult to introduce into a competitive economy, since, by the very nature of asymmetric information, economic agents do not possess equal market power and some markets may be incomplete. Recent advances in economics still use a general-equilibrium framework, but for a fragment of the economy rather than for the economy as a whole.

The enhanced interest in market failures in the form of monopoly, externalities, and public goods also makes economywide general-equilibrium representations problematic owing to incomplete markets. In the case of monopoly, firms are price makers (subject to market demand), so that their supply relationship is not well defined – that is, each price may be associated with more than one quantity supplied depending on the shape and position of market demand. Without a supply relationship, there is no well-defined excess demand relationship, and hence the search for prices that make all excess demands equal to zero loses its value in identifying a general equilibrium. Thus, the construction of a microeconomic foundation for macroeconomics, where the behaviors of firms and consumers are aggregated to give a macroeconomic representation, has been fraught with difficulties.[16] These shortcomings are exacerbated because dynamic notions of expectations have not been adequately woven into micro-based representations of macroeconomics.

Any "wish list" for general equilibrium would include the introduction of more dynamic elements, including a better analysis of disequilibrium positions and the associated pathways (if any) to equilibrium. Such an extension would require more universally accepted adjustments to disequilibrium relationships. Another element of this wish list would be to integrate transaction costs into the adjustment process. A third wish is the introduction of noneconomic factors. For example, biological and atmospheric equilibria are essential when studying many environmental problems (see Chapter 11); similarly, political equilibria are important for public choice issues. If the interrelationships among markets are important, then so too are the interactions among markets and the germane noneconomic relationships and equilibria that influence, among other things, supply.

The laying of the foundation of general equilibrium has occupied the greatest minds in economics, because its complexity has required nothing less than the attention of the best thinkers. By the same token, this complexity limits its overall appeal. To make much headway, modelers have to employ rather extreme assumptions that greatly limit its applicability and policy orientation, which, in turn, will curtail future activity unless some ingenious means for streamlining its analysis is devised. Many of the extreme assumptions of general equilibrium also hamper its testability, thus further curtailing future interest. Despite its shortcomings, the general-equilibrium revolution has taught us a crucial lesson: not to ignore interrelationships among relevant markets. Partial-equilibrium analysis can serve only as a first attempt to get our thinking straight in an elementary setting before accounting for other relevant interactions among markets. Although novel during its heyday in the 1950s and 1960s, the novelty of general equilibrium has worn off, underscoring its diminished hold on economics.

---

[16] On the microeconomic foundations of macroeconomics, consult Leijonhufvud (1968).

9   Laboratory Economics: Of Rats and Men

In the mid-1970s, I chanced upon a fascinating article by Kagel and associates (1975) that used male albino rats to test some basic properties of demand curves; namely, whether or not animal consumers would abide by a negative substitution effect when the price of one commodity rose relative to another. Apparently, rats enjoy drinking both root beer and Tom Collins mix, even without the alcohol. The subjects had been trained to press a left lever for root beer and a right one for Collins mix. The number of bar presses for an equal quantity of one drink versus the other drink determined the *relative prices* of the drinks. If, therefore, two presses on the left lever give .05 milliliters (ml) of root beer, while one press on the right one gives .05 ml of Collins mix, then the relative price of root beer in terms of Collins mix is two.[1] The total number of bar presses available to a rat represents his income. With income and prices operationalized, a budget constraint is thus defined.[2] By holding purchasing power constant for a price change in, say, root beer, these researchers isolated the influence of changes in the drinks' relative prices on the purchases of root beer, and, in so doing, identified the substitution effect. As anticipated, the rats displayed a textbook negative substitution effect – they "bought" more of the drink whose price fell, even when the increased purchasing power implied by the price reduction had been removed.

One of these researchers' most clever experiments was to show that *equal proportional changes* in the rats' income and prices led to *no* change in their purchases of the two beverages. When, for example, income was doubled along with all prices, the rats still consumed the

[1] Relative price can also be changed by varying the amount of liquid given out for the same number of bar presses.

[2] A budget constraint consists of the sum of the expenditures on the available goods set equal to income – that is, total expenditures equal income. Expenditures on any good equals the good's price times the number of units purchased.

same commodity bundle. Thus, the rats displayed no money illusion and abided by the "zero degree homogeneity property of demand," which serves as the foundation for indexing income to price changes in some economies, such as Israel.[3] This esoteric-sounding property of demand merely implies that for unchanged relative prices and purchasing power, there is no reason to alter one's purchases. Doubling all prices means that relative prices or price ratios are unchanged, because the common factor of two cancels. Moreover, doubling income and prices simultaneously results in no change in purchasing power, because the new income can buy the same market basket – no more and no less.

Although some experiments in economics have involved rats and pigeons, most experimental evidence has come from human subjects.[4] The roots of experimental economics involved consumer choice problems: in an early study, L. L. Thurstone (1931) tried to determine an individual's indifference curves[5] in an experimental framework where the subjects responded to a large number of hypothetical choices without actually consuming the market baskets. This pioneering paper was strongly criticized by W. Allen Wallis and Milton Friedman (1942), who were unconvinced that the hypothetical nature of the experiments was a legitimate procedure for constructing an indifference curve or displaying consumer choice. In these authors' view, specific reactions to real choices needed to be recorded in an experimental setting to cast any light on consumer choice. This emphasis on real choices is a hallmark of modern experimental economics, where subjects are motivated to take their actions seriously by means of monetary rewards.[6] An astute subject can earn a good deal of money, compared to his or her market wage, in experiments involving payoffs for allocating one's assigned budget among alternative actions that might involve strategic interactions, the purchase of a public good, profit maximization, or decision making under uncertainty. During the last three decades, there has been a tremendous growth in the literature in experimental economics, fueled in great part by the insightful work of John Kagel, Charles Plott, Alvin Roth, Vernon Smith, and others.[7] This

---

[3] With indexing, wages, rents, social security payments, and other remunerations increase in proportion to increments in the general price level to adjust for inflation.

[4] With animals, environmental factors can be better controlled, but at the price of having to generalize from animal behavior to human actions.

[5] An indifference curve displays all bundles of goods that a consumer views as giving the same satisfaction.

[6] An important early paper was by Mosteller and Nogee (1951), who tested expected utility analysis with real money gambles. This use of real money was motivated by the criticism of hypothetical choices raised by Wallis and Friedman (1942). See Roth (1995) and references therein on the history of experimental economics.

[7] Key articles include Kagel and Roth (1995), Plott and Smith (1978), and Smith (1962, 1980, 1982).

growth has been greatly supported by the National Science Foundation (NSF), which has allocated a significant portion of its economics research budget to funding laboratory economics since the 1970s (Roth 1995, p. 20). With its recent growth, experimental economics has gained legitimacy and wide acceptance and is now firmly entrenched in modern economics.

Experimental economics provides a means for testing the validity of economic models in terms of their specification. By investigating the influence of variables, experimentalists can guide theorists either to include more variables or to omit noninfluential ones. Much as empirical economics helps economists to evaluate theoretical models, experimental economics can serve a similar function. By uncovering anomalies in behavior in the laboratory, experimental economics can present outcomes that new theoretical models and approaches must explain. Thus, it can guide economists toward improved theoretical representations and predictions. Laboratory economics can also allow for a dialogue between experimenters and policy makers when the laboratory setting is used to test the impact of alternative institutional arrangements, incentive structures, or regulatory policies (Roth 1995, p. 22).

Experimental economics has been applied extensively to study consumer choice under certainty and uncertainty. The convergence to equilibrium under alternative market institutional arrangements has been investigated since the early 1960s. Another area of intense activity has been the study of voluntary contributions to public goods (see Ledyard 1995) and free-riding behavior. Experimental economics has also examined market failures associated with common property resources. From the origins of game theory, experimental economics has been applied to evaluate game-theoretic models and their equilibrium concepts. This interest has extended to the analysis of bargaining theory in its myriad forms. Another area of investigation for experimentalists has been the study of industrial organization, including profit-maximizing behavior under alternative scenarios and the strategic interactions of cartel members. Many other applications of experimental economics exist, including the study of auctions, externalities, and institutional design. Interest in experimental economics has spilled over into other social sciences, including political science and sociology. In the former, public choice and collective action concerns have been scrutinized with experimental procedures, while in the latter, group behavior has been examined in an experimental setting.

ADVANTAGES OF EXPERIMENTAL ECONOMICS

As a methodology, experimental economics possesses a number of advantages, which makes it an important tool for economics and other social sciences. First, researchers can investigate hypothetical situations in a controlled environment from which intervening influences have been removed. Second, experimentalists are able to derive their data within a relatively short time, since they do not have to wait years, or even decades, for market-generated data. Third, with experiments, there is typically consistent coding of data because a single set of individuals can be employed, which is often not the case for empirical data covering a long interval. For example, when coding the empirical data for the attributes of terrorist incidents (such as the number of terrorists or the type of incident) from 1968 to 1999, the coders changed every ten years or so as the data was generated.[8] Fourth, the experimental approach provides latitude to vary key aspects of a problem studied, at the discretion of the investigator. When studying voluntary contributions to public goods, the experimenter can vary group size, the marginal payoffs from contributing, the type of public good, the per-unit price of the public good, and the manner in which individual contributions determine the overall quantity of the public good.[9] Given the ability to control some influences, the experimenter can isolate and highlight specific variables, as demonstrated in the rats experiments by Kagel and associates with their clever procedures to remove income effects associated with a price change. Fifth, experimental economics can be used to draw policy conclusions. If, for example, alternative institutional arrangements for a collective action problem are investigated in a laboratory setting, then experimental results can assist governments in their subsequent design of institutional structures such as treaties and international organizations. Sixth, experimental economics can direct theorists to new theoretical directions by identifying omitted variables or problems with equilibrium concepts.[10]

Experimental economics also lends itself to classroom applications. At the start of this book, I indicated the daunting challenge that confronts college faculty members teaching large, impersonal sections on economic principles. Even simple experiments can illustrate the applicability and relevancy of economics, while diversifying classroom activities. For example, the impact of fiscal policy can be shown by having students separate into firms that make production decisions so as to maximize profit. If I choose parameters for the consumption function that permit only a low-level equilibrium where aggregate demand equals aggregate supply

[8] The relevant data set is known as International Terrorism: Attributes of Terrorist Events (ITERATE). Edward Mickolus coded the data for 1968–77, while Jean Murdock (my wife) and my students coded the data for 1977–87. Subsequent updates have been done by Peter Fleming, myself, and others.

[9] For further details, see Cornes and Sandler (1996, pp. 512–6) and Ledyard (1995).

[10] For example, Nash equilibrium has been subject to much experimental investigation (Kagel and Roth 1995; Ledyard 1995).

(or the sum of the firms' production), unsold goods will accumulate in the firms, cutting into my students' profits. I found students, even those who dislike government, clamoring for government expenditures to raise aggregate demand. These hypothetical firms even formed a lobby to get me to raise government purchases. In a computer laboratory, students can experience firsthand how their independent maximizing decisions can lead to market equilibrium in double-price auction scenarios where participants are randomly assigned to buyer and seller roles. In short, the experimental environment provides students with insights into economic behavior that no amount of lecturing can impart.

People possess innate economic intuition and ability to barter and trade. The use of an experimental environment in teaching allows students to tap their natural abilities prior to being given the economic explanation of their behavior. When they have acted in the predicted manner before being given the underlying principles, the theory makes more sense.

DISADVANTAGES OF EXPERIMENTAL ECONOMICS

Experimental economics must contend with some difficulties and methodological problems. Some parameters may be particularly difficult to vary in an experimental setting; for example, consider efforts to alter group size when investigating voluntary contributions to a public good. Standard theory indicates that as group size increases, people display less interest in contributing to a public good whose benefits are received by both contributors and noncontributors owing to nonexcludability. To investigate the effects of large groups on public good contributions, an experimentalist would require a sizable research budget, so that the large numbers of subjects would be properly motivated by monetary incentives. I have heard of experiments involving upward of 100 subjects, but these are rare. Moreover, many interesting public good scenarios involve thousands, or even millions, of people (for example, contributions to the nonprofit sector) and can be studied only with empirical data. Some experimental studies, in which actions of a small number of subjects have been multiplied by some factor to simulate a large-numbers problem,[11] have misrepresented group size to the subjects. When such misrepresentations are discovered by future subjects, they are apt to disbelieve the scenarios portrayed in the experiment, which in turn can affect their behavior. Moreover, the ratcheting up of individual behavior by a constant multiple to simulate a larger group introduces a regularity into the results that is unlikely to have been recorded had actual subjects been used.

[11] This was true of studies by Bohm (1972), Kim and Walker (1984), Marwell and Ames (1981), and others.

Unless an underlying theory is specified, it is easy to misinterpret the experimental results. It is essential that the theory specified be the one tested by the experiment. Seemingly innocuous aspects of an experimental design can cause a deviation from the theory that the experimenters think they are testing. If, for example, a threshold level of public good contributions must be surpassed prior to benefits being received, then the experiment does not really apply to the standard public good, for which no such threshold is required. With thresholds, contributors may have higher motivation to contribute, especially if shortfalls from the thresholds are refunded to the contributor. The strategic structure of the underlying game is greatly influenced by such thresholds (Sandler 1992, 1998). Over the last decade, experimentalists have done a better job of making the underlying theory explicit when designing their experiments; but, at times, it may be exceedingly difficult to formulate an experiment that strictly reflects the theoretical construct. In addition, it is important to ensure that alternative theories are not consistent with the same predicted outcomes, an observation that also applies to empirical studies.

Another potential problem can arise if subjects try to please the experimenter by behaving as they think the experimenter wants them to behave. For example, subjects may be more willing to contribute to a public good than they would in real life if they think that is expected of them. Obviously, this problem does not arise with animal experiments.

Yet another difficulty concerns the so-called *framing problem*, which refers to the fact that the subject's action is sensitive to the way the choice is posed, so that theoretically equivalent choices may result in quite different responses for alternative presentations. For example, one manner of soliciting a public good contribution may be more conducive than an alternative (equivalent) solicitation. The psychological framing problem is particularly difficult to anticipate beforehand. In fact, the backgrounds of the subjects may themselves lead to different framing biases. This problem has been aptly indicated in a series of experiments by Andreoni (1995), in which he presented the subjects with essentially the same choice – that is, spending on a private versus a public good – with a positive and a negative frame. For the positive frame, Andreoni told his subjects that contributing to a public good will help everyone's payoffs; while for the negative frame, he informed his subjects that purchasing the private good will make everyone else worse off. In the latter case, he emphasized the opportunity cost of buying the private good, which is not buying the public good. The positive frame was associated, on average, with about twice as much cooperation as the negative frame, even though the underlying choice was the same; hence, the context in which the experiment is presented makes a difference.

Surely, expense is another drawback to experimentation, one that involves both the fixed costs of equipment, software, and training and the variable costs associated with each experiment. I have already mentioned the costs associated with experiments involving large numbers of subjects. The large fixed costs involved in setting up well-equipped laboratories limit the ability of independent researchers to replicate some experimental results and confer monopoly power on some research sites. Such power poses some real worries. Fixed setup costs also imply that these laboratories will have to conduct many experiments if per-unit experimental costs are to be kept down. One must not lose sight of the fact that many experiments can be performed inexpensively without massive amounts of equipment if the researcher is clever in designing them.

EXPERIMENTAL VERSUS EMPIRICAL ECONOMICS

Empirical tests are part of the scientific method that characterizes economics. Economic theories are evaluated periodically by empirical tests of their predictions. Those theories that perform badly under the empirical magnifying glass are either replaced or revised. These new theories must also be evaluated empirically. The rise of experimental economics has given economists another means for testing theoretical hypotheses. Unlike empirical data, which is environmentally, institutionally, and historically determined, researchers have much greater control over environmental and other factors in an experimental framework. There are, of course, limits on the ability to quickly generate experimental data by which to judge a theory; surely, to evaluate negotiation strategies in terrorist hostage-taking situations, social scientists must rely on empirical data. It would be ludicrous to try to simulate such intense situations in a laboratory. Thankfully, limits are imposed on human experimentation by the legal system that inhibit such experiments.

In those situations where both empirical tests *and* experimentation can be applied, both procedures are employed for cross-validation purposes. At other times, only one of the two procedures will be appropriate, as in the terrorist example. Econometric procedures, developed for statistical inference in empirical studies, can and should be used to analyze experimental data, so that confidence intervals can be placed around the conclusions drawn from the data. In many of the animal experiments in economics, there are so few subjects – as few as three or four – that statistical inference would achieve nothing. Human experiments do not have such limitations and should be tested.

SPECIFIC EXAMPLES

To illustrate the usefulness of experimental economics and its findings, I shall briefly consider a few specific examples.

Public Goods and Free Riding

In the last two decades, there has been a great deal of experimental work examining various aspects of voluntary contributions to public goods.[12] The notion of a public good and free riding was introduced in the early chapters of this book – see, in particular, Chapter 1. Free riding results when individuals fail to support the public good, relying instead on its nonexcludable benefits that are freely available from the contributions of others. Free riding often takes the form of easy riding, where the individual contributes less than what is necessary to equate the associated marginal benefits (conferred on the entire group) to marginal costs. In an experimental setting, subjects are endowed with income to spend on a private good and a public good, each of which has its own price. Thus, subjects are confronted with a budget constraint defined by income and prices. Money spent on the private good benefits only the contributor. The benefits derived from the public good, however, depend on both the subject's own contributions and those of the other subjects. In many experiments, an individual's public good benefits decline with the *number* of individuals, n, receiving the good's benefits, so that an implicit crowding or consumption rivalry is introduced. One essential experimental parameter, a, indicates how much benefit the subject receives from each unit of aggregate contribution.

To illustrate, suppose that $a = 5, n = 10$, and that 20 units of the public good, Q, are purchased in total. Then each subject receives $(a/n)Q$ or $10 = [(5 \times 20)/10]$ in benefits from the aggregate level of the public good. The experimenter can vary marginal gains, group size, and the public good's price at will. Given the basic experimental setup, the outcome associated with independent behavior can then be compared to some efficient ideal or Pareto optimum. Independent behavior or the Nash equilibrium can be identified by relating the subject's marginal costs of contributing, or the relative price of the public good, to his or her marginal benefit of a/n, received from each unit contributed. Additional parameters at the experimenter's discretion involve the possibility of communication among subjects, the relationships among subjects (that is, their previous interactions), and the number of runs or plays permitted.

---

[12] For a summary and list of references, consult Cornes and Sandler (1996, pp. 510–16) and especially Ledyard (1995).

Thus far, experimental results for public goods have been mixed; some have found strong evidence of free-riding behavior (Kim and Walker 1984), while others have not (Bohm 1972; Marwell and Ames 1981). In general, these free-riding experiments tend to display three common features.[13] First, in a single-shot interaction, subjects tend to contribute toward the public good at a performance level that is about halfway between free-riding and Pareto-optimal levels. As more trials or interactions are permitted, this halfway result applies just to the initial interactions. Second, the contribution level approaches that of free riding as the number of repeated interactions increases, so that free riding appears to have a learning component. Third, when communication is allowed among the subjects, contribution levels improve substantially. In another set of experiments, the presence of a threshold level of contribution, prior to the public good giving benefits, served to limit free riding, as theory predicts.

There are a number of cautions to raise about these findings that may affect how much one can truly relate the experimental results to the theoretical predictions of the pure public good model. One caution involves the way that subjects have been homogenized by their underlying payoff function and budget constraint. When deriving the standards for independent behavior and the efficient ideal, the experimenter assumes that subjects in identical situations will behave identically. This is not always the case in real-world interactions. There is also the worry that an implicit rivalry exists, because each subject receives only one nth of the aggregate benefits of the public good. In the case of a *pure* public good, everyone receives the entire benefit without division by group size. There is also the problem that, unlike the real world, subjects have an incentive to spend their income in each period – there is no return to savings. I raise these concerns to highlight the fact that even slight deviations in the experimental design from the theory that the experiment seeks to validate may be behind the unexpected behavior uncovered. It takes a great deal of skill and insight to achieve a near-perfect match between the theory and the experimental design. This match is frequently lacking in public good experiments.

In the future, it is important that experimentalists isolate the true influence of the rivalry identified earlier. There is also a need to examine club goods, where exclusion of nonmembers and/or noncontributors is feasible, and increased membership creates greater crowding. Can such groups devise a toll scheme in an experimental setting and achieve efficient results as predicted by the theory of clubs? A host of market failures should be subject to experimentation.

---

[13] On these common features and other insights, see Ledyard (1995).

Experiments and Game Theory

Since the 1950s, there has been continuous activity in examining game theory in a laboratory setting. Unquestionably, the game receiving the most attention has been the Prisoner's Dilemma, discussed in Chapter 3 and displayed in Figures 3.1 and 3.2.[14] In a two-person, single-shot Prisoners' Dilemma, each agent is anticipated to use the dominant strategy to confess or defect, thereby leading to a Nash equilibrium where payoffs are low. Both agents would be better off had they agreed to cooperate and honored their agreement. Repeated Prisoners' Dilemmas may or may not result in cooperation. If a limited (known) number of iterations are to be played, then in the last period each player has a dominant strategy to defect. This is also the case in the next-to-last period, at which time the players reason ahead and assume that everyone will defect in the last period. Cooperation unravels from the known last period up through the initial period of play, so that the theory predicts defection in each and every period. Cooperation may, however, arise in two kinds of repeated games: those where the game goes on in perpetuity, and those where the end point is not known with certainty.[15] For these repeated games, punishment-based tit-for-tat strategies, in which defections by the other player are met with one or more periods of defection, may result in an equilibrium. This means that the gains from a defection must be compared to the losses associated with the threatened withdrawal of cooperation by the other player(s). If a player values the future sufficiently, so that he or she is concerned about future retribution, then cooperation may ensue at the equilibrium. The same may be true if the last interaction is unknown, so that a longer-run view must be assumed on any round insofar as any defection that one's own defection causes can hurt for an additional but unknown number of periods.

Much as in the case of public good experiments, the experimental results are somewhat mixed (Roth 1995). In many one-shot games, the extent of cooperation is somewhere between mutual defection, as predicted by the theory, and mutual cooperation. Because many of these experimental single-shot games actually involve multiple, but unknown, rounds of plays, some cooperation is not really against theoretical predictions. For repeated games with a known number of iterations, initial periods of mutual cooperation are followed by noncooperation thereafter. Although the initial cooperation calls into question the Nash equilibrium notion upon which defection in every period is anticipated,

---

[14] For references, see Roth (1995, pp. 26–30).

[15] These are standard results for repeated games and can be found in any text on game theory – see, for example, Binmore (1992) or Dixit and Skeath (1999).

play *after a certain number of rounds* supports the theory. With a large number of (known) repeated interactions, the initial phase of "learned" cooperation may last quite some time, before concluding close to the final rounds. These experimental results strongly suggest behavior not in keeping with a Nash equilibrium. Thus, as indicated earlier, experimental economics can identify behavior that indicates the need to rethink and refine the theory. At times, post-trial questionnaires administered to the subjects as to what their thinking had been in reaching their strategies can suggest new variables and relationships to pursue theoretically.

In recent years, experiments have been an integral part of the study of evolutionary game theory, which investigates the population dynamics of repeated games. Unlike standard repeated games, evolutionary games allow the number and type of players to change over time. If each player type is identified with a strategy (for example, tit-for-tat), then evolutionary game theory predicts that the "fittest" players will survive, multiply, and eventually take over a population. Fitness is based upon relative payoffs that a player receives through his or her strategy;[16] player types earning high payoffs will replicate more often and may come to dominate a population. Successful strategies or player types are initiated and "learned" within the population. For example, punishment-based strategies that are more forgiving than tit-for-tat strategies may do better and, in so doing, may be replicated or copied more often. An *evolutionary stable equilibrium* is not only a Nash equilibrium, but also one able to resist "invasion" by strategies not previously present in the population at its equilibrium. Evolutionary game theory provides a method to study dynamics within an experimental game setting. This same study is not practical in an empirical setting, where the researcher cannot introduce the so-called "mutant" or out-of-equilibrium innovative strategies.

Experiments can be applied to virtually any form of game including chicken, coordination, and assurance. The initial fetish with Prisoners' Dilemmas involved a misallocation of resources, since many interesting real-world strategic situations are not Prisoners' Dilemma games. For chicken, coordination, and assurance games, there are multiple equilibria with no obvious means for determining which is the "focus," or the one that subjects will favor. Experiments can identify factors that direct attention to one equilibrium over another. Additionally, experimentation should help the profession to develop new equilibrium concepts, much

---

[16] Weibull (1995) is an advanced textbook introducing the concepts of evolutionary game theory. Also see Axelrod (1984), Vega-Redondo (1996), and Maynard Smith (1982). Experimental results for evolutionary games are discussed in Skyrms (1996).

as experiments have helped psychologists and economists to build new theories for choice situations involving uncertainty.[17]

Bargaining and Experiments

Experiments have also involved myriad aspects of bargaining where two or more agents are deciding how to divide some mutual gain. In game-theory parlance, bargaining solutions are often in the *core*, a bargaining outcome from which no subgroup can do better on its own. Even in the standard two-person bargaining situation where exchange equilibria are identified, the core involves many equilibria, giving rise to a great deal of indeterminacy.[18] To address this indeterminacy, the relative bargaining strengths of the opposing agents would have to be known. These strengths depend on such factors as the agents' impatience, information about their counterparts' preferences, the sequence of offers and counteroffers, and other negotiation aspects. These factors are extremely difficult to observe in the real world or to infer from data on past bargains. Insofar as the experimenter can control the bargaining situation in terms of the information provided to each agent, the experimental setting can perform tests on the theory not necessarily available to standard empirical procedures. In the case of agents' impatience, an experiment can test whether or not this impatience works against an agent's bargaining outcome. Similarly, the impact of risk aversion on a bargainer's payoff can also be tested in the laboratory – that is, whether more risk-averse agents do better when their disagreement prize is higher, as the theory predicts. The disagreement prize is what each party gets in the absence of an agreement and is known as the *threat point* of the negotiation.

Experiments in a bargaining setting have shown the importance of both the information possessed by the agent and the threat point.[19] For example, more equal bargaining outcomes characterize situations where the less-endowed player at the threat point had information about the other player's endowments, while this better-endowed player was uninformed about his opponent's endowments. A common theme in these experimental results is that information significantly affects the outcome of the negotiations. Asymmetric information, where one side to the negotiation has knowledge not possessed by the other side, gives informed

---

[17] One such example is "prospect theory," developed by Kahneman and Tversky (1979), where individuals respond differently to losses and gains of equal value.

[18] In the Edgeworth-Bowley box for two goods and two agents, the core is depicted by the contract curve where the two agents' indifference curves are mutually tangent, so that each agent's marginal willingness to trade one good for the other is equated. Without some distribution assumption there are an infinite number of points in the core.

[19] See the discussion in Roth (1995, pp. 40–9).

players a real advantage that they capitalize on. Another theme is that risk attitudes also matter. A third interesting finding is that deadlines serve to speed an agreement, with many settlements being reached just prior to such deadlines (Roth 1995, p. 48). This is often observed in real life, with threatened strikes being averted minutes before the deadline after months of fruitless negotiation. This finding makes me reflect on the monthly faculty meetings I attended at one university, which commenced at 4 P.M. and were expected to conclude shortly after 5 P.M. Given the lateness in the afternoon, I was always amused that the most inconsequential matters, those with virtually zero gain, were afforded so much discussion. Once the meeting passed 5 P.M., faculty members were willing to pass judgment on any matter, even the most controversial in terms of distributional effects, with little or no discussion. I have even joined in on meaningless discussion involving trivial proposals prior to 5 P.M. to ensure that my controversial proposal would come up for a vote well after 5 P.M., when its passage was assured.

Given the number of contingencies involving bargaining among sovereign states germane to today's world, insights gained from these experiments can be crucial in facilitating such negotiations and predicting their outcomes. Such bargaining situations include India and Pakistan ending their nuclear arms race and their conflict over Kashmir, the world reaching agreement to cut back greenhouse gas emissions, the global community limiting the proliferation of weapons of mass destruction, and the United States and Canada agreeing to limit acid-rain-producing sulfur emissions. Clearly, experimental economics can enlighten policy making.

The "Winner's Curse"

Although there have been many experiments devoted to auctions, I shall consider only those based on the winner's curse, where the winning bidder pays "too much."[20] Because the winner is the bidder whose estimate of the object is the highest, this potential for bidding too much may not be accounted for when he or she offers the bid. These experiments are worth highlighting because they aptly illustrate how simple experiments can enlighten complicated theoretical models. Economic theory, however, suggests a more calculated response, especially among skilled players such as oil companies bidding for drilling rights; but even these oil companies have been observed to bid too much.

In one set of experiments,[21] subjects were instructed to estimate the number of pennies in a jar which in fact held 800 pennies. The motiva-

---

[20] This subsection draws on material from Bazerman and Samuelson (1983), Kagel and Levin (1986), and Roth (1995, pp. 60–5).

[21] These were conducted by Bazerman and Samuelson (1986).

tion to give accurate estimates was a prize for the closest guess. This prize was given only after the jar was auctioned off to the subjects, who were asked to bid for its contents; the highest bidder would pay the bid value in exchange for the contents of the jar. Since the jar was typically won by bids in excess of $8, the winner's curse was observed. In fact, the *average winning bid* was $2 over the value of the contents, despite an average estimated bid of $5.

Insofar as this first set of experiments was conducted with just single bids being solicited, the subjects remained inexperienced. In a subsequent set of experiments by Kagel and Levin (1986), subjects were allowed to bid in multiple auctions and were given information *after* each auction about all the bids and the true value of the object acquired by the highest bidder. Thus, they were allowed to gain experience and knowledge about the procedure. Generally, these experiments showed that the winner's curse diminished with experience, a result at odds with the behavior of many oil companies.

EXPERIMENTAL ECONOMICS: AN EVALUATION AND ITS FUTURE

When I first learned about experimental economics in the early 1970s, I was very skeptical. My skepticism grew during the early 1980s, when I read and served as a reviewer for many papers, because either the theoretical underpinnings were not clearly indicated or the experiments did not appear to test the intended theory owing to intervening variables and experimental design flaws. Public good experimental papers that misrepresented the group size to the participants concerned me greatly, as did the large number of papers that came to contradictory results for free riding with no attempt to explain or rectify the differences. Today, I have a much greater respect for experimental economics and sincerely feel that its place in economics as an important methodology is assured for decades to come.

Experimental economics fulfills my four criteria for sustained success. It can be used to formulate propositions that can be subsequently tested by both experimental and empirical methods. With sufficient ingenuity, the experimental method can be applied to a limitless number of economic concerns, including institutional design, auction procedures, market failures, public choice issues, and competitive behavior. The winner's curse example aptly illustrates the fact that experiments can be made feasible and, as such, can be brought into the classrooms as an important pedagogical device. Moreover, experimental economics remains ingenious in creating novel applications. For example, much more can be done in investigating the role of learning and the design of institutions in a wide variety of economic scenarios. The development of better software and hardware will facilitate further laboratory and classroom applications. An essential message is to focus on the theoretical linkage and to make this theoretical underpinning of the experiment clear. If this is done, experimental economics will have a bright future and will contribute a large and growing literature of significant influence.

10   Before Yesterday and Beyond Tomorrow: Intergenerational Economics

I have always been fascinated by the interrelationships and interactions among generations. In airports, I enjoy looking at children and parents and seeing how similar they appear in both looks and actions. After my son was born, I closely observed him as a baby and a toddler to discern the innate character that he had inherited from me or my wife. Of course, whenever he did something that epitomized one of our annoying traits, one of us would knowingly glance at the other with raised eyebrows and think, "Yes, he is definitely *your* son!" As he grew older, it became more difficult to identify the distinction between genotype and phenotype, that is, between his inherited and his environmentally determined characteristics. And just when I became convinced that he displayed a random mix of our collective genetic backgrounds combined with an imitation of our behavior, he would say or do something completely foreign to both my wife and me. I then pondered whether this novel behavior was some atavistic characteristic of a long-lost relative or an innovation all his own.

Clearly, each of us possesses a particular identity – a unique mix of genetic code, mimicked behavior, and random innovations. I recognize this better than most people because I am a clone – an identical twin – who grew up with my brother in the same household. Despite our shared genetic makeup and virtually identical environment, we are not the same. Although even our mother had to put different colored ribbons on our wrists when we were babies to keep us straight,[1] and we did everything together, we do not think alike. When he became a Marine officer and I a conscientious objector during the Vietnam War, our difference finally became all too clear to everyone.

[1] Our mother undoubtedly mixed us up at times, especially after a bath, so that whether Todd or Tom is the true author of this book depends on whether this error occurred an even or odd number of times.

161

It is this difference in tastes and endowments, which characterizes each generation and even identical twins in the same generation, that makes the study of intergenerational economics so interesting and challenging. Even if one wants to be altruistic toward the next generation, how does one know what the next generation will want? While it is safe to assume that no one wants to live in a polluted, unhealthy environment, the desired trade-off of the next and ensuing generations between gleaming skyscrapers and pristine rain forests teeming with species is much harder to know. As generations advance into the future, such altruistic intentions become even more difficult to implement, with fewer of our tastes being shared by more distant generations. The study of economics as it applies to intergenerational choices presents one of the most daunting and important challenges to economists of the twenty-first century. Even though economists started studying such choices early in the last century, beginning with F. P. Ramsey's (1928) study of savings, the analysis of intergenerational economics is still in its infancy.

The basic economic problems of allocation, distribution, growth, and stability also apply to an intergenerational setting, in which decisions made yesterday and today by the past and current generations affect the choices of tomorrow's generations. For example, investment decisions today determine, along with the initial capital stock and depreciation, the capital stock of tomorrow. A myopic generation that saves and invests little leaves less capital to the subsequent generation. Similarly, today's accumulation of debt to foreign interests can restrict the options of the next generation, as they must transfer assets to pay off this debt. Efforts that result in research advances in medicine, the sciences, and the social sciences shape the endowments, essential constraints, and destiny of future generations. The composition of an uplifting aria, the painting of a masterpiece, or the writing of an enduring novel (economics book) enriches not only the current generation but also innumerable subsequent generations. What is the value that later generations derive from the collected plays of Shakespeare or the novels of Dostoevsky? Is it priceless? Consider what the creation of the computer has done for our way of life or what the discovery of a cure for cancer would do for the well-being of our children's children. How does society promote such enriching innovations and discoveries?

Each generation also inherits the *natural capital*, which consists of the biosphere on which human life and economic activities depend and includes air, land, minerals, atmosphere, fauna, flora, and the forces of the solar system. The way in which this natural capital is used today determines how much is passed down to our children. Patterns of unsustainable development can reduce this inherited natural capital, as in the case of deforestation or agricultural practices that degrade the fertility of the soil.[2] The accumulation of man-made capital (henceforth called just capital, in distinction to natural capital) in the form of dams and cities may come at the expense of this natural capital.

In recent years, we have acquired the ability to monitor the planet from Earth-based observations (for example, ice cores drilled in Greenland and pollution-collection stations) and remotely from satellites.[3] What emerges from such observations is a picture of the planet's ecosphere under siege and in a state of stress from pollutants (for example, greenhouse gases, chlorofluorocarbons, and sulfur emissions) and an expanding population. There may soon come a time when gains in capital will not compensate for losses in natural capital, so that future generations will be impoverished by their ancestors' consumption decisions. Consequently, economic choices by one generation influence allocation outcomes as well as the distribution of income among generations.

Given these impacts on the planet, one must wonder whether policies can be implemented to make today's choices more farsighted from an intergenerational perspective. How does the natural sequence of generations affect the possibility of intergenerational exchange that could allow for more farsighted actions? Can overlapping and even nonoverlapping generations engage in games with efficient and equitable consequences, and, if this is possible, what is the likely outcome of such games? These games must account for evolutionary changes in tastes and learning over time. Do markets properly adjust for intergenerational implications of today's actions? Are accepted practices of discounting future benefits and costs desirable for the evaluation of decisions with deepfuture considerations?

This chapter is devoted to addressing these questions and to raising related concerns of intergenerational economics. My intention is focused on identifying crucial intergenerational issues of an economic nature that must be resolved through analysis. At the end of the day, this chapter will pose more questions than it will answer. Given the state of knowledge in this area, this is the best that I can hope to do. Problems abound at every juncture. For instance, the appropriate institutional environment for addressing these intergenerational issues is yet to be created. That is, the rights of the unborn are not currently recognized by the US courts

---

[2] On the notion of sustainability, see Howarth and Norgaard (1992), Pearce and Atkinson (1995), Toman (1994), and Toman, Pezzey, and Krautkraemer (1995). On alternative definitions of sustainability, see Doeleman and Sandler (1998).

[3] Ice cores drilled in Greenland can reveal information about Earth's climate going back as far as 100,000 years (Alley and Bender 1998). Atmospheric monitoring stations atop Mauna Loa in Hawaii indicate the accumulation of greenhouse gases, while satellites track the density of the stratospheric ozone layer.

and, without such rights, there is no legal basis for protecting the natural-capital heritage of future generations, giving sustainable development a dubious legal basis. My goal in writing this chapter is more to stimulate a search for improved insights into intergenerational economics than to criticize the profession for the lack of progress to date. The latter failing is understandable, because our concern for the distant future has only recently surfaced with the creation of man-made substances, such as plutonium, with long lifetimes and with our newfound ability to gauge the consequences of past economic activities. It is time for economists to address the hard questions that impinge on allocative choices and distributional justice.

INTERGENERATIONAL PUBLIC GOODS

Although the international aspects of public goods have received much attention in recent years, particularly with respect to environmental activities,[4] intergenerational public goods have received relatively scant attention. Just as benefits from international public goods cross territorial boundaries, the benefits of intergenerational public goods transcend generational boundaries. An intergenerational public good (bad) provides benefits (costs) that are nonrival and nonexcludable within and among generations. For example, a genetically engineered medicine that impedes the progress of Parkinson's disease provides benefits to people worldwide during the discovering generation's lifetime and for generations to come. The preservation of biodiversity and the stability that it gives to ecosystems as well as the promise that this diversity holds for new medicines represent other instances of intergenerational public goods. Still other intergenerational public goods include eradicating a disease, restoring the stratospheric ozone shield, mapping the human genetic code, establishing enduring institutions (for example, universities, churches, and social organizations), contributing to the arts, and cleansing the ecosphere.

Table 10.1 depicts a taxonomy of public goods based on temporal, spatial, and publicness considerations, in which eight categories are identified. In the two right-hand columns, public goods are distinguished based on purely and impurely public benefits. A pure public good possesses benefits that are completely nonrival among users and excludable only at a prohibitively high cost. In contrast, an impurely public good displays benefits that are either partially nonrival (for example, subject to crowding) or excludable at a reasonable cost, or *both* partially rival and partially excludable. Impure public goods can be further subdivided into

---

[4] Examples include Barrett (1993), Helm (1991), Kaul, Grunberg, and Stern (1999), Runge (1993), and Sandler (1997, 1998).

Table 10.1. Taxonomy of public goods

		Purely public	Impurely public
Intragenerational	Regional	• Forest fire suppression • Cleansing groundwater • Flood control	• Interpol • Extension service • Waterways
	Global	• Weather satellites • Controlling organized crime • World Court adjudication	• INTELSAT • Electromagnetic spectrum • Internet
Intergenerational	Regional	• Culture preservation • Curing river blindness • Curbing lead emissions	• Peacekeeping • Immunization programs • Pest eradication
	Global	• Ozone shield protection • Curbing global warming • Curing cancer	• Geostationary orbits • Ocean fisheries • New antibiotics

club goods and public goods with joint products, categories ignored in the simple taxonomy of Table 10.1. These pure and impure public goods are further distinguished by spatial and intertemporal spillovers of benefits. For either kind of public good, intragenerational and intergenerational public goods can yield benefits at the regional and global levels. While "region" can refer to either transnational or national regions, for the purposes of this chapter region will often be transnational. Insofar as the suppression of a forest fire yields regional purely public benefits to only the current generation, it is placed in the top purely public good cell along with the cleansing of groundwater and the control of flooding – activities whose benefits have a relatively short temporal span.

In the next cell down, global public goods that benefit only a single generation include weather satellites, the control of organized crime, and the adjudication of international disputes by the World Court. Weather forecasts of El Niño, for example, contain useful information worldwide on the consequences of warm waters in the Pacific Ocean for storm and drought patterns. Such forecasts are intragenerational because El Niño is a relatively short-lived phenomenon and its intensity varies over time, thus inhibiting the ability to generalize from one period to the next. As the Russian mafia and the drug cartels have become transnational players, their suppression offers purely public benefits to the current generation in a host of countries. Actions by the World Court to resolve disputes between nations do not limit the Court's ability to address additional disagreements between others, so its benefits are nonrival. Its openness to all nations supports nonexcludability of benefits.

At the regional level, intergenerational public goods include preserving culture, curing river blindness, and curbing lead emissions. Each of these examples displays nonexcludable and nonrival benefits that favorably influence at least two generations. Maintaining cultural integrity enriches present and future generations, while curing a disease such as river blindness improves the health of present and future generations. In the case of a long-term stock pollutant like lead, emissions can remain in the environment for a sufficiently long time to harm multiple generations. Lead can also have intergenerational consequences owing to the way that it impairs the learning capacity of the very young. Global intergenerational pure public goods include protecting the ozone layer, curbing global warming, and curing cancer, all of which provide nonrival and nonexcludable benefits to a series of generations.

In the right-hand column, three instances in each of four categories of impure public goods are listed. At the regional level, the Paris-based Interpol, which coordinates police activities among member states, yields partially rival benefits to its 100 or so members. Nonmembers are excluded from these coordination gains, while Interpol's limited capacity means that as it acquires cases its quality of service declines. Similarly, the provision of agricultural extension services and waterways is subject to exclusion and congestion. For all three cases, public good benefits are short-lived and do not extend beyond the current generation. The International Telecommunication Satellite Organization (INTELSAT), a private consortium with nations and firms as members, shares a global communication satellite network in geostationary orbit that carries most international phone calls and television networks.[5] Congestion assumes the form of signal interference. Given that satellites must be replaced every ten years, INTELSAT is a global *intragenerational* impure public good. Two additional cases are the electromagnetic spectrum allocation and the internet, both of which are subject to congestion in the form of interference and longer waits. Exclusion can be practiced and use can be monitored for both of these impure public goods.

The bottom two right-hand cells of Table 10.1 display intergenerational regional and global impure public goods. At the regional level, peacekeeping provides intergenerational impurely public benefits by preventing deaths and quelling grievances that, if unchecked, could fester for generations, as in the case of the Serbs, the Palestinians, and the

---

[5] In a geostationary orbit some 22,300 miles above the equator, a satellite orbits the Earth in sync with the Earth's surface. At this orbital band, only three satellites are required to provide point-to-multipoint service throughout the Earth, except at the poles.

Armenians. By eradicating a disease or strengthening a population's resistance, immunization programs result in intergenerational public benefits. Efforts to eliminate a pest can yield impure benefits over multiple generations. At the global level, intergenerational impure public goods include geostationary orbits, ocean fisheries (if fish are not harvested to extinction), and antibiotics. Congestion both at a given point in time and over time can influence the benefits derived from each of these public goods and, by so doing, result in a benefit rivalry. Intertemporal rivalry for geostationary orbits takes the form of discarded satellites that pose a collision hazard, as satellites drift up to 100 miles while in orbit. Overfishing presents an intertemporal rivalry that reduces the fishery's biomass and could result in the extinction of species. For antibiotics, an intertemporal form of congestion occurs when greater utilization of antibiotics today raises the likelihood that surviving bacteria will develop an immunity to them, decreasing the drugs' future effectiveness.

INTERGENERATIONAL PUBLIC GOODS AND SPILLOVER AWARENESS

Intergenerational public goods are assets because, once provided, they last for numerous periods and, in some cases (curing a disease, satellite orbital bands), may be infinitely long-lived. Moreover, many of these goods possess two dimensions of spillovers – spatial and temporal – that must be taken into account if allocative efficiency is to be achieved.[6] While it is tempting to blindly apply standard remedies for transnational public good problems to transgenerational public goods, this may be ill-advised and cause even greater misallocation of resources. For instance, fostering fuller international cooperation may worsen intergenerational inefficiency if it leads to an even *larger* provision of an activity that benefits the current generation at the expense of future generations.[7] A case in point concerns efforts by the United States, the United Kingdom, and France to expand the use of nuclear energy through international cooperation prior to developing proven techniques for storing nuclear wastes and ensuring against accidents. As a result, present and future generations confront an even greater containment problem (to be discussed). Actions of the World Bank and the International Monetary Fund to finance dams and roads in South America have resulted in enormous losses in biodiversity, thus impoverishing future generations. In some

---

[6] The discussion in this section is based on Sandler (1978b, 1999). The theoretical analysis and underlying models are presented in these earlier works, which an interested reader should consult for analytic details.

[7] This scenario is examined in John and Pecchenino (1997) and Sandler (1978b, 1999).

cases, the debt incurred from these projects has created burdens for unborn generations.

To evaluate the likely actions of policy makers with respect to inter-generational public goods (IGPGs), we require an efficiency criterion. There are numerous possible criteria, depending on how farsighted is the provision decision. The concept of *intergenerational Pareto optimality* is employed and corresponds to a position from which it is not possible to improve the well-being of any person at any point in time without harming someone in the current or some other generation. This criterion is a generalization of Pareto optimality to a scenario where an asset may have long-term influences over multiple generations, both domestically and internationally.[8] In particular, intergenerational Pareto optimality applies the Pareto principle over time and space, because it accounts for all relevant periods and places where the IGPGs' benefits may reach.

Suppose that, once produced, an IGPG generates nonrival and non-excludable benefits for the current generation and the next nine generations, not only in the providing country but also in four neighboring countries. To obtain intergenerational Pareto optimality, the IGPG provider must account for the marginal benefits that the long-lived public good confers on the people in the current *and* nine future generations in *all five nations*. Moreover, this sum of marginal benefits over regions and generations must be equated to the IGPG's marginal cost in the period of provision. If a policy maker truly accounts for the marginal benefits received by all relevant generations in his or her own country as well as in the neighboring countries, then *full spillover awareness* is achieved. Of course, this ideal is seldom seen in the real world owing to decision makers' myopia, whereby either future generations' gains or benefits conferred on neighboring countries are ignored. Public choice has taught us to expect a myopic response and a lack of interest in the welfare of neighboring countries.

Based on full awareness as a standard, it is easy to show that international cooperation among policy makers who are only concerned with the current generation can result in excessive provision of an IGPG with long-run *harmful consequences*. Suppose that the IGPG's marginal benefits to the current and next generation are positive, but are negative for subsequent generations, as may be true for nuclear energy development. Under these circumstances, international cooperation will increase provision of the good by accounting for just the positive marginal benefits

---

[8] Alternative intertemporal efficiency criteria are discussed in Doeleman and Sandler (1998). The intergenerational Pareto optimality criterion, used here, is analyzed in Page (1977) and Sandler and Smith (1976).

to the two immediate generations. The higher provision level will mean a greater sum (in absolute value) of negative marginal benefits to subsequent generations. In fact, the *net* sum of marginal benefits over the five generations may well be smaller with the increased cooperation than without it; thus full awareness requires smaller provision than that associated with international cooperation where longer-run harmful effects are ignored.

Other reduced levels of awareness are possible. I shall label decision makers, like those just discussed, who account for international benefit spillovers but not for intergenerational spillovers, as abiding by international awareness. A third level of awareness has a nation's decision maker ignoring interregional spillovers of benefits while accounting for intergenerational spillovers. Thus, the marginal benefits are summed only over the region's own current and future generations prior to being equated to the marginal costs for the public good. A still further reduced awareness would have the nation's policy maker failing to account for either interregional or intergenerational spillovers of benefits. Insofar as neither the residents of other countries nor future generations vote for the policy makers in charge of these decisions, a rather healthy dose of myopia and neglect of these nonvoters is the anticipated norm. This means that too little of the IGPGs that generate long-term benefits will be provided from a society's vantage point, because much of the goods' benefits are of no concern to those deciding upon the provision. By the same token, too-large amounts of intergenerational public bads (IGPBs), whose intergenerational marginal benefits are negative, will be provided.

We live in an age where technology is creating more IGPGs (IGPBs), so this inherent tendency toward underprovision (overprovision) is a real concern. In simple terms, it means fewer cures for new diseases and fewer research breakthroughs than needed, and longer waits for these discoveries. It also implies that nations are prone to adopt policies when sufficient gains are immediate despite potential longer-term negative consequences. One need only look to AIDS and malaria in Africa today, or to yesterday's rush to adopt nuclear fission reactors, to identify real-world counterparts to these predictions.

Thus far, the underlying analysis derives from an ethic of intergenerational Pareto optimality, based on equal weights being placed on the well-beings of current and future generations in the decision maker's own country and abroad. This is obviously a rather extreme awareness, worthy of a Star Trek episode. Suppose that an optimality criterion gives more weight to the current generation, which may be the case if its children are also concerned with their ancestors' well-being, as in some Eastern philosophies. With such an orientation, the associated optimality criterion will place more weight on the present generation's well-being. Each optimality criterion, which indicates how constituent preferences are aggregated or weighted when making decisions (that is, who counts and for how much), results in a different distribution of welfare among countries and generations when resources are being assigned to IGPGs. It is in the choice of these welfare standards that ethics, philosophy, economics, and religion have an important interface. The appropriate ethic depends on the cultural norms of the society and may differ across societies and within the same society over time.

At times, legal institutions may determine which generation's welfare matters for decisions involving IGPGs. In a landmark case during the early 1970s, the Sierra Club sued Walt Disney Productions to keep it from building a ski resort at Mineral King in California's Sierra Nevada Mountains.[9] The Sierra Club, maintaining that the proposed ski resort, which was to be surrounded by the Sequoia National Park, would damage the park's environment, brought suit on behalf of current and future users who would lose from the anticipated degradation of the park. These future users included yet-unborn generations. The case went all the way to the Supreme Court, which upheld the lower courts' rulings that the Sierra Club could not represent the interests of others, especially those of yet-unborn generations. Thus, the US legal system limits inter-generational awareness to the interests of the present overlapping generations in preserving nature-provided IGPGs.

When two societies with different welfare norms interact, interesting outcomes can result. This explains, for example, recent events concerning negotiations over environmental agreements to limit pollutants and preserve IGPGs. Suppose that Western countries, which display altruism and a concern for future generations' well-being, negotiate with Eastern countries, which are more focused on the current generation's well-being. The enhanced intergenerational awareness of Western countries will induce them to augment their provision of the IGPGs, thus affording the Eastern countries better opportunities to sit back and free ride. This free-riding proclivity is worsened if the Eastern countries' ethic induces them to curtail their intergenerational efforts yet further. The end result is that treaties are consummated with the Western countries pledging to underwrite the IGPGs with little or no support from their Eastern counterparts. This outcome is in keeping with the Kyoto Protocol on global warming.

The bottom line with respect to IGPGs is not very promising, inasmuch as legal constraints, political incentives, and cultural interactions

---

[9] This lawsuit and its ethical principles are analyzed by Krutilla and Fisher (1975). Also, see an empirical study by Cicchetti, Fisher, and Smith (1976).

are not very supportive of supplying IGPGs and eliminating IGPBs. The requisite collective action with respect to these IGPGs presents a supreme challenge to political economists.

LINKING GENERATIONS AND SHARED RISK

The dikes of Holland are an insurance policy that protects the current and subsequent generations from being swept away when the sea rises.[10] Why have these dams been built even though they have benefits for subsequent generations? When visiting the cathedrals of Europe, I have always marveled at how more than a century of construction went into some of these houses of worship, which represent IGPGs. One generation made farsighted decisions for subsequent generations, who were then willing to carry on construction to complete the cathedral. What is it about these two examples that resulted in such farsighted and seemingly unselfish behavior?

To illuminate such outcomes, I shall use a simple two-period game played between two overlapping generations, for which generation 1 must decide in period 1 (at node n_1 in Figure 10.1) whether or not to invest in a safeguard – heightening a levee – to protect against flooding during a subsequent period. Each generation has an endowment worth 20. Suppose that, if the flood occurs in the second period, it only destroys the endowment of generation 2, since generation 1 has retired to higher ground. The likelihood of the flood in period 2 is 50%. Further suppose that at the start of period 2 (node 2, n_2) that generation 2 has two possible courses of action if the levee has been raised, and two random outcomes if it has not. Thus, in the upper half of the tree at n_2, generation 2 experiences the flood and reimburses its predecessors the 20 that its action saved in losses, or it experiences no flood and shows no gratitude. In the lower half of the tree at n_2', the levee had not been improved, and so generation 2 owes nothing to its predecessors, who have done nothing to protect it from disaster.

At the four end points, the left-hand payoff is that of generation 1, while the right-hand payoff is that of generation 2. The improvement to the levee costs 10 to generation 1 and must be accomplished, if at all, during period 1. Once period 2 begins, it is assumed to be too late to increase the levee's height. If the levee is raised and the flood occurs, then generation 1 gets 30, which equals its endowment of 20 less its levee

---

[10] With an insurance policy, an individual pays a premium in order to limit losses during bad outcomes. That is, the person foregoes an amount of money whether the outcome is good or bad so that when it is bad he or she is protected. Insurance represents reducing one's income to reduce the risk associated with uncertain states. This payment to avoid gambles is only anticipated to come from risk-averse individuals.

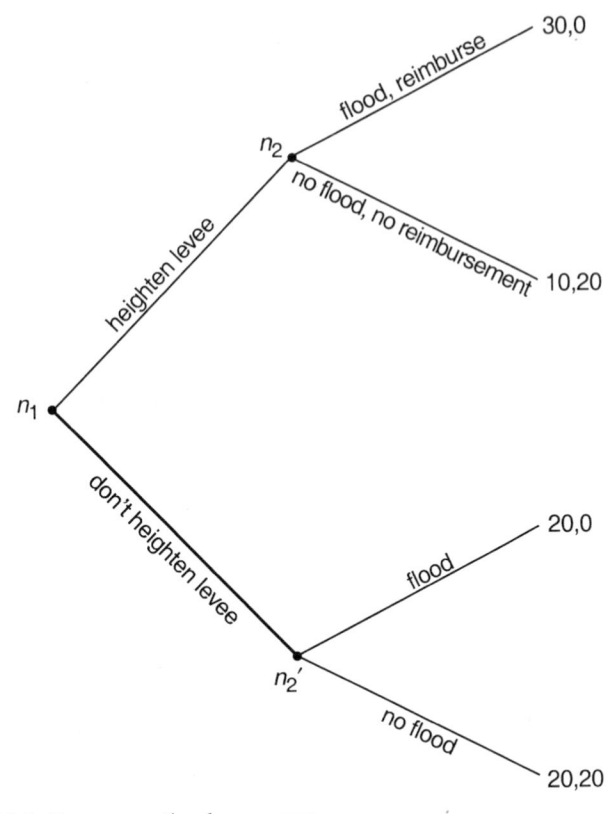

Figure 10.1. Two-generation levee game

costs of 10, plus its compensation of 20 from generation 2. The latter ends up with nothing by paying out its endowment in gratitude. If the levee is raised and there is no deluge, then generation 1 keeps just half of its endowment by expending 10 for the levee without later being repaid, while generation 2 maintains its endowment of 20. When the levee is not raised and disaster hits, generation 1 holds onto its endowment while generation 2 loses everything. If, however, the levee is not raised and there is no flood, then both generations maintain their endowment of 20.

Generation 1's decision whether or not to improve the levee at the outset hinges on how it values the certain payoff of 20 that it receives regardless of what nature dishes out when it does not improve the levee, versus the *expected* payoff of 20 ($0.5 \times 30 + 0.5 \times 10$) associated with raising the levee. If generation 1 loathes the risk (that is, payoffs that vary between 30 and 10) tied to raising the dam, then it will take the sure thing and do nothing. Thus, the thickened branch in the game tree in Figure 10.1 indicates the outcome for a risk-averse generation.

There are at least two ways to improve this situation and provide a risk-averse generation 2 with an insurance policy that would make it better off by limiting its risk. Suppose that generation 1 also suffers from the flood by losing half of its endowment when the levee has not been raised. This scenario is accounted for by changing only generation 1's payoff from 20 to 10 at the third endpoint from the top of Figure 10.1. A gamble for generation 1 is now tied to either decision. Since raising the levee gives generation 1 a greater expected payoff of 20 when compared to 15 for doing nothing, raising the levee is preferred. The upside gain from raising the levee is now greater, while the downside risk is identical for either gamble. The message here is that giving generation 1 some shared risk or a stake in the decision to raise the levee induces action. In the example, its stake does not need to be as great as that of generation 2 if the latter compensates the former for its earlier action when the flood arrives. Again consider the dikes of Holland. There is no higher ground, and every generation has an interest in keeping the dikes well maintained. Fear of Hell and the promise of Heaven tied together the generations that built Europe's massive cathedrals. Shared risks and overlapping generations are the factors that promote intergenerational trades.

A second scenario in which this intergenerational trade could take place is when generation 2 contracts with the earlier generation to cover its levee expenses no matter what. Now suppose that there are no shared risks, so that the payoffs in the bottom half of the tree are unchanged. If generation 2 commits to (or can be committed to) reimbursing generation 1 regardless of whether the flood comes, then a trade can be achieved. This requires that generation 2 reimburse 10 to generation 1 at the start of period 2 regardless of nature's outcome. Now the top end point would have payoffs of (20, 10), while the next end point below would also have payoffs of (20, 10). These payoffs are not shown in Figure 10.1. If this exchange could be engineered, the certain payoff of 10 for risk-averse generation 2 provided through the insurance of underwriting the raising of the levee, is preferred to the gamble associated with not raising the levee. Generation 1 is indifferent between heightening or not heightening, because it is assured 20 in either case. With some inducement from generation 2, generation 1 would provide this insurance by raising the levee. Can such an insurance scheme be realized in practice? The answer is maybe. If generation 1 borrows the money and commits its offspring to the repayment, a not uncommon practice, then the answer is yes. Whenever the later generation sees a moral responsibility to compensate its parents for such farsighted and altruistic actions, the answer is again yes.

Of course, the moral responsibility may be forward in time, as when the current generation displays altruism toward its children by using some of its children's future inheritance as a means for reducing their risks. There are good reasons why an inheritance may take the form of increasing the safety of one's children. Clearly, such altruistic actions improve the quality of life of the next generation, who, if given a choice, can be expected to relinquish inherited wealth in return for ensuring its safety from disaster. The problem is a sequential one insofar as seeing a disastrous flood coming leaves too little time to react if the preceding generation had not acted earlier in terms of precautions.

Next, consider a more difficult problem where safeguards must be taken today to keep something from happening many generations into the future. Suppose that the introduction of a genetically altered insect today is judged both beneficial and safe for the next four or five generations (say 200 years into the future), but that dire consequences might result thereafter. To institute the proper precautions, each intervening generation would have to act so that the insects would be monitored and sufficiently confined. If a potentially harmful mutation were to develop 200 years hence, then the at-risk distant generation could easily destroy the sport. The required intergenerational coordination is, however, too much to expect, especially when the intervening generations are not themselves at risk, which is the case when a mutation requires time to develop.[11] Another relevant example involves the storage of plutonium and other highly radioactive daughter elements from nuclear fission. The likely scenario is for the decision-making generation to institute a short-term fix that leaves future generations the chore of storing these highly toxic substances for literally hundreds of thousands of years. The required insurance is not undertaken, because the risks can be transferred to distant generations whose welfare is of no concern to the decision-making generation.

If intergenerational coordination of risky situations is to be engineered, then there must be sufficient propinquity between the generations. Additionally, the decision-making generation must share some risks with its descendants. With too much separation, altruism, risk sharing, and the possibility of coordination disappear. Later generations are disenfranchised, and the required insurance transactions or markets remain missing. As humankind enters an age where innovations and

---

[11] Doeleman and Sandler (1998, pp. 6–8) demonstrate that if there is even one intervening generation separating the decision-making generation and the generation at risk, the necessary coordination or insurance arrangement among the generations is unlikely.

actions have increasingly long-term consequences, we must become more concerned about the implied deterioration of the choices facing our descendants.

INTERGENERATIONAL CLUBS

In Chapter 6, clubs were introduced as a way of economizing on transaction costs in which members voluntarily share a public good financed through tolls or a membership fee. The essential requirement for a club is that the shared public good's benefits are excludable at costs smaller than the allocative benefits achieved by matching tastes and user fees. In an intergenerational club,[12] the members share a durable impure public good (club good) that lasts beyond the membership span of the original members, at which time new generations of members enter and share in the good's benefits until the good is worn out. Many clubs are intergenerational; these include religious groups, a city's residents, universities, professional associations, and indigenous people on a forest tract. National parks represent an intergenerational club, as does the sharing of long-lasting infrastructure such as bridges. Even a nation or a city is an intergenerational club where the required toll must account for crowding at a point in time and depreciation losses over time that use of the good imposes on current and future members (residents). Depreciation due to utilization arises when a current visit affects the quality of the club good now and into the future. Users who visit more frequently cause more crowding and depreciation and pay more in total tolls, yet pay the same toll per visit.

As for other clubs, intergenerational clubs account for taste differences by monitoring use and charging for each visit according to the associated costs imposed on the membership. If, for example, a visit to a national park on a crowded summer day causes a great deal of depreciation for current and future users, then the toll must be sufficiently high to reflect these losses. Members who visit early in an intergenerational club good's lifetime may have to pay relatively large fees for any resulting deterioration of the club good, since this depreciation will affect a large number of subsequent generations and members. As the intertemporal component of the toll rises, individuals will be dissuaded from visiting, thus preserving the good. A visitation limit can be reached where the deterioration is so severe that tolls cannot compensate the generations of members for the resulting losses. Utilization must then be capped and would-be users temporarily turned away. Thus, national parks must close their gates once the number of visits reaches a limit beyond which

---

[12] Sandler (1982) introduces intergenerational clubs.

the deterioration to the park's amenities is too great. This is a policy concern in many national parks worldwide today.

Toll proceeds are earmarked to maintain and provide a club good passed among the generations of members. If the tolls are properly designed, then tolls can finance the club good without the need for outside intervention. Clubs can be owned and operated by members (such as a tribe on a forest tract), a government, or by a firm for the well-being of its members. Clubs can assume myriad forms – there is no single blueprint for success if exclusion can be practiced and estimates computed of the congestion and depreciation that each use creates.

A subsequent generation of members can reimburse an earlier generation's investment through equity or ownership shares sold as the club good is transferred between generations, much like the way in which a house is traded from one owner to the next. The value of these equity shares depends on the residual worth of the club good. If a generation were myopic and ran down the club good's value through use and collected tolls that did not reflect this depreciation, then the myopic generation would receive less in payment to finance its retirement when the club asset was traded to the next generation. This club arrangement ties the current generation's actions to future consequences, thereby motivating more farsighted behavior. If, instead, the club investment were financed by debt, then the club's ability to repay its loan would hinge on its collecting enough tolls to offset any depreciation through maintenance. The ability to refinance the loan from generation to generation depends on the residual worth of the shared club good – the collateral on which the debt is drawn. If a generation behaves in a shortsighted manner, the shared good depreciates prematurely, and this results in less money being raised during refinancing; hence, the generation shoulders the burden of its myopia. Any combination of debt/equity financing of the shared good provides the right incentives for today's generation to collect the proper tolls.

Why is a club good that lasts for many generations a more hopeful scenario than some of the purely public intergenerational goods described in the last section? The answer lies in the club arrangement, which forces every generation to assume a shared risk because each generation's ability to recoup its club investment upon retirement hinges on how well the club was managed. Tribes are known to manage forest tracts in a sustainable fashion, passing an undiminished asset to their children, who then use the forest's abundance to support their retired parents. Nations also care for their treasured assets (for example, the Taj Mahal, the Egyptian pyramids, works of arts) so that they can be visited by present and future generations. Failure to do so would diminish an asset that brings tourists and revenue.

MARKETS FOR NONRENEWABLE RESOURCES

Some resources are fixed in terms of their stocks, so that a unit used today is a unit less available for tomorrow. These resources are called *nonrenewable* or exhaustible and pose an interesting choice problem over time. Consumption of an exhaustible resource by the current generation determines how much of the resource remains for subsequent generations. If markets are competitive and property rights to the resource are well defined, then the profit-maximizing extraction rate is related to a simple opportunity cost. Suppose that the only cost of obtaining a nonrenewable resource, such as oil, is fixed, so that the variable cost of extraction is zero. If more of the resource is required, then simply pressing a button starts the flow of the oil to the market from its underground reserves.

The firm must decide each year how much of the oil to leave in the ground and how much to sell. A barrel of oil sold today will earn revenue that can subsequently be invested where it will earn a rate of return over time. Suppose that capital markets are efficient, so that the average rate of return of an investment equals the interest rate or the cost of borrowing money. Leaving the oil in the ground is only worthwhile when its return in situ or its expected growth in price is equal to or greater than the interest rate or what could be earned over time from oil sold today and invested. If the price of oil is expected to rise by 10% and the interest rate is just 6%, then it pays to leave the oil in reserve to sell another day, since it yields a higher rate of return through its expected appreciation. If, instead, the price is only anticipated to grow by 4% and the interest rate is 6%, then it is better to sell off more oil reserves now and use the proceeds for investment that can earn 6%. In the first case, selling less oil will raise the price (because demand slopes downwards)[13] and, given next period's expected price, will result in a smaller price rise, so that an equality between the expected price rise and the interest rate is approached. For the second case, it is better to remove more oil, which, in turn, lowers the current price and results in a greater anticipated price rise. In either case, actions set into motion equilibrating forces that equate the growth in price to the interest rate – the point at which the profit-maximizing amount of oil is just being brought to the market.

What is the social optimal exploitation rate? Harold Hotelling (1931) showed that it also corresponds to where the anticipated growth in price

---

[13] Consider a standard demand and supply diagram. If the supply brought to the market decreases, then the current supply curve shifts up to the left and intersects the downward sloping demand at a higher price. Thus, the anticipated difference between today's price (which has risen) and tomorrow's expected price will decrease, leading to a smaller growth in price than originally anticipated.

equals the interest rate. This follows because the growth in price denotes the marginal social benefits from abstinence, while the interest rate indicates the marginal social costs from leaving the oil in situ or the money that could be earned from the sale's proceeds. Competitive profit maximization satisfies social optimality, a result reminiscent of Adam Smith's invisible hand. If the variable costs of extraction are nonzero, then both the profit-maximizing condition and the social-optimizing Hotelling rule require that *the growth in net price*, or price minus marginal extraction costs, equals the interest rate. In an analysis of a capital or resource asset, the interest rate serves as the opportunity costs or standard of earnings performance.

The implied intergenerational harmony in exploiting a nonrenewable resource breaks down under conditions of market failure. First, if the resource is owned in common, then the depletion rate is expected to be pushed to the point where the appreciation of the resource in situ is less than the interest rate, as exploiters race to grab the resource before someone else does. Thus, the resource is overexploited. Second, there may be externalities in which efforts by one person to extract the resource result in higher costs to other exploiters, which are unaccounted for by the user. Overexploitation is anticipated based on this crowding externality. Third, monopoly power may characterize the exploiters, which implies reduced efforts to remove the resource. Fourth, there may be uncertainties that make it difficult to know the growth in prices so as to satisfy Hotelling's rule.

RENEWAL RESOURCES

A renewal resource can be used and then replenished; for example, a stand of timber can be harvested and a new stand planted. As timber grows, its value increases. The optimal time to harvest a tree is found by equating the interest rate to the tree's growth in value. The latter depends on how fast the tree grows and how the wood is valued by society. A higher interest rate signals a greater opportunity cost from not harvesting today and putting the proceeds to work. This result is reminiscent of the Hotelling rule and again highlights the pivotal position played by the interest rate when examining decisions involving assets.

An essential concern with respect to renewal resources has to do with exploitation rates that go too far, so that insufficient populations remain for sustainable replenishment. That is, a species' numbers can be so depleted that there are too few remaining members to maintain a viable population. The passenger pigeon and the Tasmanian tiger are instances where species were literally hunted to extinction, thus creating a significant transgenerational negative externality. In many ways, the existence of a species and its ability to promote the stability of an ecosystem through diversity is an intergenerational pure public good and, as such, is prone to the kind of myopic decisions discussed earlier. Surely, the current generation can pursue its own well-being without regard to the long-term consequences for subsequent generations. Not all species are alike, since those that have more linkages to the population stability of other species are apt to be more valuable for the future than those with few linkages. Additionally, species that are more distant genetically from any other species may also be more valuable from an intergenerational perspective owing to the absence of substitutes. A gingko tree, which is a unique species, may have more value than one of the 600 varieties of eucalyptus tree. The valuing of species, not to mention their cataloging, is a necessary task if sensible economic trade-offs for such renewable resources are to be made. The allocational and distributive implications of extinction are important concerns that distinguish renewable from exhaustible resources.

ON THE SOCIAL RATE OF DISCOUNT

A little background is required to understand the issues behind the debate over the social rate of discount. If I promised to pay you $110 a year from now, how much would you lend me today? A wise person would lend me less than $110 owing to the opportunity cost of doing without this money for a year. This opportunity cost is, of course, what the money could have earned if invested. If the bank is paying an interest rate of 10%, then the foregone earnings are related to the interest rate. Suppose that an investor leaves $100 on deposit in a bank for a year. With an interest rate of 10%, this investment will be worth

$$\$100 + \$100i = \$100(1 + i) = \$110 \tag{1}$$

or principle plus interest after a year. If, instead, the investor were promised $110 a year hence in return for money sacrificed *today*, the investor would relinquish just $100 today at an interest rate of 10% to be compensated for the lost earnings of $10. Equation (1) indicates that the value of $110 a year from now is $110/(1 + .10) or just $100 today. That is, the present value (PV) of $110 in a year's time is $100 when the interest rate is 10%. In general, the present value is related to the future value (FV) or payment one year hence as follows:

$$PV = FV/(1 + i). \tag{2}$$

In (2), the greater the opportunity cost or i, the smaller is the present value of a *given* future payment. A physician, who must forego earnings for many years of schooling and residency, must receive the prospect of a high future income stream to engage in this sacrifice. Otherwise, this person would be better off putting the money in the bank.

Formula (2) can be generalized to include more years of waiting, for which an investor is willing to give up less today for a sum in the distant future. Suppose that $100 is left on deposit for two years, at which time this principal has become

$$\$100(1 + i) + \$100i(1 + i) = \$100(1 + i)^2 = \$121 \tag{3}$$

when i equals 10% per year. On the left-hand of (3), we have applied the interest rate in the first year to $100 and in the second year to $100i$ or the earnings of the first year. Equation (3) tells us that the present value of $121 in two year's time, with nothing paid in the interim, is $121/(1 + .10)^2$ or $100. In general, the present value of FV dollars t years from now is represented by

$$PV = FV/(1 + i)^t. \tag{4}$$

Quite simply, the longer the wait, the smaller the present value of the promised payment t years hence. The discount rate is the i in equation (4), whereas the discount factor is the multiplier, $1/(1 + i)^t \leq 1$, applied to a future payment that translates it into present-value terms. The formula can be further developed to allow the interest rate to vary across periods, or for it to be compounded or applied more than once during a year, but this is not needed for the purposes here.

If the current generation contemplates an investment with a short-run income stream, there is little disagreement among economists that formula (4) holds, with some market rate of interest used that reflects capital's marginal productivity. The real issue involves what to do when an investment decision has consequences, good or bad, in the far-distant future.[14] Suppose that a possible harmful effect of an innovation (for example, a genetically altered species or a new energy-generating process) occurs some 1,000 years after its introduction and creates an expected cost of $1 billion to be addressed at that time. Based on equation (4) with $t = 1,000$, $i = 10\%$, and $FV = \$1$ billion, the present value is $FV/(1 + .10)^{1000}$, which is virtually zero. For most reasonable interest rates, the discount factor approaches zero in a mere forty or fifty years, leaving society to ignore even catastrophic outcomes when they are sufficiently distant. This does not bode well for the well-being of future generations.

If, however, the present generation deposits the required sum of money in the banking system so that it earns interest and grows to

---

[14] A recent treatment of this issue as well as others in this section can be found in Portney and Weyant (1999).

$1 billion in 1,000 years, then the present generation has provided for the future contingency. For the current example, this compensatory deposit is just the present value, $1 billion$/(1 + i)^{1000}$, of the distant payoff. Of course, this practice assumes that the banking institutions will last 1,000 years and that an intervening generation will not withdraw the money for its own purposes.[15] The ability of one generation to compensate for a distant contingency depends on a sequence of generations playing a cooperative game, even though no earlier generation has any leverage on a succeeding *nonoverlapping* generation. The primary factor that mildly promotes this compensatory scheme is altruism, because generations nearer in time will display a greater interest in one another – generally, we care more about our parents and our children than about our great grandparents or our children's children. Thus, propinquity in time again plays a crucial role in engineering compensatory incentives for distant generations. The practice of discounting gives a first-mover advantage, like going first in tic-tac-toe, to the current generation over succeeding generations.

Some economists argue that the discount rate used on short-term projects should not be the same as the rates applied to long-term projects with intergenerational consequences.[16] In the latter case, a smaller discount rate is required when the payoffs are more distant, so that the welfare of future generations is included. If one subscribes to this view, then the highest discount rate is applied to projects lasting, say, 1–40 years, a lower one to those lasting 41–60 years, a still smaller one to those lasting 61–80 years, and so on. While this practice might be justified on ethical or altruistic grounds, it has some undesirable technical implications that are beyond the scope of this book.[17]

In assessing the proper social rate of discount, society must adjust for the human tendency to undervalue what future costs might be. If, say, a future generation places a greater value on its environmental amenities because of increased scarcity, then today's estimates of tomorrow's damages may be much too small. This tendency would support the use of a smaller social discount rate. The further away tomorrow is, the greater is this undervaluation and the smaller should be the discount rate. Given that capital's future productivity is more uncertain as one moves into the future, there is yet another reason to employ a smaller social discount rate for deep-future projects.

---

[15] Arrow (1999, p. 18) discusses this concern.

[16] This argument is made by Heal (1997) and Weitzman (1999).

[17] In particular, it leads to time-inconsistent choices, where a decision maker at a later time will want to deviate from the chosen decision path (Portney and Weyant 1999, p. 3).

If too high a social discount rate is used, then society will produce too few intergenerational public goods and too many intergenerational public bads. This translates into too few cures for diseases, not enough research breakthroughs, and too little preservation of Earth's natural assets. It also implies too much global warming, acid rain, and forest depletion. Even though it has been debated since Ramsey's (1928) seminal paper, the issue of the proper social discount rate is far from settled. Without a resolution, one generation's responsibility to the next is left to whim and chance.

TODAY'S TOMORROW: A PROGNOSIS

If I were to predict an area where major new insights in economic understanding will be achieved during the coming decades, I would put the study of intergenerational economics toward the top of the list. To capture the strategic interactions among sequentially overlapping generations as they make allocative and distributional decisions, a researcher must be astute in reducing a problem to its essential elements. Without such simplification, the issues are much too complicated to make much headway. A key ingredient will be modeling the manner in which tastes are transferred from one generation to the next. Another important aspect concerns the ethical norms by which one generation weighs the interests of past and future generations. The choice of the social rate of discount is just one part of this ethical determination.

Intergenerational economics is near the top of my list of areas with likely breakthroughs because of current interest and abundant applications. For the environment, the planet's ecosphere is under siege by pollutants. The accumulation of stock pollutants, such as greenhouse gases and chlorofluorocarbons in the stratosphere, has created long-run consequences that will be experienced far into the future. Technological innovations in medicine, agriculture, and industry also create long-term allocative consequences, as is aptly illustrated by genetic engineering, where both the intended useful effects and the unintended harmful consequences impact many generations. Today's tomorrow is an age for which public good benefits (costs) will increasingly span the globe as well as the generations. Technology also places in our hands the means to address some of these global intergenerational effects. In particular, geoengineering may allow humans to augment a thinned ozone shield or to sequester carbon. For example, greenhouse gases can be pumped into underground reservoirs, or the absorptive capacity of the oceans as a carbon sink can be enhanced. Fast-growing tree plantations in the tropics can be a way to store more carbon if the associated free-riding problem both within and among generations can be successfully addressed.[18] Thus, the economics of the twenty-first century must pay greater heed to inter-generational political economy.

As life expectancy increases, more generations will overlap, and this raises the question of whether more farsighted allocative and distributional decisions will be made. Certainly, a subsequent generation that lives longer will want to take a longer-term view of allocative trade-offs, given that they may survive long enough to suffer from myopic decisions. Most current economic models allow just two overlapping generations, even though a time is fast approaching when three or more generations may overlap.

Another intergenerational concern is social security and how generations cooperate to accumulate assets to provide income for an older generation during its retirement. Population dynamics can create imbalances in which a large aging generation must be supported by a relatively small subsequent generation. This scenario is especially relevant to a social security program that operates on an unfunded pay-as-you-go program, as is partly true of the current US system. In contrast, a funded system would invest a generation's contributions during its working years to support it during retirement.[19] Such a system would be relatively immune to population imbalances. Social security poses interesting issues of intergenerational equity and responsibilities.

Evolutionary game theory holds much promise as a tool for understanding intergenerational choice. Unlike the standard study of repeated games, evolutionary game theory allows tastes, population size, and composition to change over time (see Chapter 3). Moreover, population dynamics and the resulting stability of equilibria depend on the performance of different kinds of individuals. Good performers have more offspring and may come to dominate a population, but random factors, not unlike those in the real world, also play a role. Because evolutionary game theory is based on population dynamics and innovation, it represents an ideal technique for studying intergenerational economics. In essence, this branch of game theory tries to incorporate both genotype and phenotype considerations. Tests of evolutionary game theory's propositions must include field data in addition to the laboratory experiments performed to date.

If intergenerational economics is to achieve its full potential, then an accounting of natural assets (for example, the value of environmental amenities) must be introduced into national income accounting. Once a

---

[18] Tree plantations can store carbon but cannot bring back lost biodiversity.

[19] On alternative social security systems, see Bruce (2001, pp. 253–79) and Meyer and Wolff (1993).

value is computed for a country's stock of natural capital or assets, this capital's depreciation can be deducted from national income to give a more complete picture of the annual net gain in economic activity. Currently, the depreciation of man-made capital is subtracted, but not that of natural capital. Moreover, investment efforts that result in the improvement of natural capital must be included in national income, valued at the appreciation of these assets. This valuation and its annual updating for depreciation and appreciation will allow a present generation to fathom the implications of its choices for itself and tomorrow's generations. Unless this accounting is accomplished, it will be difficult to achieve sustained economic development where the options of future generations are not foreclosed.

The study of intergenerational economics presents a supreme, but essential, challenge to economists. Because this long-run thinking is alien to modern-day political institutions, the practice of intergenerational political economy necessitates significant institutional changes.

11   Fish, Space, and Spaceship Earth: Bioeconomics and Interdisciplinary Economics

Adam Smith taught us that the division of labor could keep down costs and promote economic efficiency. Thus, one set of workers cuts the wires for the pins, another straightens them, and still another attaches the heads. The ability to exploit gains from this division of labor is limited by the extent of the market; the larger the market, the greater the division of labor. Academia is also characterized by a division of labor where scholars are separated into disciplines; those disciplines are further subdivided into fields and even subfields. This division has both advantages and disadvantages in the pursuit of knowledge. Specialization has allowed scholars to become experts within a narrow range of topics, which in turn has promoted the rapid acquisition of knowledge. In the process, fields and subfields have created their own jargon, terminology, notation, and methods that present an entry barrier to others. Many problems involve relationships derived from multiple disciplines and cannot truly be understood with the tools of a single discipline. For such problems, an interdisciplinary approach is required.

In the study of a renewable resource such as a fishery, economic decisions and forces impinge on both the fishing industry and the biological relationships that influence the supply of fish. Biological forces also constrain economic decisions regarding harvesting the fish in both the short run and the long run. *Bioeconomics* investigates the interrelationship between an economic and a biological system, so that equilibria and adjustments to disequilibria account for the influences of both systems.[1] In macroeconomics, an equilibrium must account for the goods and the asset markets if a general equilibrium is to be found. Similarly, a bioeconomic equilibrium must achieve a balance of opposing forces

---

[1] A pioneering paper in bioeconomics is by H. Scott Gordon (1954) on common property aspects of fisheries. For a list of references and a careful presentation of bioeconomic modeling, see Clark (1985) and Conrad (1995).

within both the economic and biological systems. Interesting questions arise. Is the optimum concerned with maximizing the biomass of the fishery or with maximizing the profits earned from this biomass? Are fisheries prone to so much overharvesting that species are doomed to extinction? If extinction is not the norm, then what factors push harvesting activities to cause the extinction of some species? How can fisheries be properly managed so that the intended consequences of regulations are achieved?

Interdisciplinary approaches to economics continue to grow in importance and harken back to the roots of economics in political economy and moral philosophy. For example, public choice combines economic methods with the study of political questions and represents an instance where insights are gained by marrying tools and issues from two or more fields. Cliometrics applies sophisticated theoretical tools of economic analysis and econometric techniques to the study of economic history.[2] A more recent endeavor is what I like to call geoeconomics, in which economic methods and relationships are combined with those of geology to characterize an equilibrium and its adjustments to disturbances. Geoeconomics concerns such issues as the influence of economic activities and decisions on groundwater quality, the runoff of nitrogen from cultivated fields, or the use of geological structures to store carbon in order to curtail global warming. The study of the economic implications of activities to augment the carbon absorptive capacity of the oceans (for example, the use of iron filings) represents another geoeconomic case where geological relationships must be included as constraints or within the objective function of an economic model for policy purposes.

Atmospheric relationships, which determine the transport of air pollutants and the chemical reactions in the troposphere and stratosphere, must be part of economic models involving air pollutants. The study of acid rain, global warming, and the depletion of stratospheric ozone must, therefore, include atmospheric relationships if the appropriate predictive model is to be formulated. In the field of environmental economics, economic models must encompass the relevant geologic, atmospheric, hydrologic, genetic, and climatic relationships if predictive power is to be fostered.

Another interdisciplinary area of significant recent growth is spatial economics, where sophisticated tools of spatial statistics have aided the burgeoning analysis.[3] Myriad applications exist. For example, spatial eco-

---

[2] Nobel Prizes in economic history were awarded in 1993 to Robert Fogel for his work on the economics of slavery and to Douglass North for his work on the role of property rights in economic development.

[3] The two pioneers in the use of these tools of spatial statistics and econometrics are Luc Anselin (1988) and Noel Cressie (1993).

nomics is required to investigate the economics of acid rain, where sulfur and nitrogen pollutants are transported by air currents to downwind countries. The economic study of pest control also involves spatial dispersion, as does the analysis of species migration. In political economy, spatial factors influence the manner in which collateral economic damages from a civil war or other conflict disperse and infect neighboring countries and beyond. One need only look at the aftermath of the civil war in Rwanda and Burundi during the 1990s to appreciate that mass migrations, spawned by such conflicts, have had economic impacts far beyond the conflict's origin. Even the dissemination of technology and information has a spatial component that needs to be incorporated into economic models.

If much can be learned in economics from broadening partial-equilibrium analysis to that of general equilibrium, as shown in Chapter 8, then the same holds true for expanding general-equilibrium analysis to incorporate equilibria of related noneconomic systems that work in conjunction with economic relationships. For certain problems, noneconomic relationships play a pivotal role, so that a true general-equilibrium depiction must include both economic and noneconomic relationships. Impacts of the economic system on the noneconomic system and vice versa must be incorporated, along with subsequent feedbacks and spillovers among the systems, as an equilibrium is attained following some disturbance.

This kind of thinking is aptly illustrated by a recent article that develops a general-equilibrium depiction of an ecosystem (Tschirhart 2000), where plant and animal organisms demand and supply biomass based on *energy prices*. Equilibrium results for a set of energy prices for which all biomass markets clear (that is, the quantity demanded equals the quantity supplied) and all organisms are optimized with respect to their net energy intake (that is, the same energy *cannot* achieve a larger biomass by being spent in a different fashion). This creative exercise shows how economic analysis not only can further understanding outside of standard applications, but also can result in a model that can easily be integrated with another depicting economic influences.

Interdisciplinary approaches can be achieved in a couple of different ways. Either researchers from two or more disciplines can form a team, or one or more researchers can acquire an expertise in two or more disciplines. Of course, both of these paradigms can be simultaneously applied, and may be particularly effective when interdisciplinary researchers on a team facilitate communication and exchange between those trained in just a single discipline.

The purpose of this chapter is to examine a few multidisciplinary economic analyses that are growing in importance and are expected to continue to gain prominence. As someone who contributes to two disciplines (economics and political science), I appreciate the importance and power of a multidisciplinary investigation, but I also recognize its pitfalls. These include the difficulty of finding a publisher, since most journals are highly discipline-specific. Another hazard to someone doing interdisciplinary research in a university setting involves being expected to satisfy two sets of colleagues, both with a narrow view of research. Thus, a faculty member in two departments may work twice as hard to stay current and publish in two disciplines while earning half the credit, because neither department values anything but a single-discipline approach. It is therefore not surprising that polymaths with interdisciplinary expertise are so rare in today's institutions of higher learning.[4]

BIOECONOMICS

The best way to make the case for an interdisciplinary approach is to consider the classic case of bioeconomics in both static and dynamic settings. A static analysis concerns equilibrium and instantaneous adjustments to disturbances, while a dynamic analysis involves the actual movement or time path from one equilibrium to another. Is this movement rapid or slow, and is it direct or indirect? A brief overview of the bioeconomic approach will be presented in a nontechnical way, with an emphasis on concepts and defining principles.[5]

A Static Model of the Fishery

The basic biological relationship underlying the fishery model, where firms ply the seas in search of a catch, is the yield-effort curve, which indicates the annual catch that can be sustained indefinitely for a given level of fishing effort, E. Effort can be measured in terms of the number of vessels of a standard size, whereas the yield, Y, is the fish harvested. Initially, greater effort can augment sustainable yields, but eventually effort reaches a point where fish populations are so depleted that sustainable yields fall. The effort level at which the sustainable yield is the greatest is known as the *maximum sustainable yield, MSY*. In Figure 11.1, a typical hill-shaped Schaefer (1954) sustainable yield-effort curve is depicted, where E_{MSY} represents the effort level, measured along the horizontal axis, associated with the maximum sustainable yield. In some theoretical treatments, the biomass, X, of the fishery is placed on the horizontal axis, which then gives a yield-biomass curve of the same shape.

---

[4] The dual committee work that comes with belonging to two or more departments will limit research time or else kill the person with boredom!

[5] For the technical presentation, consult Clark (1985) and Conrad (1995).

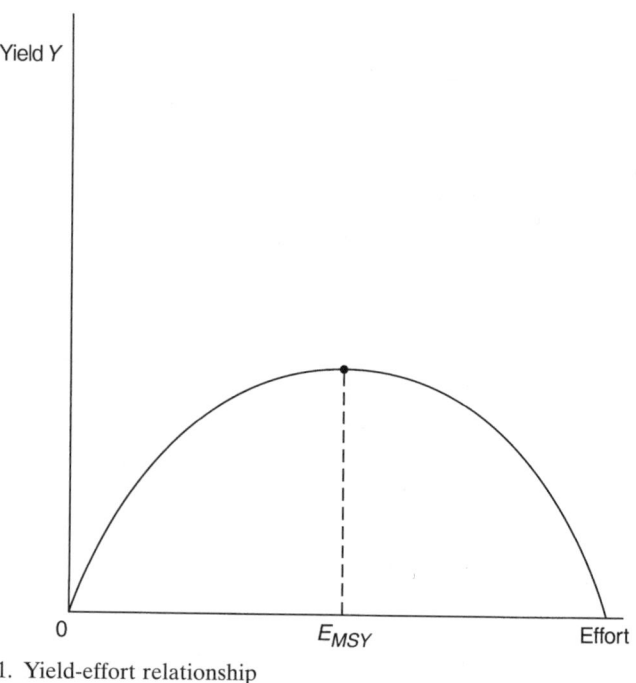

Figure 11.1. Yield-effort relationship

Because effort can be directly tied to the fishery's biomass, the problem can be represented in terms of effort or the biomass.

If the yield or catch is multiplied by the price, p, of fish, the vertical axis in Figure 11.1 now represents the fishery's revenue, pY, or the value of the harvest. The hill then displays a revenue-effort curve, in which revenue increases with effort and peaks at the MSY before declining. If revenue is the objective to maximize, then the biological objective of MSY coincides with revenue maximization. From a biological viewpoint, overfishing occurs if the yield drops below the MSY. In economics, profit and not revenue is the objective, so costs must be introduced and deducted from revenues. Things are kept simple by assuming that the fish are sold in a competitive market where the price of fish is a constant determined by the forces of supply and demand of the overall market for fish, for which this fishery's harvest is a small total of the supply.

Profits are maximized at the point where the difference between revenue and costs is the greatest. The cost is simply the money expended on fishing effort or cE, where c is the price per unit of effort – for example, the rental price of a vessel. Figure 11.2 presents a graphical

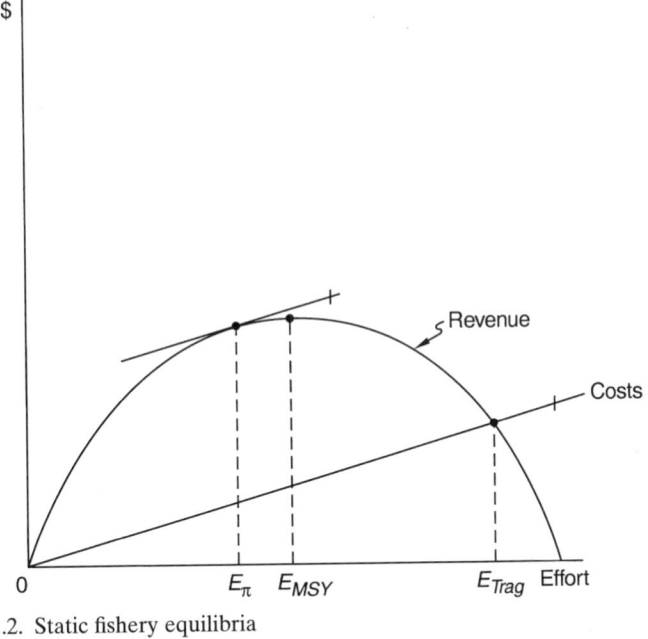

Figure 11.2. Static fishery equilibria

depiction of revenue and costs. The revenue curve is the yield-effort curve multiplied by the constant price of fish, while the cost curve is a straight line from the origin with a positive slope of c, representing the marginal costs. If there is no effort, there is no cost. As the number of vessels increases, the costs increase in a linear fashion. Profits are the largest at E_π, at which point the difference between revenue and costs is maximized. At this profit maximum, the slope of the revenue curve is parallel to that of the cost curve, so that marginal revenue equals marginal costs, which is a standard competitive solution. In Figure 11.2, the profit-maximizing effort will *not* coincide with the effort associated with the biological MSY unless variable costs are zero at all effort levels, so that the cost curve is horizontal.[6] Thus, a conflict is inevitable between the interests of economists and biologists. If the marginal costs are greater, so that the cost curve is steeper than the one displayed, then the profit-maximizing effort will be smaller (that is, lie to left of E_π in Figure 11.2) and will depart even further from the biological ideal at E_{MSY}.

---

[6] In Figure 11.2, fixed costs are assumed to be zero, since there is no cost with no effort. The presence of fixed costs would be consistent with a nonzero vertical intercept for the cost curve at the level of fixed costs.

The static profit-maximizing solution depicted is that of a sole owner of the fishery, who restricts the access of others. But what happens to the exploitation of the fishery if there is open or unlimited access? With open access, profits signal entry, and harvesting will continue past E_π until profits are driven to zero at the point at which revenue equals costs. This occurs at an effort level of E_{Trag} in Figure 11.2, where the cost curve intersects the revenue curve, and is known as the "tragedy-of-the-commons" equilibrium. Sustainable harvests are now far below MSY, since effort is far above E_{MSY}. If, however, the cost curve is steeper than that shown in Figure 11.2, then the associated E_{Trag} could be equal to or even less than E_{MSY}. Even if $E_{Trag} = E_{MSY}$, which is highly unlikely, this solution is still not economically efficient, since marginal social benefit (in terms of the price of fish) is not equal to the associated marginal social harvest costs, which account for the costs that one's efforts impose on others. The true social optimum requires that the slope of the revenue curve equal the slope of the social cost curve, and occurs at a smaller effort level than E_{Trag}.

The extent of overexploitation hinges on the ratio of the price of fish to marginal harvesting costs. The greater this ratio, the larger the value of another unit harvested relative to the harvesting costs, which then encourages a greater effort level, owing to the larger profit potential. If, say, $c = 0$, so that the ratio is infinite, then efforts will not stop until the species is driven to extinction at the point where the revenue curve intersects the horizontal axis. Policies to restrict effort work only temporarily as profit rises and induces further industry expansion, leading to overcapacity and idle boats.

Although this analysis is useful, it does not present a dynamic representation; instead, it characterizes adjustments as taking place instantaneously. If, for example, overfishing causes low sustainable yields, then it will take time for the fish population to replenish itself. A static analysis is unable to account for this temporal growth or the *required time* for a harvesting embargo to allow fish stocks to replenish themselves. Additionally, current gains and losses are not properly being compared to future gains and losses in the static model. The fishery is an asset whose biomass can increase in value if allowed to grow. When valuing an asset, the interest rate becomes a crucial opportunity cost that is thus far absent from the analysis.

A Dynamic Model of the Fishery

In a dynamic bioeconomic model, an essential biological constraint is the growth rate of the biomass, which depends on the species' growth rate, the environmental carrying capacity, and the catch rate. Each species will have its own innate growth rate based on genetic and environmental considerations; large species, such as whales, will naturally display slower growth rates. Growth is positive (negative) provided that the biomass is less (greater) than some limit determined by the ecosystem based on nutrients, species diversity, and other considerations. This limit is the *environmental carrying capacity*. The catch rate must be subtracted from the species growth rate when calculating the species' *net growth*. Finally, the *natural growth* rate $G(X)$ or the *productivity of the fish population* equals the resource growth prior to the catch rate being deducted.[7]

A dynamic model degenerates to the earlier static model *in a steady-state equilibrium where the growth rate of the key variables*, such as the stock of fish, *is zero*. At such an equilibrium, all variables maintain their values from one period to the next. The problem is to choose an effort level that maximizes the present value of a profit stream over time, which is constrained by the growth of the biomass. Thus, the size of the profit stream hinges on changes in the biomass, as effort affects both biological and economic factors. If, initially, marginal costs are assumed to be zero, then the maximum profit stream occurs when the choice of effort *equates the marginal productivity of the fish species*, or the change in its natural growth rate as the biomass is exploited, *to the interest rate*. Quite simply, the marginal productivity of the fish species indicates how the current stock of fish is adding to its numbers given current catch rates. This result should be familiar based on earlier remarks in Chapter 10 concerning the optimal exploitation of a renewable resource. In effect, the resource is exploited until the gain in its biological productivity matches the opportunity cost of leaving the resource to replenish itself. This opportunity cost equals the return from the earnings from harvesting the species now and using the proceeds to invest. This return is the interest rate. When the biomass exceeds the level at which its marginal productivity equals the interest rate, so that the species is replenishing itself relatively slowly compared to the interest rate, then effort should be at its maximum. Denote the biomass where its marginal productivity equals the interest rate i as X^*. If, however, the current biomass is less than X^*, then nothing should be harvested, and the species is left to replenish itself. This result is a "bang-bang" solution, where effort is either at capacity or nil – there is no optimal level in between.[8] This is analogous to how addicts behave:

---

[7] A standard natural growth equation is $G(X_t) = rX_t(1 - X_t/K)$, where X_t is the biomass at time t, r is the intrinsic rate of growth, and K is the carrying capacity. The overall growth rate is then $G(X_t) - C_t$, where C_t is the catch rate. The growth rate used here is a "logistic population" growth equation.

[8] See Clark (1985, pp. 19–22). When the objective is linear, as it is here, a bang-bang solution results.

if supplied with the drug, they use it until they can no longer function. If the drug is not available, they do without.

The solution of equating the marginal productivity of an asset to its interest rate is so prevalent in the study of asset management that it is known as the *golden rule of accumulation*. If the interest rate is zero, then the marginal productivity of the fish biomass must be driven to zero, which occurs at X_{MSY}, where the biomass is maximized. With a zero interest rate, the future is valued as much as the present and there is no incentive to run down the resource stock to augment consumption today at the expense of consumption tomorrow. When the interest rate is positive, X^* is now less than the maximum sustainable biomass, since the proceeds from the harvested species earn a positive rate of return. An essential insight from such a dynamic bioeconomic study is that *the higher the interest rate, the smaller the conservation in terms of the equilibrium biomass*. The higher the interest rate, the less the future is valued, and the more the species will be exploited today. The species is actually driven to extinction whenever the interest rate is always larger than the marginal productivity of the species. For pelagic whales, the marginal productivity is sufficiently small owing to these species' slow growth rate that even reasonable interest rates can spell disaster. This is also true for other large mammals, Hawaiian koa trees, desert savannahs, and some species of large fish. This result is consistent with the severe depletion of blue whales and koa trees. The extinction concern is particularly problematic when common ownership raises exploitation beyond profit-maximizing levels.

Thus far, the marginal costs of harvesting have been assumed to be zero. When a positive marginal cost is allowed, harvest rates are curtailed and extinction is less of a concern. With positive marginal costs, the golden rule now equates the *difference* between the species' marginal productivity and its marginal stock influence *to the interest rate*. The marginal stock influence arises because the marginal costs of harvesting increase as the fish stock is depleted or thins. With fewer fish, it takes more effort to land another fish. The net proceeds from harvesting the stock fall as the stock thins and marginal harvesting costs rise, and these smaller net proceeds support conservation. As the marginal stock influence grows in importance, there is an incentive to let the species replenish itself. The presence of these harvesting costs gives an optimal biomass for a positive interest rate somewhere between the tragedy-of-the-commons biomass and the profit-maximizing level of the static model. In effect, the thinning costs represent a crowding externality that limits exploitation.

Economic dynamics, as characterized by bioeconomic analysis, presents some novel features. First, the static analysis can be recaptured at the so-called steady-state equilibrium, where all variables display a zero growth rate, so that their stocks remain constant from one period to the next. Second, relevant marginal comparisons involve growth rates; thus, the interest rate, which is itself a growth rate, is ever-present. Because benefits and costs can occur at different points in time, there is a need to put net earnings into present value terms, and this brings in the interest rate. Third, stocks cannot change instantaneously, so time is a factor when decisions are made. Fourth, decisions are expressed in terms of optimal time paths for decision variables. These time paths can imply one course of action for one scenario and another course of action for an alternative scenario, thus leading time paths to involve rather abrupt changes, as the bang-bang solution for the fishery illustrates. Fifth, for sufficiently long time horizons, the solutions to dynamic problems are intergenerational in character, and this raises a host of issues discussed in the previous chapter, such as the appropriate discount or interest rate. Bioeconomic outcomes that result in severely depleted stocks or even extinction have significant intergenerational consequences.

A dynamic bioeconomic analysis indicates not only when an action should be taken, but also how it should be adjusted over time. The analysis determines whether a decision needs to be implemented immediately or delayed. I particularly enjoy the way that such investigations weave together biological relationships and economic decisions.

Management Decisions

Whenever I think about fisheries and their problems, I recall the scene in the movie *Forrest Gump* where Forrest has purchased a shrimp boat. He lands little more than old boots and discarded appliances at first, until a vicious storm destroys all of the boats except his. From that point on, his boat's hold teems with shrimp on every outing. Obviously, the storm had temporarily rectified the commons problem, thereby allowing the shrimp stock to replenish itself. With such abundance, the sole exploiter could harvest as much as he wished.

Fishery management does not need an act of God, but it does require some careful thought that is too often lacking. For example, management policies that limit the fishing period encourage greater exploitation during such periods, so that harvesters invest in additional boats and high-technology equipment (for example, sonar, radar, and satellite reconnaissance) to lay waste to stocks in a shorter time.[9] The result is an industry with overcapacity, which introduces an additional economic inefficiency and keeps the species in peril. Management policies that

---

[9] The application of modern technology and other threats to the world's fisheries are presented by Safina (1995).

raise costs by introducing impediments to fishing technologies and practices, such as the use of inefficient nets, introduce further allocative inefficiencies without addressing the underlying property rights problem associated with open access to the fishery.

What needs correcting is the perverse incentives of the commons problems, where the firms' dominant strategy in the short run is to deplete rather than to conserve. This follows because the associated game is a Prisoner's Dilemma, where it is always in one's immediate interest to harvest as much as possible no matter what the other exploiters decide to do. Management decisions must thus introduce intertemporal tit-for-tat strategies that punish those who do not take steps to implement their assigned restraint so as to achieve an efficient time trajectory for effort.

ENVIRONMENTAL AND ECOLOGICAL ECONOMICS

Environmental economics often concerns the control of a pollutant that is itself driven or transported by atmospheric, hydrological, or other forces. When these noneconomic drivers are explicitly modeled into the economic representation, an integrated analysis, not unlike a bioeconomic model, results and can yield insights unavailable when either system is analyzed in isolation.

Consider the case of acid rain produced by sulfur emissions from fossil-fueled electric power plants, vehicles, and industries. The emitted sulfur combines in the troposphere with water vapor and ozone, and forms sulfuric acid. This acid can later fall with the rain and degrade lakes, rivers, coastal waters, forests, and man-made structures. Sulfur emissions pose a transnational pollution concern, because once released into the atmosphere those pollutants can remain aloft for days and travel from their emission source to be deposited on the territory of a downwind country. The Cooperative Programme for Monitoring and Evaluation of the Long-Range Transmission of Air Pollutants in Europe (EMEP) has been collecting annual data on sulfur emissions sources and their place of deposit since 1979.[10] From EMEP data, spatial transport matrices can be constructed that indicate the amount of sulfur that each country within a region receives from each emitting country. The columns of the transport matrix correspond to the emitters, while the rows indicate the recipients. By dividing each entry by the emitter's total sulfur emissions and then multiplying by the fraction of the country's emissions that remains in the study area, a researcher generates a

---

[10] Dispersion maps can be constructed from the data provided in Sandnes (1993). For a description of the transport matrix, see Eliassen and Saltbones (1983), Murdoch, Sandler, and Sargent (1997), and Sandler (1997).

transport matrix in which each entry denotes the fraction of a country's emission deposited on another country.

This spatial transport matrix can then be incorporated into the economic model, so that each country's pollution level can be related to its own and imported emissions. Once the dispersion of pollutants is part of the analysis, participation in acid rain treaties can be related to a country's self-pollution, its imported pollution, and to economic factors such as abatement costs and national income. Essentially, the spatial transport matrix captures the "spatial publicness" of emissions or abatement efforts and, in so doing, makes for a more precise model. Spatial statistics can later be applied to estimate a demand for emission reduction, where strategic interactions account for spatial considerations. That is, a country's ability and desire to free ride hinges on its location vis-à-vis pollution sources and deposition. An upwind polluter, such as the United Kingdom, which is primarily a sulfur emission exporter to downwind Europe, gains little from the Helsinki Protocol on reducing sulfur emissions and has resisted ratifying it. Large importers of sulfur emissions have signed quickly and participated vigorously. This analysis shows that atmospheric and economic relationships can be combined to create a system of equations that provide a more accurate representation.

Global position can play a role in modeling actions to curb chlorofluorocarbons (CFCs) emission, because the ozone hole in springtime is largest at the higher latitudes in both the Southern and Northern Hemispheres. This suggests that countries at higher latitudes will do more than those at lower latitudes to limit CFCs or to draft treaties to address the problem. In the case of global warming, identifying disparities in its influence across locations is only an educated guess at this juncture. A northern country may potentially gain from global warming if it results in a longer growing season and increased rainfall. Until these locational winners and losers are identified, some nations will be reluctant to commit to greenhouse gas reductions that might limit a process beneficial to them. To predict nations' strategic responses to such reductions, a modeler would need to know the locational consequences of global warming.

Water pollution problems involve dispersion by gravity (in field runoffs), river transport, ocean currents, or reservoir mixing. As in the case of air pollution, a transport matrix can be used to incorporate spatial considerations in the representation of public good spillovers. Strategic responses in terms of emissions and/or cleanup can be made dependent on spatial dispersion. In a dynamic context, feedbacks between economic choices and the spatial distribution of pollutants can also be taken into account.

An exciting area of research, *ecological economics* includes the workings of relevant ecosystems in economic models of pollution generation and abatement.[11] Bioeconomics is in many ways the forerunner of the ecological economics approach, where equations for economic decisions account for their effects on ecosystems and vice versa. Some ecological economists think that they have a mandate to advocate environmentally friendly solutions, but that is not how I interpret this new and important interdisciplinary approach to environmental economics. From my perspective, ecological economists merely try, whenever possible, to recognize and analyze the interactions and "feedback" between the economy and the relevant ecological systems influenced by economic decisions. For some problems, a scientific background or a good understanding of the functioning of ecological systems is required. The inclusion of ecological systems often involves dynamic analysis in which ecosystems may recover gradually from harmful effects owing to regenerative abilities. Interdependencies among two or more ecosystems may mean that multiple ecological equations must be embedded in the economic model.

OTHER MULTIDISCIPLINARY POSSIBILITIES

Ecological economics is representative of a host of economic analyses that can no longer afford to exclude essential noneconomic factors as an integral part of the analysis. For example, development economists have learned after many fruitless approaches that cultural and sociological aspects must be incorporated into the design of a development strategy. Western-oriented blueprints for development may be doomed to failure, as the World Bank has recently discovered when evaluating the effectiveness of aid.[12] For example, development programs based on the donors' view of what is important lead to a "problem of ownership," where the recipient country has no interest in carrying on the program once the funding dries up. As van de Walle and Johnston (1996, p. 54) write, "Recipient government can be said to 'own' an aid activity when they believe that it empowers them and serves their interests." In other instances, the program is unsuccessful because the requisite supporting technologies or cultural norms may be nonexistent. Consider the case where a funded program depends on a distribution system for the intended final product that is alien to the recipient nation. Another mismatch occurs if the program's human capital requirements, in terms of entrepreneurial skills or technological expertise, are not available in the

---

[11] Ecological economics is described in Costanza, Perrings, and Cleveland (1997) and in van den Bergh and van der Straaten (1997).

[12] See, especially, World Bank (1998). Other relevant literature includes Kanbur, Sandler and Morrison (1999) and van de Walle and Johnston (1996).

recipient country. The effectiveness of aid may also be limited by cultural differences, such as financial markets in the recipient country that function adequately but are based on different norms of behavior than those of the donor country.

Economics and Psychology

Economists have traditionally assumed that tastes are given and therefore beyond economic analysis, leaving the study of taste formation to psychologists. Surely, past consumption behavior and experiences can have an influence on future tastes. If this were not the case, then addiction and habit formation, which are common behavioral patterns, would never occur. Moreover, people could never acquire a taste for beer or coffee. Our taste in music or the visual arts changes as we come to experience and appreciate new kinds of music or new artists. By accounting for the transformation that past consumption has on taste formation, an economist is said to *endogenize* tastes or to bring taste explicitly into the economic analysis as a variable.[13] The endogenizing of tastes is long overdue in economics and is no less important than accounting for institutions. Modeling the transformation of tastes can be aided by insights from psychology, so that psychological relationships can constrain the change in taste parameters over time.

Learning is another area where economics is now allowing for the transformation of tastes. Typically, economists have relied on Bayesian learning, where prior probabilities of possible events are updated in ensuing periods based on things learned from past observations.[14] For instance, a government's view of whether it is being targeted by a strong or a weak terrorist group can be revised based on the number and nature of earlier events.[15] Once the government determines that it confronts a strong group that can impose costs greater than those associated with capitulation to the terrorists' demands, it is in the government's interest to capitulate. Thus, it is important that the government try to ascertain the terrorist group's true capabilities. Although economics has relied on Bayesian learning models, alternative learning paradigms would be welcome.

In recent years, evolutionary game theory has provided novel learning mechanisms based on the most successful behavior either being imitated or being replicated more often in subsequent generations (periods). The fittest individuals, which are those with the largest payoffs,

---

[13] Gary Becker examines the endogeneity of taste as well as habit formation (Becker 1996; Becker and Mulligan 1997).

[14] Bayesian learning is discussed by Binmore (1992, pp. 462–7).

[15] This example is taken from Lapan and Sandler (1993).

are able to propagate more rapidly, so that successful behaviors are acquired (learned) by a growing proportion of the population. Advances in the study of psychology can also be applied to evolutionary game theory to make more precise the manner in which successful behavior is emulated. To date, the persistence of memory is not part of the process, but it should be. With memory considerations, some percentage of descendants may not display the successful behaviors, and this will slow the evolutionary process and learning dynamics, thus resulting in alternative time paths and population equilibria. From my perspective, evolutionary economics rests on a very mechanical transfer function, devoid of conscious thought, and this is worrisome for a social scientist who intends to explain behavior rather than merely to record it.

Sociology and Economics

Another fruitful marriage involves applying sociological relationships to economic models. Conventions and norms of behavior provide agents with common expectations that limit uncertainty and foster regularity in behavior.[16] The study of the formation and operation of conventions and norms is an aspect of sociology that is relevant to many economic situations, especially those involving collective action. Surely, the forces that drive societies to develop those expectations and rules of behavior that serve to minimize transaction costs have a crucial role to play in economic interactions with respect to a host of challenges, including those concerning transnational public goods (for example, fighting organized crime, limiting global warming, and curbing income disparity among countries).

The question of the enforcement of rules or the punishment of those who fail to abide by accepted norms has been afforded scant attention in economics. For example, the sociologist Heckathorn (1989) shows that free riding is more apt to characterize a society that is enforcing a collective action agreement than a society that is reaching a collective action agreement. In fact, group behavior is the subject of both economics and sociology; our understanding of it can be improved by drawing on and combining techniques from both disciplines into an integrated model.

Agents abide by conventions because it is in their interest to do so; thus, conventions avoid accidents at sea and on the highways by directing the passage of oncoming traffic. Conventions are self-enforcing and thus correspond to specific game forms where proper strategic combinations must be played.[17] The manner in which such conventions are

---

[16] Russell Hardin (1982) presents important work on the role of "contract by convention" when addressing collective action problems.

[17] Such games are called coordination games (Sandler and Sargent 1995).

agreed upon by groups of individuals can enlighten social scientists on how conventions can be instituted among nations confronting common contingencies. Progress can sometimes be achieved by identifying the ingredients that induce groups of individuals to form a convention but that are absent from negotiations carried on by a collective of nations. Once the missing catalyst is isolated, the requisite precondition can then be introduced into the transnational situation.

OUTER SPACE, THE NEW MARKET FRONTIER

With the 1957 launch of Sputnik, outer space became an available resource to be exploited. The April 1981 mission of the US space shuttle furthered the accessibility of outer space as a resource, since satellites could now be retrieved and repaired, and human habitats could be more easily constructed in low-earth orbit. To explore the economics of outer space as a natural resource, an economist must combine concepts from multiple fields of economics with an understanding of scientific principles, so that interdisciplinary approaches are required. For example, a working knowledge is needed of the electromagnetic spectrum, consisting of the entire range of wavelengths or frequencies propagated by electric and magnetic fields. This spectrum includes gamma rays, visible light, ultraviolet radiation, infrared radiation, and radio waves. The physics of space travel and satellite orbits also come into play, as do other scientific principles governing the Earth and its atmosphere.

When one thinks about outer space, the notion of infinity and lack of scarcity comes to mind, but nothing could be further from the truth in an economic sense. Consider the geostationary orbital band, where a satellite remains fixed with respect to a point on the Earth's surface, and only a single Earth-station receiver is needed to communicate with each satellite.[18] Without station-keeping devices that limit a satellite's drift (about 100 miles without such devices), approximately 1,600 evenly spaced satellites can safely populate the geostationary orbital band. As this limit is exceeded, collisions are a possibility. Since most transoceanic communications occur between North America and Europe, the most desirable orbital slots are the 375 positions over the Atlantic, which will soon be occupied. These "parking spaces" are scarce and valuable commodities. While outer space is infinite, plum satellite positions with economic value are not. When Bill Schulze and I made this point in a 1985 article in *Economic Affairs*, we were ridiculed in a political cartoon in the *London Standard*, which showed a real estate agent in a bowler hat and a space helmet. Tethered to a spacecraft, the agent is placing a "For

---

[18] Further details of the economics of outer space are provided in Sandler and Schulze (1981, 1985).

Sale" sign on a barren asteroid. Of course, if this asteroid were close to Earth and contained scarce resources, it too would have value.

Additional geostationary positions could be engineered if expensive station-keeping devices and their energy sources could be placed aboard future generations of satellites. Satellites without such devices in crowded areas of the orbital band would eventually have to be cleared or destroyed. Currently, the expense does not warrant hardware or clearances, but in time it will become economical to fit in more satellites.

The scarcity of the orbit-spectrum resource is even more apparent when the externality of signal interference along the electromagnetic spectrum is considered.[19] Such interference occurs when satellites using the same or nearby frequency bandwidths for transmissions are too close together, so that undecipherable signals or noise results. If insufficient bandwidth in the high frequency gigahertz band is allocated, as has been the case in the past, then an even smaller number of satellites can populate geostationary space to advantage.[20] Clearly, both orbital slots and spectrum bandwidths are scarce resources that must be allocated efficiently. An obvious solution to this allocative problem would be to assign property rights to these orbit-spectrum resources and to allow the respective owners to trade them with others who possess a higher-valued use for the resource. Current occupants of orbits could be assigned a squatter's right of ownership, not unlike the manner in which property rights were assigned in the American West. Although alternative assignments would have different distributional implications, whatever assignment is chosen would foster allocative efficiency as the resource gravitates through trades to its best employment. The production complementarity of the orbit position and bandwidth dictates that their property rights be assigned as a package rather than separately. That is, these two goods are consumed together and should be traded as a bundle. Externalities can be controlled and markets made complete if the assignment of these two resources limits satellite collisions and interference. Thus, the application of advanced technologies and physics principles can foster the provision of well-functioning markets.

The exploitation of extraterrestrial resources will continue to expand as space vehicles, satellites, and space colonies are perfected. For example, remote sensing by satellites has given us better maps, improved weather forecasts, enhanced monitoring of the planet's well-being, more efficient military surveillance, and novel prospecting techniques. Outer space contains much-needed resources for an increasingly stressed

---

[19] On the economics of the orbit-spectrum resource, see Wihlborg and Wijkman (1981).
[20] High-frequency gigahertz waves are better able to penetrate clouds to communicate with Earth-based receivers and transmitters.

planet. This exploitation and exploration will be associated with both positive (for example, knowledge gained from space probes) and negative (for example, satellites that crash back to Earth) externalities, and, as a result, market failures and their correction will remain relevant. Manufacturing under zero gravity will provide new products, but, because of the large fixed costs of getting started, may result in the monopolies of the future. Economics has much to say about this new market frontier.

INTERDISCIPLINARY ECONOMICS AND THE TWENTY-FIRST CENTURY

I have only just scratched the surface regarding economic fields that require an interdisciplinary approach. For instance, the field of law and economics, where such concepts as the assumption of risk, liability assignments, and compensatory payments are combined with economic principles, has not even been mentioned. Genetic engineering and advances in medicine raise a host of economic questions, ranging from the issue of property rights to the control of externalities and market failures. I view these interdisciplinary approaches as growing in applicability in today's complex world. Such approaches in economics are destined to uncover novel solutions to issues in emerging technologies such as the internet. One example is the determination of the appropriate user fees for the internet, while another involves responding to the monopolies that will surely arise. With novel applications of economics will come the need for testing. As argued earlier, these tests will, in some instances, involve new econometric procedures capable of accounting for noneconomic factors, such as spatial relationships. Although combining economics with principles from other disciplines is not simple, the rigors of economics have given its researchers the requisite reasoning skills to master the principles of other fields. Economists also possess the technical training to communicate with practitioners in a wide range of scientific disciplines that rely on similar mathematical, statistical, and reasoning skills. If my prediction is accurate, there is a justification for keeping an economist's education broad, with a good grounding in mathematics, philosophy, statistics, and the social sciences.

12 Crystal Ball Economics: Rational Expectations

When I think about the notion of rational expectations, I am reminded of a character in a Kurt Vonnegut, Jr., novel who, after becoming "unstuck in time," is condemned to live and relive his life in random order until his death.[1] In so doing, he is able to know the past and the future, though not perfectly. His omniscience is incomplete because some key factors are not revealed to this hapless character, whose futile efforts are unable to avert a horrible destiny. Ironically, his actions to escape his fate are the very trigger needed to bring it about. Thus, the long-run future is completely determined, even though unanticipated surprises may occur at any instant. With a rational expectations framework, the agents' forecasts of prices and other essential economic variables are correct in the long run, though there are unanticipated short-run surprises along the way.

Rational expectations has come to mean diverse things to different economists. To its critics, the rational expectations hypothesis casts economic agents as being perfectly informed of the likelihood of future events and, thus, capable of maximizing their well-being in the presence of random events – known as shocks. Agents are rational in the sense that they know the underlying model of the economy, which is no easy feat. According to Kenneth Arrow (1978, p. 160), "in the rational expectations hypothesis, economic agents are required to be superior statisticians, capable of analyzing the future general equilibria of the economy." The originators and the defenders of rational expectations take issue with Arrow's characterization and emphasize that information is scarce and imperfect, so that the hypothesis merely represents the agent as exploiting available information in a optimizing fashion.[2] That is, an

---

[1] This is the premise of Kurt Vonnegut's *Slaughterhouse-Five*, whose hero, Billy Pilgrim, becomes unstuck in time.

[2] See, for example, Kantor (1979) and Maddock and Carter (1982).

agent acquires an optimum amount of information in the face of constraints; the proper trade-offs between costs and benefits of acquiring information are made on the margin. In some instances, an individual may know the *distribution* of a variable – that is, its alternative values and the probabilities attached to each of these values.

The application of a rational expectations framework is particularly germane to those scenarios where market behavior is influenced by agents' expectations and their actions based on these expectations. With rational expectations, economic agents can improve their well-being if they successfully anticipate the effects of policy actions and take steps immediately to respond appropriately. Considered in this way, the notion of rational expectations is akin to the concept of an efficient capital market, where information is efficiently processed so that observed security prices represent a correct accounting of all pertinent and available information regarding the security's anticipated performance. Thus, when a new drug is finally approved, the drug company's stock price hardly budges, because informed investors have long before bid up the stock's price as the drug was going through its clinical trial and approval process. As a small investor, I have learned that when I hear "inside information," the market had long before incorporated its impact on the stock's price, so that little additional appreciation should be expected. Stock prices on US exchanges rise and fall on anticipated Federal Reserve (the Fed) interest rate changes. On the day of the actual change, little happens to the stock prices if the Fed acts as projected. If, however, unanticipated events occur, then stock prices will respond.

The rational expectations hypothesis depicts economic agents as acquiring and processing information in order to position themselves opportunistically, given their expectations. If, for example, changes in tax loopholes are anticipated, people will alter their asset portfolios prior to such changes so that, once they are instituted, agents are poised to profit from the new rules. With rational expectations, the relative knowledge among the agents represents an essential determinant of income distribution, thus highlighting the message of Chapter 7 that knowledge is power.

A rational expectations approach allegedly augments a general-equilibrium representation of the economy to include two factors not fully integrated into Keynesian economics: dynamics and uncertainty. In a Keynesian framework, uncertainty and expectations are clearly mentioned, but their *explicit role in the model* is never adequately displayed. Dynamics are appended in an ad hoc fashion to a static model by Keynes. The rational expectations framework has been characterized as achieving a methodological breakthrough by formulating a dynamic, stochastic general-equilibrium representation of the economy.[3] Although this hypothesis is most associated with macroeconomics, it is also applicable to microeconomic problems where agents must interact, process information, and act on their expectations. Strategic interactions and their game-theoretic implications are relevant to models based on rational expectations. In its macroeconomic application, the theory of rational expectations has much to say about policy and its effectiveness. These policy implications can be, at times, rather pessimistic.

RATIONAL EXPECTATIONS: ITS ORIGINS

John F. Muth (1960, 1961) is credited with first formulating the notion of rational expectations when he described firms' expectations as agreeing with theoretical predictions in a world of uncertainty. That is, firms process information sufficiently well that they can identify not only the possible outcomes confronting their alternative actions but also the likelihood of these outcomes. Muth envisioned that these firms' information processing capabilities and subsequent actions match the best theoretic representation of the uncertain choices confronting them. It is important to emphasize that uncertainty applies to the final outcome *but not to a knowledge of the probabilities* attached to these outcomes. Decision makers are really operating in an environment with risk but not uncertainty; the latter term is reserved in traditional economic parlance for those situations when even the odds attached to possible outcomes cannot be estimated. These risks are revealed as a result of conscious efforts by agents to ascertain knowledge about these probabilities. Muth's faith in agents' abilities to achieve theoretic standards has motivated critics to brand agents as superior statisticians. In characterizing Muth's analysis, Brian Kantor (1979, p. 1424) states that: "Muth seems to be saying no more and no less than that the observed empirical regularities that serve as the basis for, or the confirmation of, economic theory also form the basis of economic action."

While this depiction does not say that agents are omniscient, it does imply that they know quite a lot and, clearly, more than a bounded rationality viewpoint would espouse. Based on rational expectations, the subjective anticipated value of a random variable[4] is equal to its optimally chosen average outcome, conditioned on the available information. As such, only unanticipated events or shocks will cause the actual value of the variable to deviate from its average value or stated course. A

---

[3] Stochastic refers to the inherent uncertainty where alternative outcomes occur with different probabilities. Chari (1998, p. 172) characterizes the main methodological contribution of rational expectations theory in these terms. Also see Lucas (1972, 1996).

[4] A random variable can assume alternative values with certain possibilities.

recurrent theme of rational expectations concerns the alternative impacts and responses attributed to anticipated versus unanticipated changes.

Robert E. Lucas (1972, 1973) applied rational expectations in two seminal contributions that have altered the way that policy effectiveness is viewed. His clever and celebrated analysis earned him the 1995 Nobel Prize in economics. Another goal of Lucas's analysis was to lay a microeconomic foundation for macroeconomics, so that individual behavior formed the basis of macroeconomic theorizing and predictions. In the 1960s, there was dissatisfaction among economists with this lack of an apparent microeconomic foundation in either the classical or the Keynesian representation of macroeconomics. Aggregate demand and supply relationships were abstractions that seemed to come from nowhere, and their optimizing underpinnings were not at all apparent. A second spur to the origin of rational expectations was the absence of dynamics in macroeconomics. Classical economics was a timeless, mechanical representation of a general equilibrium in a set of aggregate markets. Keynesian economics also consisted of a static equilibrium representation, with alternative speeds of adjustment and rigid variables mentioned at judicious places. No internally consistent Keynesian dynamic model existed. A third motivation for the rational expectations hypothesis concerned the deterministic representation of earlier macroeconomic models – expectations and uncertainty had little role to play.

RATIONAL EXPECTATIONS AND ECONOMIC POLICY

When I was a graduate student in the late 1960s and early 1970s, the Phillips (1958) curve was a guiding principle of the perceived workings of some policies to stabilize the economy. The Phillips curve indicates a downward sloping statistical relationship between a country's unemployment rate (on the horizontal axis) and its growth in wage rates (on the vertical axis) or its rate of inflation. Based on this curve, a decrease in the unemployment rate comes at the expense of some inflation. The Phillips curve is asymmetric, with virtually no fall in unemployment being associated with sizable increases in wage rates and prices once some "natural rate of unemployment" is reached, while wage deflation may result in large additional unemployment past some threshold of deflation. This natural rate varies among countries and is tied to *structural* features in the labor market – such factors as people requiring retraining, practices inhibiting hiring (for example, large fringe benefit packages), and market frictions. If one ascribes to the Phillips curve, then monetary policy can reduce unemployment at a level greater than the natural level by allowing for more inflation, say, through increases in the money supply.

Milton Friedman (1968) and Edmund Phelps (1968) took issue with this policy recommendation by arguing that continued inflation would not affect the economy because in the long run agents are concerned only about real quantities (that is, nominal or money expenditures divided by the price level). In simple words, "real" quantities imply an absence of money illusion, so that only inflation-adjusted values matter to the agents. In the long run, rises in nominal expenditures would be in proportion to the rise in prices, so that real output would remain unchanged. The Friedman–Phelps view was that the long-run Phillips curve was vertical – the monetary authorities' efforts to raise or lower prices or wages through changes in the money supply would have no influence on the long-run unemployment level, which would remain at a country's natural level. This emphasis on real effects is reminiscent of the *quantity theory of money*, which indicates that proportional changes in the money supply result in equal proportional changes in prices, leaving real magnitudes unaffected. In the long run, a doubling of the money supply doubles prices and, thus, expenditures in money terms, but will not influence real output. With no long-term change in real output, there can be no long-term influence on employment – there is no reason to hire more people when output does not change. The Friedman–Phelps analysis does not, however, explicitly incorporate dynamic or informational aspects, thus setting the stage for Lucas's innovative analysis.

The Lucas framework consists of an overlapping-generations model in which at every instant there exist both a (young) working generation and an (old) retired generation. Each generation of identical individuals lives for two periods: in the first, they produce goods for themselves and the retired generation; in the second, they live on the first-period earnings. These earnings come from the money that they have received from the older generation's purchases, who, in turn, pay with money they have accumulated from sales to the now-deceased parent generation. Members of the young generation must decide how much to consume and how much to sell based on their forecast of prices, which depends on the succeeding generation's accumulation of money and the actions of the monetary authority to increase the money stock through additions to the stock given to the older generation. In this stylized model, markets are assumed to be perfectly competitive in the sense that each youth views prices independent of his or her production and selling decisions. An equilibrium is achieved when expected prices and variables coincide with their actual values.

Based on this equilibrium notion, Lucas establishes that certain anticipated changes in the money stock have no *real* influence, leading instead to an equal proportional change in prices or reduction in the value of money, so that the same output is produced and changes hands between overlapping generations.[5] If the older generation is given an injection of money from the monetary authority *in the same proportion as they carried over from their youth*, then there is no influence on their money-holding decision. This follows because each generation foresees the rise in prices (fall in the value of money) that the monetary authority's decision creates. The rate of return to holding money remains unchanged, because the adverse influence on earnings coming from the inflation is just offset by the equal proportional gain coming from the monetary transfer. With no change in savings' rate of return, there is no reason to adjust behavior, and the anticipated change in monetary policy results in the neutrality of money. Lucas thus provides a microeconomic foundation for the quantity theory of money based on the optimizing decisions of overlapping generations.

Lucas goes on to show that *unanticipated* policy changes by the monetary authorities can, however, have an influence on output and employment in the short run. However, as the new policy persists, economic agents learn its influence on expected prices and, in so doing, nullify any influence that the policy can have on long-run output and employment. In a rational expectations framework, deviations between actual output and its natural rate are proportional to differences between expected prices and actual prices. If agents' rational expectations have eliminated any differences between expected and actual prices through experience and subsequent forecasting, then there can be no deviation in output from its natural rate in the long run.[6] In the long run, systematic or anticipated policy has no influence on the key macroeconomic variables – output and employment – meaning that the long-run Phillips curve is vertical at the natural unemployment rate, and monetary injections are neutral. Thus, policy effects are traced to the random or unanticipated actions of the government that surprise the public and alter expectations. These changes are, however, transitory and disappear as the public acquires a new, informed set of expectations that can be used to correctly forecast future prices.

I certainly sympathize with any reader who finds rational expectations reasoning rather abstract. It is unquestionably an ingenious theoretic construct whose sophistication is difficult to teach to students – who, along with others, are supposed to display this behavior. A few illustrations are instructive to show how rational expectations in its ideal form can stand in the way of policy effectiveness. Suppose that a government intends to introduce an investment tax credit to stimulate investment. If,

---

[5] For details of the model, consult Lucas (1972, 1996) and Chari (1998).
[6] See Maddock and Carter (1982, pp. 43–8) and Lucas (1972, 1996).

however, the public incorporates this expectation into its actions, then it may hold off investing until the announced tax credit is instituted and, by so doing, curtail investment. This expectation-induced reaction creates an outcome that is precisely the opposite of the intention of the announced policy.

As an illustration of rational expectations reasoning applied to a non-macroeconomic setting, consider a policy that the Israeli and US governments have tried to institute with respect to hostage-taking terrorist events. If the government announces that it will never concede to terrorist demands when a hostage is abducted, and *if this pledge is believed* by potential hostage takers, then no hostages would be abducted in a rational expectations equilibrium, since there is no payoff from doing so.[7] If, however, the terrorists correctly believe that the government may make exceptions for some highly valued hostages (say, a CIA agent, an Israeli pilot, schoolchildren) and may concede to demands, then the terrorists will act on these expectations and apprehend such hostages so as to pressure the government to deviate from its stated policy. As a government reneges (for example, the Reagan administration's actions in response to the capture of William Buckley, a CIA agent, in Beirut), these past inconsistencies influence terrorists' expectations of the government's future actions. Thus, past events shape expectations. This example illustrates that the institution of a mechanism to enforce adherence to policy rules may be advantageous over discretion, where an agent may rethink his or her committed course of action at a future date. Rules can make someone stay the course, as in the case of a student who drinks to excess at a bar but has followed the university's rule of leaving his car keys in the dormitory. Limiting one's options may improve welfare.

As another non-macroeconomic rational expectations response to policy, consider the Soviet Union's construction of the doomsday machine in the movie *Dr. Strangelove*, directed by Stanley Kubrick. The machine was intended to be the ultimate deterrent, since if it detected a nuclear bomb exploding on Soviet territory it would automatically fire off, without any possible discretion, the entire Soviet nuclear arsenal, thereby causing Armageddon. If would-be aggressors knew of this device, then they would never attack and thereby set in motion their own annihilation. Thus, the rational expectations equilibrium results in no nuclear attack. In *Dr. Strangelove*, Armageddon nevertheless occurs, because the Soviets do not want to disturb the American

---

[7] Lapan and Sandler (1988) address these terrorism-thwarting policies. The text implicitly assumes that the terrorists get no other payoffs (for example, publicity or martyrdom) from taking hostages.

president with information about the doomsday machine over the weekend after its installation on a Friday – so much for politeness and best-laid plans!

These examples illustrate that behavior is influenced by the policy environment. *An essential message of rational expectations thinking is that the parameters and structure of models of behavior are not policy independent.* Agents' behavior and the models to describe their behavior must account for the influence that policies have on people's actions. This is a novel way of thinking, which, when introduced, was at odds with the standard view that policy effectiveness could be ascertained from behavioral models that ignored any anticipation of or response to the policy.

AN EVALUATION OF RATIONAL EXPECTATIONS THEORIZING: STRENGTHS AND WEAKNESSES

The analysis of rational expectations represents a novel and, at times, useful way of thinking for a variety applications. It is particularly helpful as a thought experiment that presents an idealized reaction by sophisticated, farsighted agents; however, its extreme demands on agents' rationality should not be forgotten when drawing policy conclusions. The notion that behavioral models must endogenize policy responses is a crucial insight. An understanding of rational expectations forces economists to rethink the nature of policy effectiveness. Additionally, Lucas's distinction between responding to anticipated and unanticipated policy changes is more enlightening than earlier distinctions between long-run and short-run responses, since the latter did not explain why there are such differences.

Rational expectations analysis provides a logically consistent theory along with testable hypotheses concerning how well-informed agents will act in alternative policy environments. In so doing, it presents a stochastic, general-equilibrium alternative to the deterministic framework of earlier macroeconomic models. It is noteworthy that a microeconomic foundation underlies the analysis, where agents optimally choose decision rules in light of uncertain outcomes. Consequently, an agent's information relative to that of other agents is an essential consideration. Rational expectations modeling draws on many of the theoretical breakthroughs of the last fifty years, including the role of information, general-equilibrium analysis, game-theoretic strategic responses, intergenerational economics, and the inclusion of new variables. Even the importance of institutions is germane, insofar as the different ways in which monetary and fiscal authorities announce and institute their policies can have vastly different impacts. Thus, policy formation and predictions are not independent of institutional arrangements, which becomes clear in the debate over rules versus discretion.

The works of Lucas and others represent elegant theoretical constructs with wide-ranging applications. It is the type of modeling that I admire and wish that I had had the insight to discover. Nevertheless, there are aspects of rational expectations modeling that are troubling and even annoying. The proponents of rational expectations characterize the model as dynamic and, at places, even mention the convergence of the equilibrium. Yet the hypothesis is silent about the actual speed of adjustment over time. This is troublesome, because a true dynamic theory must be concerned with an explicit derivation of the time path of adjustment. In his seminal paper on money neutrality, Lucas (1972) focuses on the existence, optimality, and form of the equilibrium. While random factors are clearly displayed in the model, the problem is presented as a *static, intertemporal-optimization* problem involving two overlapping generations. The so-called dynamics of rational expectations is appended ad hoc, without an explicit formulation; on this score, Lucas does not really accomplish the alleged improvement over the Keynesian discussion of dynamics. A rational expectations equilibrium is really a steady-state representation, in the spirit of Gordon's static model of the fishery discussed in Chapter 11. In the rational expectations model, there is *no equation of motion* constraining the system's movement of variables nor any of the other trappings associated with a true dynamic representation. It may make a great difference in the design of policy if the equilibrium is approached directly and quickly or through a series of oscillations requiring a lengthy convergence.

Although I am sympathetic to the rational expectations representation of agents as flawless calculating entities in a best-case thought experiment, I am less comfortable when this representation is intended to guide policy. If, however, some policy announcements are misinterpreted, then how will the economy be influenced? In game theory, Selten (1975) has introduced the possibility of errors in his trembling hand equilibrium concept, so that even the game theorists, who champion rational choice, permit the possibility of mistakes. As a modeler, I cannot claim that my own forecasts always coincide with theoretical predictions, whether or not I use simple rules of thumb.

As mentioned at the outset, agents are supposed to have mastered the underlying macroeconomic models, thus anticipating the actions of the policy makers. I can only surmise that students at the University of Chicago are a lot smarter than those whom I have taught, who have had difficulty understanding such models. But even if the public can master these models, are the policy makers, who are being second-guessed, sufficiently clever? What if these policy makers are driven by their own self-interest, as in a public choice model? When policy decisions are modeled in a game framework, there are numerous instances where the policy maker's best strategic choice, regardless of the choices of others, is irrational in the sense that it leads to a low-payoff outcome – recall the Prisoners' Dilemma representation of an arms race.[8] The alleged "inflation bias" of policy makers is another instance, where the dominant strategy of high spending leads to low payoffs as an economy inflates.[9] The underlying game-theoretic framework of rational expectations has been left vague, with catchall terms such as asymmetric information substituted for well-defined concepts of imperfect or incomplete information. The result is very unsatisfying – a sophisticated public whose theoretical skills outclass those of the policy makers whose "rational" behavior the public is supposed to predict.

The rational expectations model really only distinguishes individuals by their generations. Within each generation, optimization is with respect to a representative, presumably identical, individual. Thus, differences among individuals in their ability to acquire and process information are never addressed. Additionally, there is no cost to becoming informed, so that each individual possesses incentives to become fully informed. With costly information, the rational expectations equilibrium may then involve less-informed agents, and this has implications for the equilibrium.

In any social group, some individuals wield disproportionate influence over others as the collective's opinions converge to some average view of the future. If these opinion leaders are persistently wrong in their forecasts, then the equilibrium will depart from the theoretical ideal. Errors will then be systematic and correlated among agents. After fourteen years in an economics department where the majority of voting members were influenced or intimidated by an opinion leader who regularly misjudged the best course of action and misjudged the future, I am uneasy with theories that place too much faith in crystal-ball outcomes, particularly when complex ratiocination is required.

Another facet of the rational expectations framework that could profit from further development is the influence of learning. When a monetary shock occurs, individuals must judge whether the shock is a one-time change or a continual one. Clearly, an individual's perceptions of possible outcomes and their likelihoods must be updated with new

---

[8] I thank Dan Arce, who suggested this line of reasoning and criticism of the rational expectations hypothesis.

[9] Players are rational in the sense that they know the appropriate macroeconomic model, but they are not sufficiently rational in the sense that they adjust for the underlying game with the policy makers and the resulting low-level equilibrium.

information, and this process constitutes learning. The manner in which an individual accomplishes this task and how revised forecasts diffuse throughout the economy affect the equilibrium and the convergence. I appreciate the fact that such theoretical fine tuning is very difficult to accomplish in the complicated modeling environment of rational expectations.

There is also the matter of testing various aspects of the rational expectations hypothesis – for example, the prediction that only unanticipated changes in the money supply influence real output and employment, which requires distinguishing between unanticipated and anticipated changes. Anticipated monetary growth can be tested by first fitting a statistical model to forecast monetary growth, and attributing unanticipated changes either to shifts in the estimated relationship or to residual random error. The pitfall of this procedure is that individuals are indeed viewed as superior statisticians equipped with statistical skills in fitting such models. Some tests of the rational expectations approach are based on whether systematic components of a variable, say consumption, are fully explained by its lagged value (Hall 1978). The argument is then made that this lagged value encompasses any other *economic factors* that influence the consumption decision. If the variable is related only to its lagged value, then unanticipated influences can be attributed to the random residual. There is an extensive literature on testing rational expectations hypotheses, whose evaluation lies beyond the scope of this book.

FUTURE PROSPECTS OF RATIONAL EXPECTATIONS

In a recent article, William Baumol (2000) provides an assessment of the twentieth century's contributions to economics. He identifies three major areas of progress and upheaval: (1) the formalization of macroeconomic theory, (2) the creation of useful tools of empirical evaluation, and (3) improved understanding of macroeconomic and public finance policy (Baumol 2000, pp. 2–3). The development of the rational expectations hypothesis interfaces with all three of these upheavals in economic thought: stochastic elements are brought into the formal equilibrium representation of macroeconomics; tests of the hypothesis rely on new tools of empirical evaluation; and the study of rational expectations has much to say about policy effectiveness. There now exists a sizable community of macroeconomists who address issues related to rational expectations in their research. This community includes both theorists and empiricists. Given the large number of such researchers, the study of rational expectations is a sure bet to remain an active area for some time to come.

My earlier criticism of rational expectations' reliance on a static framework should not be misconstrued. A strength of the Lucas formulation is its relative simplicity, which would be lost if recast in a dynamic framework. My remarks about the lack of dynamics are motivated by the literature's misrepresentation of the model as dynamic. The insight that behavioral models are not invariant with respect to policy changes is simple and easily understood, which enhances the appeal of rational expectations. Its notion is rather subtle, and this explains why different economists have used rational expectations in different ways.

The rational expectations concept is applicable not only to macroeconomics, but also to other fields of economics reliant on policy prescriptions, including industrial organization, public finance, defense economics, environmental economics, and labor economics. It is applicable anywhere that the interplay between agents' behavior and policy is relevant. In the last thirty years, economists have paid more attention to policy failure, after an initial faith in economic policy following the Keynesian revolution. While public choice indicates that the incentives of the policy makers could lead to policy failures, the rational expectations approach emphasizes that policy-induced behavioral changes can impede policy effectiveness. Welfare economists put policy in a negative light by highlighting whether the existence of incurable distortions would eliminate the need to address correctable ones.[10] After so many years in the crosshairs of economists, policy may soon experience greater favor with the profession, since fashions in academic disciplines also seem to be cyclical. Whether or not this swing comes, rational expectations reasoning is apt to have a longer-term impact if its proponents highlight how policies can be redesigned to be more effective.

Despite its many strengths, I still worry whether the rational expectations hypothesis assumes too much sophistication on the part of a typical economic agent, who must distinguish monetary from real changes and short-run from long-run influences. This overly optimistic faith in the capabilities of economic agents may eventually cause economists to question the theory's foundation and to look elsewhere.

---

[10] Still another attack on policy effectiveness comes from the social choice theorists, who show how difficult it is to institute policies that really reflect society's viewpoint.

13   How Do We Get There from Here?
       Transition Economies and Policy Reforms

With the Velvet Revolution in Czechoslovakia, the world awoke in November 1989 to a monumental economic experiment – once never dreamed possible – involving the engineering of a transformation from a command economy to a market-based one. An entire economic system of coordination needed to be replaced by a vastly different system based on the pursuit of profits, price signals, and independent actions. A socialist economy is characterized by state ownership of enterprises, central control of production, and trade by state agreements, while a market economy is characterized by private ownership of enterprises, decentralized market coordination of production, and international trade by private agents. If Czechoslovakia had been the only economy confronting such a transition, the problem might have been less poignant, but other countries quickly rejected socialism, including East Germany, Romania, Yugoslavia, Poland, Hungary, Bulgaria, and the fifteen former Soviet republics. In 1996, there were twenty-nine transition countries attempting to transform their Soviet-based planned economic systems to a market economy. Still other communist regimes (for example, China, Cuba, and Vietnam) are currently experimenting with market reforms.

Peter Murrell (1996, p. 31) aptly describes the transition attempted from 1990 to 1996 as "the most dramatic episode of economic liberalization in economic history." The transition involved freely fluctuating prices, trade liberalization, enterprise reform (including privatization), the creation of a social safety net, and the construction of the legal and institutional framework of a market economy.[1] There was also a need for macroeconomic stabilization in terms of reduced inflation, greater employment, and smaller budget deficits.

The transition took everyone, even the experts, by surprise. When the upheaval occurred, there was no blueprint on how to transform an

[1] On the preconditions and required liberalizations, see Fischer, Sahay, and Végh (1996).

economy from a centrally planned to a market economy. Lessons learned from the original transformation from a market economy to a command economy after World War II provided no real insights. Consider the magnitude of the problem. A typical Soviet-type planned economy relied on administered prices for millions of goods and services, while the state controlled almost all retail sales and over 80% of agricultural output.[2] Not only were there no entrepreneurs, but institutions to support a market economy (for example, laws and courts for contract enforcement, banks for financial backing) were also absent. State-owned enterprises (SOEs) accounted for much of the employment and social security of the workers. Such enterprises were motivated to fulfill state plan requirements rather than to make profits. If the SOEs ran into financial difficulties, the state could be relied upon to bail them out, so that SOEs' budget constraints were "soft" in the sense that additional funds were always accessible. Consequently, there was little incentive to operate within the constraints or to be efficient. SOEs tended to be large enterprises with bloated labor forces. Communists were staunch believers in economies of scale that never ended, and thus built huge SOEs, leaving command economies in 1989 with a plethora of monopolized industries. Firms became so large that they surpassed the point of the lowest per-unit cost of production.

A search began for the best *pathway* for transition. Two alternative viewpoints existed: (1) a "big bang" where everything is done at once, and (2) a gradual approach where there is an optimal sequence for transition.[3] Under either view, institutions must be created and economic liberalization instituted. As a complement to market liberalization, there was also the need for democratic reforms that would return political and civil freedoms to a generation who knew little about such rights. Market signals and institutions had to be introduced to people who had never experienced the harsh competitive realities of a market-based economy, where those with the "wrong" skills or in unfortunate circumstances are apt to be destitute. Although communism often provided a low standard of living, it also came with lots of certainty, unlike a market economy where fortunes can be made or lost quickly. The switch of systems would be psychologically devastating to those who had known nothing else. A safety net was thus needed to care for those without the proper skills.

Transition presents a dynamic problem: how to proceed to dismantle an entire economic system and replace it with another. This era of tran-

---

[2] Ericson (1991) and Brada (1996) provide good descriptions of a Soviet-style planned economy.

[3] On alternative views for transition, see Ericson (1991), Fischer and Gelb (1991), Fischer, Sahay, and Végh (1996), Murrell (1996), and Wolf (1991).

sition has also heightened economists' interest in policy reforms, which not only involve the transition economies but also the less-developed countries (LDCs). For LDCs, the issue of foreign assistance has become important, along with the design of development plans. As in the transition economies, there is now an interest in the design of capital markets and other institutions that will support market economies in LDCs. Transition economies and LDCs share many similar concerns, including the search for a pathway to development. Policy reforms also touch the developed economies as they adapt to global markets and to a greater set of transnational externalities and public goods – a topic mentioned often. Additionally, policy reforms involve institutions and, for transition economies, the design of SOEs and their alternatives.

There are also political economy issues tied to transition and policy reform. Are democratic reforms complementary to economic reforms? Must democratic institutions precede economic reforms, or vice versa? On the positive side, democracy promotes peace and reduces the proclivity for war, and it also heightens interest in the environment.[4] On the negative side, it leads to more special interest groups that can reduce efficiency.

The primary purpose of this chapter is to examine the issues raised with respect to an optimal pathway for transition. A secondary purpose is to investigate questions raised by the study of policy reforms, including the design of SOEs. Finally, the implications of democratization are briefly addressed.

HOW DO WE GET THERE FROM HERE?

The events of the 1989–91 communist upheaval became a wake-up call to economists. Apparently, the experts who study comparative economic systems were so convinced that these systems would persist that the question of how to address such sweeping changes had never been investigated. This neglect is even more difficult to accept because there had been earlier attempts at limited market-oriented reforms. Hungary introduced more market-based prices while maintaining state ownership and central planning.[5] In effect, Hungary allowed its enterprises to trade among themselves for inputs and outputs, where some prices were flexible and others were partially or wholly fixed. Enterprise "profits" were intended to direct managerial discretion as well as resources toward earning higher returns. Still earlier reforms were instituted in Poland in

---

[4] The link between democracy and the demand for environmental quality is shown in Murdoch and Sandler (1997) for the ozone shield and in Murdoch, Sandler, and Sargent (1997) for sulfur emission reduction.

[5] Wolf (1991) provides an excellent overview and evaluation of these early reform efforts.

1956–57, and again in 1980–81, to boost an ailing economy. Unlike Hungary, Poland tried to reduce central planning, but did little to allow market-based prices. SOEs faced soft budget constraints in both countries and, thus, assumed little responsibility for bad decisions.

These and other piecemeal reforms accomplished few long-lasting effects in either of these economies. According to Wolf (1991, p. 55): "Virtually no industrial restructuring had taken place, market imbalances persisted (and in Poland had even been growing),·product quality still lagged considerably, and neither country had been very successful in selling on world markets." Markets had been given an ambiguous role in each of these reform packages – prices were not liberalized, and there was little privatization of SOEs.

Command economies are *systems* of interconnected parts that work to mutual advantage. Changing some features without adjusting others may merely exacerbate poor economic performance by transmitting distorted signals. It is this view that has led reformers and some economists to recommend a holistic big-bang approach, where the entire system is dismantled and replaced by a market economy, complete with private ownership and supporting institutions. Property rights are thus defined, protected, and traded through market-based prices. If only select market reforms are instituted, then market prices, which also depend on demand and supply considerations in *related markets*, will not truly measure opportunity costs. As such, these prices will *not* serve as proper signals for channelling resources to their most valued use. International transactions will be very limited whenever prices are out of line with prices in the rest of the world. When, however, prices are universally liberalized and private ownership instituted, agents either prosper or suffer based on their economic choices, and the tenets of a market economy have been instituted.

Such a wholesale change of systems, even if feasible, would be extremely disruptive and costly, as workers are thrown out of work and inefficient firms are closed en masse. Given that most firms in these ex-communist countries had antiquated capital and techniques, many would not be able to compete with a hard budget constraint, nor would they be attractive investment opportunities for foreign or domestic investors. Realistically, any transition is expected to be a trade-off between immediate and gradual change so as to limit adjustment costs and to augment feasibility, but at the expense of lost efficiency. Partial transitions are also associated with the presence of vested interests that try to impede market reforms so that the transition will be judged a failure.

Thus, the question remains whether there is an optimal time path for instituting market reform in a step-by-step fashion. A sequential approach raises the concern of time inconsistency, where a pathway of reform, once taken, is later altered when viewed from a different perspective as reforms are achieved. Clearly, there is no single optimal pathway of transactions that applies to all Soviet-type economies. Consider the experience of Hungary, which has been more successful than many of its European counterparts in making the transition to markets in the 1990s. This is probably due to its past experience with price reforms and its subsequent successful privatization of a sizable portion of its industrial sector. Additionally, Hungary managed to achieve macroeconomic stability by controlling inflation and limiting deficit spending fairly early on, so that its economic environment was a fertile area for further reforms. A transitional country with less experience with flexible prices might require a more gradual introduction of reforms if adjustment costs and outcomes are to be favorable. Surely, the pathway of transition must be tailored to each country depending on its initial conditions, its past experience with market reforms, and the receptiveness of its people. If the reforms are intended to benefit a wide class of citizens, then this will further their implementation.

From December 1992 to October 1997, the Czech Republic began a bold experiment to privatize almost a thousand SOEs through a sale; eligible citizens were given vouchers, at almost no cost, to bid on SOEs directly or on Investment Privatization Funds (IPFs). The IPFs, controlled by the banks, could then bid for shares on investors' behalf. A second wave of privatization followed from August 1992 to November 1994. Within three short years, between two-thirds and ninety percent of Czech assets had been transferred to private hands, where the profit motive provides discipline, by means of such voucher purchases and by outright sales to domestic and foreign buyers.[6] Transition schemes elsewhere used alternative means of privatization with varying degrees of success. Some countries (for example, Belarus and Tajikistan) transferred as little as 15% to the private sector, while other countries transferred over half (for example, Hungary, Poland, and Estonia).

Even though alternative sequences exist for transition, some rules of thumb have gained consensus based on recent experience with transitions. The first efforts at reform must be quite substantial and should involve four areas: macroeconomic stabilization, price liberalization, trade reforms, and institutional change.[7] Macroeconomic stabilization is needed early on to set the proper stage for reforms by limiting

---

[6] Further description on the Czech Republic's privatization scheme and those in other transition countries can be found in Brada (1996).

[7] On the optimal sequence of reforms, see Fischer, Sahay, and Végh (1996), Fischer and Gelb (1991), and Rapaczynski (1996).

hyperinflation and deficit spending. Actions are needed to address any "monetary overhang," which arises from cash reserves accumulated by citizens during years when there is little to buy. If unchecked, this monetary overhang can fuel inflation, an unpopular means for eliminating the pent-up demand engendered by the overhang. The rising price level decreases the purchasing power of accumulated cash reserves, thereby destroying wealth. Equally unpopular is a devaluation of the currency, which wipes out wealth by reducing the value of existing cash holdings. A more popular alternative is to permit the cash reserves to purchase shares in state enterprises as they are privatized, so that wealth is maintained.

Additionally, policies need to bring balance to trade deficits, where the value of imports exceeds the value of exports. Trade imbalances represent another form of indebtedness. Macroeconomic policies must also limit government deficit spending, which arises partly from the support of inefficient SOEs with their soft budget constraints. Interest rates also need to reflect the productivity of capital, so that capital markets function efficiently.

Another aspect of the initial push toward transition is price reform, which can be combined with trade liberalization. If trade barriers are eliminated so that world prices direct the exchange of goods and services, then domestic firms must compete against foreign producers. When prices are no longer administered by a governmental bureaucracy, prices for millions of goods must be set initially, and this presents a near-impossible task. The use of world prices is a clever way to provide a starting point for instituting market prices. Obviously, world prices for resources and output can be devastating for some SOEs, which have had no competition or discipline prior to transition owing to the absence of international trade and the presence of soft budget constraints. As inefficient enterprises are competed out of business, their resources will be rechannelled to better profit opportunities signaled by prices and profits. The use of world prices is especially appropriate for SOEs that are monopolies and will exploit their monopoly position domestically through high prices without competition from abroad.

Another consideration is the time that it takes for prices in a transition economy to converge to world market prices. A lengthy process is required before relative prices reflect relative scarcities and opportunity costs following major upheavals. Such was the experience during the Latin American transitions from hyperinflation in the 1980s and early 1990s. The realization that the convergence to market prices is not instantaneous illustrates my earlier-mentioned concern that the rational expectations hypothesis ignores adjustment time. During this transition period, people's predictions are going to be ill-directed by prices. Latin

American experience with the privatization of its SOEs can also provide guidance for Eastern Europe.

A final aspect of the first wave of required reforms concerns institutional restructuring that supports a market economy. These structural innovations are best established after stabilization policies and the introduction of flexible prices, which set the proper stage for the operation of private enterprises, motivated by high returns on their investments. Institutional reforms involve laws conducive to contracts and the exchange of property rights, regulatory institutions to oversee natural monopolies, and programs for the needy. Privatization of many SOEs is another of these structural changes. In short, the infrastructure for a modern mixed market economy needs to be put in place soon after stabilization is achieved.

Each of these structural changes has its obstacles. Vested interests – for example, plant managers – may resist efforts at restructuring if they see their power eroded. Similarly, large-scale efforts to privatize industries may be opposed by party elites, who also see their power and wealth diminished as a consequence. The institution of contract laws may not amount to much if courts are not able to enforce such laws and if agents do not understand the intent or the intricacies of these laws. It may take a generation to gain the requisite experience with such laws and institutions before they function as intended, but without them, foreign investment will not be attracted. An interchange at a conference that I attended in Prague in March 1991 prior to the implementation of the voucher program illustrates another obstacle to such structural reforms. In attendance were high-level government officials from Czechoslovakia. I remember raising the need for laws to regulate natural monopolies in the electricity industry and in *a few* select industries where scale economies were prevalent over a wide range of output, thus leading to per-unit cost savings from large-scale production. A number of Czech officials were very annoyed at my suggestions and indicated that a major cause of the inefficiencies of their command economy inherited from the Soviets was the prevalence of monopolies. Although I agreed that Soviet-instituted monopolies were a major source of inefficiencies and, in general, required dismantling, I held to my statement that a few monopolies were best maintained and regulated. Small-scale production in industries where unit costs would be significantly elevated owing to reduced scale made no sense.

After the first big push toward stabilization and structural reforms, still further adjustments must follow. The second step should involve deregulating labor markets and carrying on with the privatization of SOEs. A third step is to liberalize financial markets and the banking system.

A TRANSITION STRATEGY

Transition between economic systems represents a dynamic challenge that does not neatly lend itself to economic models owing to its complexity and the importance of initial conditions in an economy. I cannot envision an analytical model that could in fact identify an optimal time path or best sequence of events. The sequential path recommended here is derived from observing steps taken by those transition economies that have made the greatest progress toward sustained growth.[8] This is probably the best that can be hoped for in terms of an overall path – that is, some rough rules as to what to do first, second, and so forth. As economists acquire experience with transitions, models will be developed that identify at a specific transition position what further adjustments would have the highest likely payoff. Essentially, analysts face a problem of second best, or what to fix when some distortions within the economy must await correction at a later point. Additionally, there is a time inconsistency problem, because a chosen pathway may look different at a later decision point, leading decision makers to alter a chosen path over time. Such behavior can result in waste as plans are revamped.

Transition policies that are complementary or tend to reinforce one another's productivity are best bundled together and, thus, should come at the same point in the sequence of actions. At the start of the transition process should be those policies that provide a conducive environment for yet further progress. Thus, macroeconomic stabilization and the creation of market infrastructure should come as early as possible. Actions that address collective action difficulties by making transactions self-enforcing, so that a positive response by one trader leads to a reciprocal response by another, should also be instituted early. If, for example, the quality of a product can be evaluated after its purchase, then the seller has a long-run incentive to deliver a quality product, or the buyers will not come back.[9] Thus, the repeated nature of some transactions leads to incentives to behave honestly without the need for costly litigation – that is, the underlying repeated game properties of the transaction provide the proper incentives. In other instances, the underlying strategic interaction may make a cooperative response the best reaction to a cooperative overture. Even capital markets possess some self-enforcing aspects: if, for example, a firm acquires a reputation for repaying loans, then it will have greater access to financial markets in the

---

[8] See, especially, Fischer and Gelb (1991) and Fischer, Sahay, and Végh (1996).
[9] See Rapaczynski (1996, p. 96) on self-enforcing aspects of markets. It is interesting to note that in tourist resorts inferior restaurants on main streets may deliver poor quality meals and still survive, because they do not depend on repeat buyers.

future. These self-enforcing properties mean that the entire market infrastructure does not have to be instituted at once, provided that those facets of the infrastructure that do the most to facilitate exchange are implemented first.

Economists' recent work on transition economies has relied on many of the concepts of economics presented in this book, including institutional design, game theory, public choice, collective action, general equilibrium, and dynamics. As progress is made on these concepts, our understanding of the transition process will be improved, but a science of optimal transition paths is nowhere in sight.

POLICY REFORMS

Since the Velvet Revolution, a new field of economics has emerged that refects the new interest in transition economies. In particular, this field examines how to accomplish more efficient and informed *changes* in an economic system or institution. Unlike the study of economic policy making, policy reform involves changing the institutional environment in which economic agents operate. Thus, the rules of the game are being altered by such reforms. This field of study is especially interested in the incentives embodied in an institution – for instance, can institutions be designed to offer supportive incentives for agents to abide by the rules? That is, are incentives compatible with the way in which agents are intended to act? Additionally, the transaction costs of the reforms are germane to this new area. Obviously, only those reforms whose anticipated benefits outweigh the costs of instituting them should be enacted. The study of policy reforms focuses on the motivation of the agent making the decisions and, as a result, applies the methodological philosophy of public choice. Agents' responses to reforms must account for strategic considerations, information patterns, and inter-institutional interactions.

The same policy reform may elicit vastly different reactions depending upon the identity of the agents and their environmental influences, both institutional and human. Some agents have vested interests in the status quo and will do anything possible to divert the reforms. This has certainly been the experience in Russia and China. In China, efforts to reform state enterprises have met resistance from party members, who exercised much power and were relatively well-off prior to reforms.[10] For example, Chinese enterprise reforms in the late 1970s and the late 1980s were inhibited, in part, by a *nomenklatura* system, where the party-appointed managers tried to preserve the established system and its

---

[10] This resistance and the various forms that it has assumed are discussed in Cauley and Sandler (1992).

reward structure rather than introduce a new system with a different distribution of rewards based on productivity.

Policy reform involves a wide range of issues. In developing countries, these reforms focus on how best to promote development and growth through institutional design. The role of infrastructure and the establishment of property rights to facilitate market transactions in LDCs are two relevant reform concerns. Financial and capital markets represent another concern; there is now a greater appreciation that such markets may be more informal and subject to different rules than those in advanced industrial countries. As a related issue, policy reforms are concerned with how foreign assistance can be more supportive of development. Issues include how to get the recipients more actively involved with the development strategy, so that they have a vested interest in the plan. It is essential that foreign assistance help develop bureaucratic and entrepreneurial skills needed by LDCs to sustain their growth. A heavy reliance on foreign technical assistance, a requirement imposed by some donors, can inhibit an LDC from acquiring the requisite skills to support an expanding economy.

Policy reforms also involve institutional innovations to address market failures both within and among nations. Over the last eighty years, economists have come to appreciate that externalities must, *at times*, be controlled and some forms of public goods provided by governments. An understanding of when to intervene and institute governmental solutions is an important policy reform issue, one that concerns the choice of alternative policies or institutional arrangements or both.

STATE-OWNED ENTERPRISES AND POLICY REFORMS

In recent years, a great deal of attention has been directed to the design of SOEs and other enterprises in transition economies. The key to how SOEs or other firms behave depends on the distribution of returns among enterprise workers and managers.[11] If workers *equally share* in the net gain of the SOE or enterprise, there is an incentive to shirk in the hope of free riding on the efforts of others. If, instead, rewards are based on the *proportion* of effort expended, then there is a tendency to exert too much effort in an attempt to gain a greater share. Each type of sharing arrangement will imply a different incentive structure and thus different reactions on the part of the agents. Incentive mechanisms that favor more equal distribution tend to be inefficient owing to shirking, whereas those that differentiate among heterogeneous stakeholders

---

[11] For a theoretical treatment, see Cauley, Cornes, and Sandler (1999).

based on effective effort are more promising.[12] Economists are learning that the structuring of incentives influences the operation of enterprises.

China instituted enterprise reforms, mentioned earlier, in the 1970s and 1980s to provide more incentives for workers and managers. The intent of these reforms was to spell out the property rights within SOEs so as to motivate workers and managers. Unfortunately, the reforms did not accomplish their goals because property rights remained ambiguous owing to weak enforcement and bureaucratic interference that did not hold the manager responsible for the profits and losses of the enterprise, so that budget constraints remained soft. Collusion between managers and high-level officials severed the link between profits and performance; similarly, collusion between managers and workers cut the tie between wages and productivity. A bonus system was instituted to connect job performance and rewards, but much of the bonus became a fixed payment unrelated to productivity.[13] Even the small flexible portion of the bonus wage was equally divided among the workers and thus independent of productivity. In practice, these reforms failed because the bonus became a wage supplement that did not distinguish among the contributions of workers.

Component institutions constitute incentive structures essential to successful policy reforms. Insights about asymmetric information can assist our understanding of the design of those institutions. For example, workers are agents who are better informed than the managers or principals who must establish an incentive scheme to induce high effort from the workers. The design of these incentive arrangements guides the necessary reforms. Moreover, recent findings from collective action theory can provide information on how to address free-riding problems when workers in a team cannot be differentially treated.

DEMOCRATIZATION: POLITICAL AND ECONOMIC CONSEQUENCES

A proper study of transition and/or policy reform must involve not only institutional considerations and economic incentives, but also political concerns. Transition and developing economies experience accompanying political change. For Eastern Europe, the fall of communism also brought significant increases in political and civil freedom, as many of these nations adopted democratic principles. There is certainly a

---

[12] Effectiveness accounts for the productivity of the effort rather than just the actual time expended.

[13] Those fixed payments accounted for a baseline wage, seniority, the task difficulty, and skill requirements (Cauley and Sandler, 1992, p. 48).

complementarity between privately owned firms and democracy. As citizens gain control of economic activities, they demand more freedoms and a say in the government that taxes their profits and wages. With freer markets, a social safety net is needed to assist those unable to contribute to production. In market economies, governments must redistribute income and provide for public goods, which not only supply the infrastructure for a market economy but also address market failures. It is not unusual to experience a drive toward democracy in countries that introduce liberal economic reforms. Such was the case in Iran prior to the Islamic revolution and in China prior to the Tiananmin Square incident.

The interactions and synergism between economics and various political systems are poorly understood. In recent work, Mancur Olson (1993, 2000) has characterized autocracies as jealously guarding their monopoly rights to tax and only willing to supply public goods if the resulting gains in tax revenues justify their provision. Even the actions of autocrats differ depending on whether they have a vested interest in the society that they rule. A "roving bandit," who moves on after extracting a maximum surplus from the people, provides no public goods, unlike a "stationary bandit," who stays to rule and therefore has a long-term interest.[14] Transition economies are experiencing a variety of political, social, and economic responses. Those countries that have privatized large sectors of their economies and instituted a wide range of civil and political freedoms are generally doing better than those that have not. In some countries, corruption and criminal activities have interfered with the protection of property rights and the enforcement of contracts – two prerequisites for growth and prosperity.[15] Surely, the interaction between economics and politics is a two-way street: privatization and prosperity will lead to democratic demands, while democratization will create a conducive environment for market transactions. Untangling their interactions is an important political economy agenda for researchers.

Democratic values and economic prosperity also influence the environment. The end of communism in Eastern Europe brought the sad realization that the environment had been afforded zero value as a resource during communist rule. Myriad environmental disasters on a mammoth scale came to light with the collapse of communism. In advanced market economies, there is a demand for environmental protection as GDP grows, making environmental quality an income-normal

---

[14] The terms "roving" and "stationary" bandits are those of Olson (1993).
[15] This view is developed in Olson's (2000) *Power and Prosperity*, where he examines the interface between economic and political systems.

good.[16] A slightly different picture emerges in terms of income per capita, where the demand for environmental quality first decreases as income per capita rises and then, after a threshold, increases.[17]

The manner by which nations address transnational environmental concerns is partly dependent on their underlying political and economic characteristics. There is a general tendency for democratic market economies to be more willing to participate in treaties than are more autocratic nations (Congleton 1992). If, however, the autocratic country is a recipient of much pollution from abroad, then it may be a more willing participant in order to limit this importation. Even cultural norms regarding how generations view their responsibilities to one another (for example, whether the welfare of the children takes precedence over that of the parents) can have an influence on economic and political choices at the transnational level (see Chapter 10).

Democracy may also influence the level of conflict and, hence, the allocation of resources to defense. A popular line of research has tried to establish that democracies tend not to fight one another, so that democratic values are conducive to peace.[18] Some caution needs to be exercised here, because the effect of peace on democracy may be as large as the effect of democracy on peace; the two-way interaction must be taken into account when empirically identifying the relationship between peace and democracy. Other empirical concerns include the relatively weak relationship between democracy and peace demonstrated to date, and the small amount of variation in peace explained by democracy (James, Solberg, and Wolfson 1999).

CONCLUDING REMARKS

The inclusion of the study of transition economies and policy reforms as a separate chapter in this book posed a real dilemma for me. On the one hand, the analysis of these issues is just an application of the methods of the new institutional economics, collective action, and other topics covered in earlier chapters. This suggests that a full chapter may not be warranted. On the other hand, the amount of interest in these topics shown by researchers since 1990 suggests that they deserve more than a passing reference. This heightened interest eventually swayed me to devote a chapter to their analysis. Additionally, the concern with

---

[16] See, for example, Murdoch and Sandler (1997) and Murdoch, Sandler, and Sargent (1997).

[17] This nonlinear relationship is established by Grossman and Krueger (1995).

[18] A good summary of the vast literature on democracy and peace is Russett (1993). For an interesting attack on the methods of this literature, see James, Solberg, and Wolfson (1999).

transition economies will be around for some time to come as we learn from pathways currently being taken. Virtually every transition economy is following a unique dynamic path. These myriad experiments should yield some better rules of thumb regarding the sequence of changes that best promote the switch from a centrally planned system to a market-oriented system.

At this point, there is still much to learn about what should be optimized along a transition path. For example, should adjustment costs be minimized, or should the time before returning to positive growth be minimized? The objectives and even the constraints that are relevant in choosing an optimal transition strategy or in instituting policy reforms are not at all clear. Lessons learned from transition economies can also be applied to developing economies. The study of transition also has much to tell us about other systemwide changes, such as the optimal response to globalization. There is no dearth of applications for what we learn from the study of transition and the policy reform process. As the transition process progresses, there will be a lot of data generated that will assist in testing propositions. Although interest will persist for the next decade or two, the novelty of the study of the transition process will diminish as fewer centrally planned regimes remain.

14   Economic Growth: Endogeneity, Institutions, and Other Concepts

Of the four basic economic problems – resource allocation, income distribution, stability, and growth – economists still have the most to learn about growth. If this were not the case, then it would be difficult to fathom why foreign aid has not been more successful in achieving sustained growth in less-developed countries (LDCs) over the last half century (World Bank 1998). Once the growth process is understood, it should be relatively easy to target aid to achieve the most sustained growth in recipient countries.[1]

Throughout much of the last century, economic analysis has focused on static equilibria, which has done little to foster an understanding of economic growth, a process that requires a dynamic framework where the time path of variables are examined. There is no doubt that economist readers will disagree with my simple characterization of the profession's preoccupation, even obsession, with static models, and will point to an extensive neoclassical literature on growth associated with the analyses of Nobel laureates (for example, Tjalling Koopmans, Simon Kuznets, and Robert Solow) and others (for example, Trevor Swan, Roy Harrod, and Evsey Domar). This literature has enlightened us about some determinants of growth, but it does not adequately explain why some nations grow faster than others or *how economic decisions* determine a country's rate of growth. Most important, this earlier literature fails to account for the role of *individual* decisions and the influence of institutions on growth. Neoclassical models attribute growth to capital accumulation and technical change, where decisions behind these processes are treated as outside or exogenous to the analysis.[2] In many

---

[1] It is not my intention to equate growth and development: the latter requires institutional and social changes that go beyond growth of GDP. Growth is necessary but not sufficient for development.

[2] On the failures of the neoclassical growth models, see Aghion and Howitt (1998, pp. 11–24). Their book is also an excellent source for a mathematical representation of neoclassical growth models.

ways, we remain in the dark about the essential determinants of growth and, in particular, about how institutions, government policies, customs, and other factors influence growth.

In recent years, there have been two active research paradigms that hold promise for enhancing our understanding of the growth process. One paradigm involves the formulation of *endogenous growth theory*, while the other concerns the application of collective action principles. The first paradigm is the more influential and has spawned a vast and growing literature. Endogenous growth theory shows how structural characteristics of an economy affect individual decisions that, in turn, determine capital accumulation, technical change, and thus growth. The essential feature of endogenous growth theory that sets it apart from its predecessors is the incorporation of individual decisions into the determination of growth-promoting processes. Even actions to open up an economy to trade and foreign investment may foster a country's acquisition of new technologies through individual responses.

Endogenous growth theory is yet another instance of the *endogenizing* revolution that provides a unifying vision for the latest era of economic thought (see Chapter 15). A similar endogeneity involves the new institutional economics (Chapter 6) and recent efforts to explain taste formation (Chapter 11). As economics matures as a discipline, there are further efforts to explain important phenomena, once taken to be outside the purview of economic analysis.

The second paradigm is associated with Mancur Olson's (1982) *The Rise and Decline of Nations*, in which Olson argues that the growth of special interest groups results in efforts to capture "rents," or group-specific payoffs, which do not add to the overall well-being of the economy. Actions by lobbies representing trade, ethnic, business, and other interests promote income redistribution to their members and use up scarce resources without augmenting national income. This redistribution may be direct in terms of subsidies, tax reductions, or transfer payments, or indirect in terms of the maintenance of a monopoly position (for example, unions keeping out nonunion labor) or the passage of a favorable piece of legislation.

The purpose of this chapter is to review previous models designed to explain growth and to indicate why these paradigms fall short of a satisfactory explanation. A second purpose is to provide an overview and evaluation of the two new approaches to understanding growth. A final purpose is to predict the lasting power of these paradigms and the possibility of new approaches. My purpose is to focus on explanations of growth and not to judge whether or not growth is a reasonable end in itself. There are real concerns about growth on a planet with a shrinking natural resource base. Some of these concerns have been recognized in Chapter 11.

OVERVIEW OF STANDARD GROWTH THEORY

Neoclassical growth theory relies on two primary ingredients: a production function and a transition equation for investment. The production function relates output to a technology parameter and alternative combinations of inputs. If one input increases while other productive influences are held constant, then diminishing returns occur, so that every additional unit of the input results in a *smaller increment of output.* Diminishing returns is a hallmark of neoclassical economics that, in the absence of technical change or population growth, implies no income growth in the long run. The transition equation describes the rate of increase in the capital stock or investment. In such a basic model, net investment is the difference between savings, which fund new investment, and the depreciation of the physical capital stock (for example, machines, factories, and inventories). When the addition to the capital stock just equals the rate of depreciation, net investment is zero and national income is stationary.

National income grows when the capital stock begins at a low level for which the rate of savings exceeds the rate of depreciation, so that *net* investment is positive. As the capital stock accumulates from this initial level, national income growth lags investment depreciation owing to diminishing returns, and growth eventually ends.[3] An increase in the savings rate or a fall in the rate of depreciation will temporarily augment investment and lead to income growth; however, there will be *no long-run effects on growth.* As capital accumulates, the rate of depreciation will again catch up with the savings rate owing to diminishing returns, and net investment and growth will return to their stationary zero values. In the process, the new equilibrium levels of output and capital will be pushed higher.

The basic model can be embellished by allowing for population growth and/or technical change. With population growth, the economy's production function must now include both labor and capital as inputs. Constant returns to scale are assumed for the aggregate production function, where a proportional change in all inputs gives the same proportional change in output. Thus, a doubling of both capital and labor results in a doubling of output. When a single input is varied, diminishing returns still apply. For the two-input case, the model is transformed to per capita

---

[3] This follows because depreciation increases in proportion to the capital stock, while savings or investment increases less than proportionally to the capital stock because of diminishing returns (Aghion and Howitt 1998, pp. 12–13).

terms, where output per person is related to capital per person. This transformation is possible because of the constant returns assumption, which allows the analysis to be in terms of one choice variable – capital per person or the capital-labor ratio. The transition equation now relates the rate of change in the capital-labor ratio to the difference between the savings rate and an augmented depreciation rate, which is the sum of depreciation and population growth. An increase in the latter reduces the capital-labor ratio and, thus, has the same influence as depreciation of the capital stock on the capital-labor ratio. Population growth spreads the capital stock more thinly over more people, so that each has less capital with which to work. Qualitatively, population growth and depreciation both reduce the rate of increase of the capital-labor ratio. Despite the change of variables and the use of per-capita terms, the basic pessimism about long-run growth remains. Net investment, in the form of an increase in capital per person, ends when savings just offset the sum of depreciation and population growth, at which point long-run growth vanishes. Diminishing returns drive the neoclassical economy to this stationary state.

If long-run growth in output per person is nonzero, then technical change must *continually counteract* the forces of diminishing returns. The production function now includes the two inputs and a technology or productivity parameter, which captures the current state of technological know-how. At times, the technology parameter is attached to one of the inputs, thus implying that technical change is embodied in the input. If, for example, technical change is associated with labor, L, then AL denotes the effective supply of labor. Suppose that this technical change parameter grows at a rate of h, so that the effective labor supply increases according to the sum of the population growth plus h. At the stationary state where output per capita and capital per capita are constant from one period to the next, it can be shown that output and the capital stock grow at the same rate as the effective labor supply, so that capital per person and, hence, output per person grows at the rate of technical progress.[4] In the final analysis, the rate of technical change is the *sole* determinant of growth in a neoclassical growth model; it has served to explain growth for much of the twentieth century.

Although the neoclassical representation is neat and elegant, it puts forward a rather unsatisfactory explanation of long-run growth for a number of reasons. First, it is a mechanical, noneconomic representation

---

[4] This follows because capital per person must grow at the rate $(n + h) - n$, where n is the population growth rate and $n + h$ is the growth of effective labor. The growth rate of a quotient is the difference between the growth rate of the numerator and the growth rate of the denominator.

that hinges on a transition equation whose genesis is never really addressed. It is more of an exercise in mathematics than in economics. Second, the analysis is entirely at an aggregate level where the behavior of the decision makers – firms, consumers, and government – is never made clear. There is no microfoundation for the exercise. Third, the driving force for positive long-run growth, which is technical change, is completely exogenous to (outside of) the model. This means that growth analysts for years have chosen to take as given, and beyond economic analysis, the key influence that could explain the observed positive *long-run rate of income growth*, and thus could not explain long-standing differences in growth rates across countries. Fourth, the neoclassical model depicts technical change as capturing any change in output growth not attributable to capital accumulation or population growth. Thus, empirical studies identified the residual determinant of growth, unrelated to input growth, as technical progress.[5] The nature of technical progress – that is, whether it came from human capital, capital-embodied technological advances, or noninput-specific causes – was left unaddressed empirically. Fifth, the neoclassical world ignores any externalities that might arise from R & D on technical progress. By ignoring externalities and by assuming a competitive world, the neoclassical model incorrectly implies that the long-run stationary state is allocatively efficient. This is worrisome, because the failure of innovators to exclude free riders from prospering from their discoveries surely results in market failures in terms of too little innovation. In the short run, monopoly gains could be expected to be earned by innovators, and these gains also mean inefficiencies. Sixth, the neoclassical growth model has not led to many policy recommendations other than to promote technical progress due to its exogenous representation as the key factor behind growth. Thus, the analysis does not provide much insight regarding how best to stimulate growth in LDCs. The model does not tell us whether aid should go to education, nutrition, public infrastructure, or somewhere else. By making technical change dependent on elapsed time, neoclassical analysis offers few policy recommendations except patience.

One empirical implication of the neoclassical growth analysis concerning conditional convergence has been of great interest.[6] Suppose that there are two identical economies with the same parameters associated with savings, depreciation, technical progress, and population growth. If these economies begin with different initial capital stocks, then the country with the lower initial capital stock will grow faster, given its

---

[5] See, for example, Solow's (1957) analysis of technical change and the aggregate production function. Also see Mankiw, Romer, and Weil (1992).

[6] Recent papers on convergence include Barro (1991) and Barro and Sala-i-Martin (1992).

smaller diminishing returns, and will catch up with its capital-rich counterpart in the long run. Convergence is conditional on the factors determining the countries' stationary levels of output per capita, so that cross-country income per capita growth depends on these factors and the initial capital stock. Absolute convergence does not require the same underlying values for the growth-determining parameters in the two countries.

Toward a Theory of Endogenous Growth

Thus, it has become clear that the determinants of innovation and technical progress must be identified and incorporated into the analysis if growth theory is to enlighten us on why countries grow at different rates. Technical progress can no longer be treated as a rite of passage. An important forerunner of the modern formulation of endogenous growth was Joseph Schumpeter's (1934) *The Theory of Economic Development*, which viewed transitory monopoly profits as the motivator of innovation. Schumpeter characterized technical change as coming from a process of *creative destruction*, whereby one monopoly is replaced by another through the invention of new products or procedures. Short- to medium-run monopoly profits fuel the process of creative destruction, whereby entry barriers are overcome in the long run through human ingenuity. Thus, Schumpeter saw monopoly profits and the process of creative destruction that they encourage as key influences that promote technical change and economic growth. The rate of technical change can be affected by the structure of the economy and by policy choices that influence this structure. Because of their growth-promoting incentives, Schumpeter characterized monopolies as having an advantage over perfect competition and so argued against regulatory policies that break up monopolies. He was the first economist to recognize that the rate of technical change is determined by conscious economic and policy choices. As such, technical change is not exogenous or outside the theoretical explanation.

Economic history is replete with examples of creative destruction. Hand calculators eliminated the monopoly position held by slide rules prior to the 1970s. In transportation markets, the railroads obtained a monopoly position in the later 1800s when they replaced barge and wagon travel. During the next century, trucks challenged the monopoly position of the railroads, followed by airplanes, which took some freight business from trucks. Innovations in computer software and hardware have resulted in sufficient profits to encourage yet further discoveries. These computer-related innovations have spilled over into all kinds of manufacturing and service industries and revolutionized the way business is done – for example, "just-in-time" inventory systems have cut expensive inventory investments, thus limiting entry barriers based on such holdings. In 2000, Microsoft's defense against monopoly accusations from the Justice Department hinged on the process of creative destruction. This defense might have worked initially had Microsoft not engaged in alleged unfair practices, deemed monopolistic by the courts, to stifle competition by dictating terms to computer retailers and by supplying Microsoft's internet browser along with its office software. In the entertainment industry, compact diskettes replaced records during the late 1980s and early 1990s, while DVDs are poised to replace videotape.

Early modeling attempts to endogenize growth by adding a technical change choice parameter to the production function often resulted in *increasing returns to scale*, where doubling all inputs, including technical change, gave more than a doubling of output.[7] With increasing returns, myriad problems arise. When, for example, the inputs are paid their marginal product, the real wage bill or factor earnings in a competitive economy will more than exhaust the entire output. Increasing returns present insurmountable problems for determining a dynamic competitive equilibrium for the economy, since there is always a gain from increasing the size of the economy. Related problems affect the profitability of competitive firms. Obviously, a different way of introducing technical change needed to be devised, or else monopoly elements in the economy had to be permitted. Modern endogenous growth theorists allow for monopolies and increasing returns.

Precursors to modern endogenous growth models were those where other growth-promoting factors, such as technical change or labor, grow in proportion to capital so as to counter the effects of diminishing returns. When these effects are completely offset, output can grow at the rate of capital accumulation and economic growth can be sustained.[8] Endogeneity comes about in an indirect fashion, as the choice of capital determines the choice of technical change as a "tied decision." These early endogenous representations were still highly aggregated, and there was little in the way of economic factors behind the decision leading to growth.

Among the modern endogenous growth theorists, Paul Romer (1986) rediscovered these early models and placed them in a framework where an individual chooses consumption over time while taking account of an investment transition equation, in which investment equals the

---

[7] The discussion in this paragraph derives from Aghion and Howitt (1988, pp. 23–4).
[8] One such model is by Frankel (1962). These models are known as AK, where K is capital and A represents other influences.

difference between income and consumption, and income accounts for the capital stock *and* technical change. In Romer's representation, diminishing returns are just counterbalanced by advances in technology, which is treated as an external effect beyond the individual's control. Sustained growth increases with a fall in the discount factor, which augments the desire to save, and so finances investment.[9] An increase in technical change and/or a decrease in diminishing returns will also increase growth.

An interesting feature of Romer's representation surfaces when individual behavior is aggregated to represent the economy as a whole. The number of firms or the scale of the economy becomes a positive influence on growth, because the number of firms is an important determinant of the extent of innovation as externalities arise from firms' actions to augment technology. Such externalities are a defining feature of endogenous growth and were absent from neoclassical growth representations. As has been discussed in earlier chapters, externalities play an important role. Anything that augments the scale of the economy promotes growth through these externalities. Thus, free trade is growth-promoting owing to these scale effects and their positive influence on technical externalities. The presence of externalities also points to under-provision of technical change and the need for government policies to promote these externalities. Each firm only considers its own gains, ignoring the benefits that its technical breakthrough creates for others, when allocating funds to R & D.

ENDOGENOUS GROWTH: FURTHER DISCUSSION

Once individual decisions and externalities are introduced into the endogenous growth framework, growth theory takes on a greater, but useful, complexity. For example, efforts to reward technical externalities add a new role for government policy in its desire to foster growth. Such rewards can lead to imperfect competition and high profits if one or more firms come to dominate a market. Schumpeter's creative destruction is a driving force behind monopolies' role in advancing technical change, so that public policy to support these monopolies and to subsidize their research may be an engine for growth. Increasing returns to scale may be part of the landscape and a factor behind sustained growth. Once differences in the rate of diminishing returns, the discount factor, the scale of the economy, and the process of technical change are allowed among countries, conditional convergence in income per capita may no longer be assured. With sufficient differences, divergence is apt to be the norm.

---

[9] The discount factor is inversely related to the interest rate. A decline in the discount factor means a rise in the interest rate and thus a greater return to saving.

At this juncture, my goal is merely to give a flavor of the endogenous growth literature and its implications for understanding and promoting growth. In simple language, endogenous growth theory indicates that there is more to growth than accumulating physical capital at a sufficiently high rate. One of these other considerations may assume the form of human capital or investment in training and education.[10] Growth now equals the sum of the population growth and technical progress, where the latter also accounts for human capital growth. Once the accumulation of human capital is introduced, growth convergence is problematic because countries make vastly different investments in people, with rich countries often making the greatest investments, thereby staying ahead of the pack. In this endogenous approach, human capital is added to the aggregate production function along with technical progress that can increase the effective supply of labor. In other instances, a positive influence on growth may come from still other forms of capital, such as public investment in the form of social capital or infrastructure. Increases in knowledge can also stimulate growth.

Endogenous growth analysis also recognizes that decisions with respect to human capital formation, innovative inputs, technical change, and other growth-promoting activities must be addressed in order for growth to be understood. The real issue is to determine what is behind the decisions to engage in these activities. For example, are monopoly profits the motivating force for the creation of innovative inputs and processes? If this is the case, then an economy that does not allow an innovator to tap into these profits through patent protection will experience fewer innovations and reduced growth. Another influence that links innovations and the rate of growth involves the publicness of knowledge, whose benefits are nonrival and partly excludable. This nonrivalry implies that knowledge can be used by one person or firm without detracting from the benefits still available to other potential users. A better process or organizational form for manufacturing a product can, for example, be applied in an almost limitless fashion to other producers. This publicness has two implications for endogenous growth: (1) knowledge spillovers can be a cause for increasing returns; and (2) knowledge creation is apt to be undersupplied. Economies with better policies for addressing this undersupply through subsidies and other inducements (for example, prizes or tax incentives given for discoveries) can achieve better growth. Most patents are filed by a relatively small group of advanced industrial countries, a concentration that impedes both absolute and conditional convergence.

---

[10] In this approach, human capital is added to the aggregate production function along with technical progress that increases the *effective* supply of labor.

Innovations spill over not only among firms in the same industry, but also among sectors. *General purpose technologies* (GPTs), which include the steam engine, the computer, the internet, the laser, and the internal combustion engine, create benefits for a wide range of industries. In many cases, GPTs may be involved with growth reduction and loss of income when human capital obsolescence is accelerated, as old skills are no longer useful and new skills must be learned. As the GPT is eventually adapted to a wide range of applications and activities, the new skills are acquired and growth takes off.[11] Countries that are slow to adopt a new GPT will be at a decided long-run disadvantage, and this will cause a divergence of income and growth in the long run, even though some convergence may occur in the short run as adopters wrestle with the new technology and experience an initial erosion of human capital in the process.

Another distinguishing feature of many endogenous growth models involves microeconomic-level choices, where the decision maker is either a representative individual or a firm. The advantage of such a formulation is that the optimizing calculus of the agents is apparent. Agents are represented as rational individuals who make farsighted and informed intertemporal optimizations. At this level, endogenous growth has incorporated the theoretical advances of the last few decades, including asymmetric information, the new institutional economics, and market failures, into the explanation of growth. For example, the actions of borrowers and lenders will depend on their relative information – that is, on who is better informed. Capital markets will be affected by moral hazard, in which the incentives of borrowers regarding repayment may be perverse.[12] The forms of existing institutions will have an influence on individuals' constraints and objectives, thus affecting their behavior: an economy with fewer bureaucratic obstacles to entrepreneurs who want to start firms is expected to grow faster than economies with more such impediments. If, moreover, property rights to inventions are protected, then these safeguards foster growth. Institutions can also promote growth when they ensure stability and limit volatility. At the same time, institutions must allow for flexibility, so that the labor force can be adjusted in response to market forces. Market failures in the form of externalities and public goods influence the manner in which technical advances diffuse throughout the economy and, in so doing, affect growth.

Political stability is also viewed as a stimulant to growth by endogenous growth models.[13] If political instability calls into question the

[11] On GPTs and their implications, see Aghion, Caroli, and Garcia-Peñalosa (1999, pp. 1640–6).

[12] For example, see ibid., pp. 1625–7.

[13] See, for example, Alesina and Rodrik (1994), Aghion, Caroli, and Garcia-Peñalosa (1999), and Barro (1991).

enforcement of contracts or the return to human capital, then investments from sources at home and abroad will not materialize. Foreign direct investment, which serves as an important source of savings, will be driven away if the political environment is unstable. For example, countries plagued by transnational terrorism directed at foreign interests have been shown to have experienced a significant negative effect on foreign direct investment.[14] As an extreme form of instability, civil wars and conflicts with neighboring states will negatively affect growth, because the returns to human capital become highly uncertain. The World Bank has in recent years devoted more attention to investigating the causes and consequences of civil wars. This is an important effort spearheaded by Paul Collier. Surely, foreign aid is unlikely to have much impact on development in countries torn apart by conflict.[15] The empirical literature has identified political instability as a significant negative determinant of growth (Barro 1991).

Endogenous growth theory has been associated with numerous empirical exercises that are intended to verify its hypothesis. These exercises demonstrate that education level (a proxy for human capital), life expectancy, investment, political stability, and the terms of trade are positive determinants of growth.[16] Even the decision to liberalize trade has a positive influence on growth[17] owing to a scale effect that augments the positive externalities arising from technological spillovers. In the case of human capital, endogenous growth analysts point to a lowering of fertility rates as women attain higher education levels; with greater education, women exercise more autonomy within the family in deciding when to have children. They tend to delay having children during the education process and immediately thereafter so as to gain a return from their education. The resulting reduction in population growth augments capital per worker and growth.

In many ways, endogenous growth theory is the rational expectations paradigm applied to factors that determine technical change and, hence, growth. As mentioned earlier, the microfoundation is ever apparent in many endogenous growth models. Individual behavior is so often stressed that I have wondered in recent job seminars whether the candidate was applying for the department's microeconomic or macroeconomic opening. In endogenous growth models, agent-level decisions are then aggregated in some fashion to give an economywide explanation of

---

[14] This has been shown for Greece and Spain by Enders and Sandler (1996).
[15] Relevant papers include Collier and Hoeffler (1998, 2000).
[16] Such results can be found in Barro and Sala-i-Martin (1992).
[17] A recent empirical study on the effects of trade on growth is by Frankel and Romer (1999). Also see Aghion, Caroli, and Garcia-Peñalosa (1999). Empirically, it is very difficult to isolate the influence of trade on growth.

growth. The aggregation process is typically a simple sum of individual behaviors with no adjustment for agent interactions that may violate the summation assumption.

MANCUR OLSON'S COLLECTIVE ACTION THEORY OF GROWTH

Mancur Olson (1982) presented a different explanation of why growth rates differ among countries.[18] His formulation is based on notions of collective action and public choice. In his institution-based theory, growth is impeded by special interest groups that seek income redistribution, an activity that wastes scarce resources as groups vie for influence with the government. Such self-promoting activities represent rent seeking, in which agents' actions expend resources without adding to national income. In the process, the production possibility frontier recedes and growth is impeded. These redistributive activities may take the form of groups that lobby for legislation favoring their interests over others' (for example, relaxed pollution standards). Other instances may be efforts to achieve tax breaks, union shops, import restrictions, export subsidies, or outright income transfers. Some of this rent-seeking activity by special interest groups preserves monopoly positions and results in allocative inefficiencies that impede growth.

If such collective actions are harmful to the economy, then why do such groups engage in these activities? Relatively small groups suffer just a tiny fraction of the loss in economywide efficiency while gaining the net redistribution that their efforts achieve. Typically, the calculations are such that groups capture a net benefit if successful, despite the overall harmful effect on the economy. Such negative impacts on others are of no concern to the lobbies, which do not account for these negative external effects. Thus, a classic externality problem is behind these lobbies' growth-inhibiting actions. Olson also views these special-interest lobbies as opposing any change that could adversely affect their relative position in society. Some lobbies may even oppose the adoption of new technologies, thereby reducing the rate of growth.

As a nation grows older, it acquires more special-interest lobbies that seek these redistributive gains and that oppose change. Long eras of social and political stability are conducive to the growth of such lobbies, as new ones appear and old ones gain strength. According to Olson (1982, p. 73): "The accumulation of distributional coalitions increases the complexity of regulation, the role of government, and the complexity of understandings, and changes the direction of social evaluation." Just as cholesterol forms atherosclerotic plaque that clogs arteries and causes

---

[18] For a complementary approach, see DeSoto (2000).

heart disease, special-interest coalitions slow the workings of economies and inhibit growth-promoting activities. Economies with fewer such coalitions can, other things being constant, grow faster, so that countries devastated by war or other catastrophic events can grow at faster rates, once stripped of many of these coalitions, than more stable countries. The rapid growth displayed by Germany, Italy, and Japan during the post–World War II period is credited by Olson to these nations' limited number of distributional lobbies. By contrast, a long-stable democracy, like the United States or Australia, has its growth impeded by myriad distributional concerns.

Although both Olson's approach and endogenous growth theory place importance on the economy's organizational structure and its ability to adopt technical innovations, the underlying analyses bear little resemblance. In particular, Olson never puts forward a mathematical depiction of the growth process, nor does he explicitly display the individuals' optimizing process. There is no transition equation or production function in Olson's representation. Ironically, both analyses are heavily dependent on externalities as a driving force, but their impacts are quite different. In Olson's analysis, the externalities induce agents to take actions that worsen the well-being of the economy. For endogenous growth theory, the externalities are a positive influence on technological dissemination and on society's welfare. Olson's externalities inhibit growth by slowing progress, whereas endogenous growth's externalities foster growth through spillovers.

Although Olson's theory suggests a number of testable hypotheses, these tests have not been conclusive. One test involves whether some time-dependent measure of institutional sclerosis is a significant negative determinant of income growth per capita.[19] In particular, institutional sclerosis is related to some measure of the time since a nation's inception, or since some catastrophic event involving the destruction of special-interest coalitions. For example, the end of World War II is appropriate for Germany, Italy, and Japan, while the end of the US Civil War is relevant for the Confederate states of the United States. Tests to date have provided weak evidence that is not immune to alternative explanations. Because countries may have institutional safeguards to protect them from the accumulation of interest groups, the actual number of interest groups is a more direct way to proxy institutional sclerosis than some variable that indicates the time since statehood or rebirth. An even better proxy is some measure of the actual influence wielded by the interest groups, which can be in terms of campaign contributions or even some redistribution variable.

---

[19] This is the test performed by Kwang Choi (1983).

Olson's theory of growth is noteworthy because of its reliance on institutions as a directing force. Nobel laureate Douglass North (1961, 1990) also formulated a theory of growth based on institutional considerations. In North's analysis, the establishment of property rights is depicted as an essential factor in promoting sustained growth. Property rights allow for the expansion of markets and the specialization of labor that such expansion brings about. North (1961) argued that the railroads served an important role in the assignment of property rights in the United States, an assignment that furthered US growth prior to the Civil War. In Europe, the enclosure acts, which required private lands to be fenced off from commons, served a similar purpose and led to the growth of private ownership of land. By displacing the peasants who had relied on commonly owned lands, the enclosure acts also created a large labor force in the urban centers that could be employed in the factories.

EVALUATION OF RECENT THEORIES OF GROWTH

Clearly, neoclassical growth theory is an unsatisfactory representation for at least three reasons. Its reliance on capital accumulation as the prime determinant cannot provide an explanation of sustained growth, because diminishing returns to capital means that long-run growth is zero. Thus, growth must depend on either population growth or technical change, two influences that are taken as given and outside of the model. Finally, decision-making behavior of the agents is never addressed by neoclassical growth models owing to their aggregate level of analysis.

As an alternative to neoclassical growth theory, endogenous growth theory in its modern formulation appeared at the start of the 1990s. Its emphasis on explaining technical progress and its role in growth is both welcome and novel. The developers of this analysis have kept the models elementary and accessible to a wide audience of practicing economists.[20] Also, the theory's guiding principles are easy to understand by policy makers and the public. Such efforts to maintain transparency should ensure that the theory's influence will continue to grow. Endogenous growth theory embraces a wide array of models that rely on alternative influences such as human capital, market failures, process innovations, population growth, institutional structure, and knowledge spillovers. The theory is not dependent on a single modeling technique, which adds to its richness and novelty. In fact, endogenous growth analysis incorporates many recent theoretical advances, including game theory, asymmetric information, and public choice. These alternative paradigms apply to a

---

[20] This is not to imply that the analysis is easy. Any analysis concerning a dynamic relationship such as growth is demanding from an analytical viewpoint.

wide range of questions that involve stabilization policy, employment practices, public-sector investment policy, and development assistance. By focusing on what explains growth in terms of agents' optimizing decisions, endogenous growth theory is well equipped to identify where to direct foreign aid in order to obtain the greatest payoff. For example, endogenous growth theory and its empirical tests highlight the importance of political stability and human capital formation.

Another desirable aspect of endogenous growth theory is its large set of testable hypotheses. Analysts have applied a host of state-of-the-art econometric techniques to test these hypotheses. Most of the theoretical analyses are inextricably linked to accompanying empirical tests, which is a desirable development. Because the theory and empirics are developed by the same researchers, more attention is given to the specification of measurable variables in the theoretical analysis.

Much remains to be done. For example, further work is needed to distinguish whether empirical findings are more consistent with neoclassical or endogenous growth theory. An understanding of the diffusion process for new technologies – that is, how technical advances spread throughout the economy – can benefit from additional analysis. To date, the externality influences of knowledge spillovers have been examined with rather broad strokes. For instance, appropriate policies and procedures for internalizing these externalities have received scant attention. It is also essential that aggregation from the individual agents to the economy as a whole be given more attention.

Olson's collective action theory of growth, while an important addition to the literature, is much narrower than endogenous growth theory. His analysis is overshadowed by developments in endogenous growth theory, owing to the latter's greater richness and its easier-to-test hypotheses. In many ways, Olson's institution-based theory is a precursor to endogenous growth theory. Both theories concern how individual choices impact growth. The absence of a formal structure limits future extension of his theory. Interest in testing Olson's provocative hypotheses has waned; recently, the primary use of his theory has been to explain what institutional features in transitional economies and LDCs facilitate or inhibit growth. This is an important contribution that can be incorporated into endogenous growth explanations.

15   Economic Visions of Future Horizons

Over the last century, economics has become more analytical and quantitatively sophisticated, making it even less accessible to nonspecialists and requiring a greater "entry fee" for those wanting to be professional economists. Even for those interested in just a rudimentary understanding of economics, the cost may seem excessive, as many college students discover when taking courses in the principles of economics. There is no reason that economics needs to be so arcane, because with a little effort on the part of economists it could be made understandable to a wide audience. With its myriad applications to fascinating topics (for example, the internet, the alleviation of poverty, economic development, the adoption of new technologies, and outer space resources), the task of interesting students and making the subject relevant could not be easier.

Too often I read or review articles in which the argument and analysis have been made very complex, when a much simpler and more transparent presentation would serve just as well. Many years ago I worked with a bright junior colleague who gave me a five-page proof for a paper that we were collaborating on. With some thought, I managed to reduce the proof to just one line. When shown the simpler and more intuitive proof, he lost his temper and stormed out of my office, not to return for two days. The paper with the shorter proof was later published in a top journal; and my colleague applied what he had learned and went on to a very successful career. Robert Heilbroner and William Milberg (1995, p. 5) describe this disturbing tendency among economists to become obsessed with technical details as follows: "Analysis has thus become the jewel in the crown of economics. To this we have no objection. The problem is that analysis has gradually become the crown itself, overshadowing the baser material in which the jewel is set." To read some modern economic analyses, one must wonder what has happened to the *social* in economics, the queen of the social sciences. All too often, the institutional, political, and societal details have been so sanitized to facilitate the mathematical presentation that what remains possesses little real-world relevancy. I am an advocate for theoretical presentations and base my own papers on analytical models, but economists must not lose sight of their social purpose – to enlighten policy makers and to improve society by making the most of scarce resources. If economics is to continue to contribute to society and maintain its relevancy, it must return to its political economy roots. Economists must also become better at communicating the subject's guiding principles and concepts to the society at large. These recommendations are particularly valid in today's world of momentous change, where more economic decisions possess an international dimension; increasingly, resource decisions have transnational consequences owing to new technologies.

One of my primary goals in writing this book has been to show that even economic concepts at the frontier of the discipline can be made understandable and interesting to a wide audience. I have tried to reach this goal without the use of fancy mathematics and have employed graphs sparingly. The logic of economics is both clear and intuitive when some thought is given to its presentation. Economics is also an elegant way of reasoning, even without the mathematics showing. At times, highly mathematical models of economics will rediscover an economic principle already made clear by Adam Smith, David Ricardo, or another classical economist, who employed no mathematical or statistical tools and relied instead on logical arguments.

Economic thought has blossomed in the twentieth century. For the first three-quarters of the century, general-equilibrium analysis of economic issues was a unifying and driving force, stemming from the work of Walras, Pareto, and Edgeworth. This analysis treats an economic transaction as embedded in an interrelated system of markets: the influence of an economic policy – say, the institution of a luxury tax – is better understood when the reactions of related markets are brought into the analysis. In the last quarter-century, economics has begun to scrutinize many of its basic assumptions. Thus, institutions and even tastes are not always taken as given and beyond economic analysis. Markets and other modes of allocations may now be allowed to have a transaction cost for doing business. Additionally, economists have moved away from their obsession with competitive equilibrium and allowed for market failures of myriad kinds. Even the once-benign view of government has changed, because public choice theorists recognize that policy makers have their own agendas to satisfy, which may conflict with the social good. Information is no longer assumed to be complete; modern economic thought permits agents to a transaction to be differentially informed. In other scenarios, earlier actions may signal an individual's type, thus curtailing the degree of asymmetric information.

The purpose of this concluding chapter is to review some key findings of the book. A second purpose is to evaluate the contributions of economics in the last century. A third purpose is to predict the likely focus of economics in the coming decades. Finally, this chapter attempts to define some visions for economics.

MAJOR DEVELOPMENTS DURING THE LAST CENTURY

It is not a trivial task to identify the major developments in economic thought during the last hundred years, since there have been many relevant changes. Certainly, general-equilibrium analysis in its varied forms represents a prime achievement, as the relatively large number of Nobel Prizes suggests. The contribution of general-equilibrium analysis must include the study not only of a closed economy without trade, but also of an *open* economy with trade. In fact, the Nobel Prize in economics in 1977 was awarded to Bertil Ohlin and James Meade for their path-breaking work on international trade. More recently, the Nobel Prize in 1999 went to Robert Mundell for his investigation of the influence of monetary and fiscal policies under alternative exchange rate (for example, fixed and flexible) systems and his examination of optimum currency areas. The European Monetary Union is an instance of a currency area where a group of countries adopt a single currency along with a set of rules for maintaining the stability of the currency's value. Optimum currency areas are associated with the creation of a common market where trade barriers are eliminated between members, leading to both trade creation among members and trade diversion away from nonmember states. The welfare of participants is as high as possible if an optimal size is chosen.

The profession's focus on general equilibrium has come at a price. Although general-equilibrium analysis is a masterpiece – a beauty to behold – it rests on a set of very restrictive assumptions. First, there is its reliance on perfect competition, a reliance that greatly limits the ability of the analysis to allow for increasing returns, transaction costs, incomplete information, or monopoly pricing – features that are prevalent in all economies. Second, general equilibrium is a static analysis that is best equipped to analyze the final equilibria arising from changes in parameters, but ill-suited to investigate the path of adjustment from one equilibrium to the next. An intertemporal representation offered by theorists enlightens us about some decisions involving assets (for example, inventories, capital accumulation), but this depiction remains a static study that does not address the actual path of adjustment or its timing. Third, there is virtually no strategic behavior, where agents try to predict their counterpart's behavior and respond optimally to these anticipations.

Fourth, general-equilibrium analysis does not provide much insight into disequilibrium positions, especially those that persist for some time.

This last shortcoming was particularly evident during the Great Depression, when a general deflation of wages and prices did nothing to rectify the involuntary unemployment. If prices can adjust downward to eliminate excess supply of labor and unwanted inventories, then general-equilibrium analysis predicts that unemployment will be fixed, but this was not the case. Prices and wages fell throughout the Great Depression, but the excess supply of labor and products was not eliminated.

Thus, Keynesian economics was born, with its emphasis on expectations and disequilibrium. When aggregate demand for goods and services is insufficient owing to pessimism on the part of consumers and investors, the economy can remain in disequilibrium, with high levels of unemployment despite deflation. The Keynesian remedy is fiscal policy in the form of deficit-financed government spending or tax reductions. Unfortunately, Hicks's graphical depiction of the Keynesian revolution in terms of the IS-LM diagram diverted Keynes's insights concerning disequilibrium and dynamics.[1] Hicks's diagram reduced Keynesian analysis to a *static* general-equilibrium representation of two aggregate markets: a goods and services market or the investment-savings (IS) equilibrium, and a money market for liquidity (LM) equilibrium, devoid of any expectations or disequilibrium. As explained in Chapter 12, there is much more skepticism today regarding the usefulness of policy, and of fiscal policy in particular; so Keynesian economics is no longer a ruling vision.

Although Keynes's mark on economics has faded, the interest in macroeconomics remains an important innovation of the twentieth century. William Baumol (2000) chooses the formal analysis of macroeconomics as the most important addition to modern-day textbooks of economic principles when compared to Alfred Marshall's *Principles of Economics*, first published in 1890. In the *Principles*, the prime focus had been microeconomics, with macroeconomics related to some summing up of industries' demand and supply curves. In his list of the achievements of the twentieth century, Baumol (2000, pp. 2–3) also includes the development of sophisticated tools of econometrics and the many applications of theory and econometrics to public policy.

While I agree that developments in macroeconomics, econometrics, and applications are among the more significant achievements of economic thought during the last century, I would place different emphasis on these developments and include some others at the top of the list. I would not put macroeconomics anywhere near the top, because there is

---

[1] See the discussion in Heilbroner and Milberg (1995, Chapter 3) which provides an insightful treatment of the Keynesian revolution and its undoing.

so much disagreement today about its general principles. For example, some theorists insist on a microeconomic foundation for macroeconomics, so that the optimizing choices of individual agents are evident. Other theorists, such as Keynes, are content with abstracting to some aggregate representation without tying everything back to the behavior of individual agents. Many different schools of thought exist, including the Keynesians, the monetarists, the neo-Keynesians, and rational-expectations theorists. For some economists, macroeconomics is the application of advanced econometrics to data, with little in the way of formal theory.[2] Advances in macroeconomics seem to be more a matter of fashion than of agreed-upon principles, which is a pity because there is no lack of important macroeconomic issues. This lack of coherence undermines the profession's achievements in macroeconomics.

Surely, the many advances in statistical testing and modeling of economics, known as econometrics, represent important methodological contributions to twentieth-century economics, but I consider these techniques to be tools that help move the frontier of economic knowledge outward, but do not constitute novel economic principles. It is necessary to look beyond the tools to identify the true advances in economic knowledge.

At the top of my list of economic achievements is the study of the public sector. In any modern-day society, the public sector has assumed an enhanced importance since the end of World War II, and now constitutes somewhere between a third to over one-half of all economic transactions. Vibrant economies have public sectors that facilitate exchange, while stagnant economies have poorly functioning public sectors. Russia, for example, will continue to struggle until it develops an operational public sector with the ability to collect taxes to fund public expenditures on schools, social infrastructure, and property rights protection. I view newly developed principles of taxation (including the study of taxes on imports and exports), government expenditures, and government-directed income redistribution as the supreme advance in economic thought over the last century. Thus, I share Baumol's emphasis on developments in the analysis of public finance as a highlight of recent economic thought.

These new insights were made possible by the study of market failures, stemming from A. C. Pigou's *The Economics of Welfare*, first published in 1920. The notions of externalities, public goods, market imperfections, and missing markets have directed economic thought over the last half of the twentieth century. In an Adam Smith paradise of perfect competition, there is little need for market intervention or public

[2] This characterizes some macroeconomists who use advanced time-series techniques.

policy, except to provide some public goods and to leave things alone. The real world is, however, not so nicely behaved – smoke belches from factories, some markets do not exist, some willing and able workers remain unemployed, and the achievement of farsighted technological breakthroughs may require assistance. Smith's vision of an economy is analogous to a precious diamond whose myriad facets reflect a perfect unity of purpose, a gem of immaculate beauty. In reality, a market economy is a semiprecious stone with all kinds of imperfections. Polishing or tinkering with one blemish may result in far-worse consequences, and thus the correction of market failures requires deft action that recognizes economic interrelationships. As the world economy becomes more globalized, market interdependencies within *and* among autonomous countries grow in importance.

The pivotal role of public sector economics and its underlying concept of correcting market failures in the development of modern economics is why I made market failures the focus of four of the first five chapters. Virtually every chapter addresses an economic concept that depends, in some way, on market failures such as externalities. For example, asymmetric information involves missing markets and externalities, so that goods and services either are not traded to those who value them most, or are traded at prices that do not reflect their true value. Similarly, intergenerational economics concerns market failures across generations. One of the new insights into market failures and their correction is the realization that policy makers do not always have the public interest at heart – an insight gained from the study of public choice. So the motivation of policy makers is now part of the evaluation of corrections.

A second major achievement of modern economics is the inclusion of strategic behavior, in which agents are thinking and reactive entities who try to attain the greatest advantage over an equally capable opponent. In a strategic environment, an agent's optimizing payoffs depend on what his or her counterpart thinks that the agent knows, and vice versa. Information, the sequence of actions, the strategic choices, and the signals given assume an importance previously absent from the timeless, nonstrategic setting of classical and neoclassical economics. Rational expectations has, for example, applied game-theoretic tools to demonstrate that policies may not have their intended outcomes if rational agents anticipate policy consequences. Game trees teach that the order of moves and what is known at every decision point have implications for the outcome.

During the last century, a third fundamental achievement has involved the development of economic dynamics, where pathways from disequilibrium to equilibrium are investigated. The study of economic dynamics is a twentieth-century phenomenon because the requisite mathematical tools only then became available. At first, economic dynamics was applied to the study of exhaustible natural resources and, later, to economic growth. Economic dynamics now involves issues in macroeconomics, public sector economics, international economics, labor economics, and other subfields.

A fourth significant feature of twentieth-century economics is the development of interdisciplinary models that include relevant biological, social, political, atmospheric, or other noneconomic processes and considerations. Given a new modeling task, I gain the greatest pleasure when I must master some concepts from another discipline and integrate them into the economic analysis. Statistical and mathematical tools shared by economics, the sciences, and the other social sciences provide the common ground for splicing together these interdisciplinary approaches. With such approaches, economics has come full circle to rediscover its interdisciplinary roots.[3] Economists have thus realized that the precision and insights gained by accounting for the interrelationships of markets can be pushed to yet a higher level by incorporating relevant noneconomic interactions.

WANING AREAS OF ECONOMIC ANALYSIS

I am only too aware that to single out areas of waning interest is controversial and will surely enrage those with vested interests. Ironically, I place the area of economics with the greatest dominance over the profession during the last century – static general-equilibrium analysis – at the top of the list of waning areas of activity. This is *not* to say that economists will not practice general-equilibrium analysis; rather, it is to imply that the basic principles of such static analysis are now sufficiently well understood that attention will be redirected to strategic and dynamic representations. The notion that everything ties together is now uncontroversial. Additionally, the requirements for existence, uniqueness, and stability of equilibrium have been identified by Arrow, Samuelson, and other intellectual leaders of economic thought in the last century. Extension of these requirements to systems with strategic and dynamic elements should be straightforward. A need to move beyond static general-equilibrium analysis is apparent from the current state of macroeconomics, the absence of a blueprint for development, ignorance of desirable transition paths between alternative economic systems, and the need to design enduring institutions for a changing world.

The current surge of interest in the examination of asymmetric information will diminish unless new paradigms are developed that provide novel findings. Currently, there is a sameness of results in the plethora

---

[3] Economics had its roots in philosophy and physics.

of recent papers on asymmetric information whose novelty rests on the application. Someone knowledgeable in the methods could easily intuit the findings without the technical details. Too many resources appear to have been allocated to building these models over the last decade, where even the simplest require elaborate structure before any results are generated. The cost of the needed scaffolding for such problems sometimes outweighs the benefits from the model's findings.

A third candidate for diminishing interest is rational expectations, whose analysis involves application of rational choice to explore policy ineffectiveness. In some ways, rational expectations theory takes static general equilibrium a step further. It remains, however, rather static, with emphasis on the final equilibrium rather than on how long it takes to achieve. A second worry concerns the failure to focus on aggregation from the representative individual to the economy as a whole. The process of aggregation may alter the findings and policy recommendations. Rational expectations' prevalence in the literature is partly due to authors' using the term in vastly different ways – a problem that needs to be fixed.

The profession's fixation on game theory is also slated, I believe, to diminish somewhat. As with any new tool that adds insight, economists seeking to embrace new paradigms have rushed to adopt game theory. When I was a graduate student from 1968 to 1971, microeconomics texts contained a single reference to game theory in the section on oligopolies, and macroeconomics texts made no reference to it. In recent years, things have changed dramatically, with some microeconomics texts giving the impression that every aspect of the topic depends on a game-theoretic explanation,[4] and modern macroeconomics texts frequently mentioning game theory. Game theory will continue to dominate economic models as a methodology in the foreseeable future, but such exercises that do not really reflect key elements of an application should decrease in prevalence. For example, some cooperative game-theoretic models, when applied to the study of environmental treaties, require assumptions to identify the core (or the coalition from which no subgroup can do better on its own) that do not capture crucial environmental considerations – for example, wind or water flow direction. It is imperative that identifying the core does not become the sole purpose of the exercise. As a social scientist, I want to know the kind of agreement that we can expect rather than some unobtainable ideal.

If game theory is to maintain its hold on the profession, then less effort should be expended on equilibrium refinements or on the development of alternatives to Nash equilibrium. An alternative is, however, required,

---

[4] Perhaps the two best examples are Kreps (1990b) and Schotter (1994b).

owing to problems with this notion and its poor performance in experimental settings. In the past, too much effort has gone into these refinements, with only a few capturing economists' imagination.

A force that could maintain economists' interest in game theory would be additional empirical testing of the models. Although I have sympathy for some theory without empirical application, sufficient empirical tests of game-theoretic models must be developed if such a large proportion of theoretical effort is to be devoted to such models. There are many game-theoretic applications (for example, labor strikes, oligopoly behavior, and charitable giving) that address essential economic and social concerns, for which empirical analysis can provide some important policy guidance.

My final prediction of decline involves highly mathematical exercises that appear driven more by a pursuit of elegance than by applicability. Economics has always attracted a large set of technically trained individuals who are prone to abstraction. Because of this, there will always be a large number of highly rigorous theoretical exercises. However, my prediction does suggest some decline in such abstract exercises with greater effort given to applications, where the analysis is kept sufficiently simple that it can be used and tested on issues of current concern. Many of the current superstars in economics, who began as theorists, have redirected their attention to more applied and testable problems. This trend is expected to continue and is also reflected in new journals, such as the *Journal of Economic Perspectives*, that are widely read.

WHERE THE FOCUS WILL BE

The predictions here are no less controversial than the hypothesized areas of decline. My guesses are based on three considerations: social and economic problems confronting society, areas of economic analysis needing further development, and subfields attracting much recent activity. In identifying these candidates for greater activity, I shall not attempt to rank them in importance insofar as I have no means for judging this.

Given the large number of transnational interactions and contingencies, advances must be made in the area of understanding collective action at the transnational level. These contingencies involve security, environmental degradation, health, exploration of Earth and its solar system, knowledge creation and dissemination, and others. Specific examples, mentioned frequently, include peacekeeping, curbing the spread of weapons of mass destruction, thwarting transnational terrorism, limiting global warming, controlling the spread of disease, and promoting discoveries. Recently, many international organizations – the

World Bank, the United Nations, the European Union, and NATO – have begun to study means for promoting transnational collective action. These efforts and the funds for research that they generate will attract economists. As globalization continues, driven in part by technological advances, transnational collective action will grow in importance. Collective action at the supranational level confronts difficulties not necessarily associated with action at the national level, where laws support such action and provide the means for enforcing agreements.

Work on institutional design is another area where much activity is anticipated. In some instances, institutional architecture is sufficient to address collective action problems both nationally and transnationally. A properly constructed treaty or supranational structure may induce participants to cooperate or, at least, to respond in kind to a cooperative overture by another agent. Institutions define the constraints under which agents operate and, as such, determine the set of possible consequences from optimization decisions. The design of institutions draws on many of the advances in economic theory, and embodies the rules that determine the underlying game presented to the participants. The construction of these institutions represents a choice that may obviate the need for other policy decisions.

The study of intergenerational economics is another potential growth area. One generation's responsibility to another involves the four basic problems of economics. For example, the social security question of how a generation is supported during its retirement is an intergenerational distribution issue of current concern in many industrial countries, especially those for which the country's demographics imply an aging population. Allocation issues involve the provision of intergenerational public goods and the correction of intergenerational externalities, which appear to be growing owing to population growth and new technologies. Even the choice of a social discount rate has allocative implications for investment decisions. Sustainable growth is an intergenerational concern in cases where the sequence of births provides one generation with an advantage over another. Intergenerational economics also involves stability issues – for example, the rate of exploitation of a species can be so high as to cause extinction. If intergenerational issues did not pose such difficult problems, then further progress would have been made by now. To confront such questions, economists will have to utilize every trick and tool available, especially those involving dynamics. Evolutionary game theory is particularly suited to intergenerational interactions of a strategic nature.

The study of economic growth and development is sure to experience significant activity in coming years. Much is still unknown about the forces that support growth and development. Based on contributions during the last century, technological change, investment, and increased productivity are recognized as growth-promoting factors. Yet the profession is only beginning to understand what causes technological change and increased productivity. Although there have been recent attempts to explain why one country grows faster than another, much remains to be done to understand this phenomenon. For economic development, social and cultural influences are also essential considerations and, as such, highlight the importance of an interdisciplinary approach.

Interdisciplinary representations of economics will generally become more prevalent. In environmental economics, further collaboration between the biological and earth sciences is essential if models are to accurately predict policy consequences. For example, unless the dispersion of pollutants among countries is known and incorporated into the analysis, it is difficult to forecast how nations will react to actions of other nations in the control and generation of pollutants. As part of this interdisciplinary interest, spatial factors will play an increasingly important role, partly motivated by recent innovations in spatial econometrics. Interdisciplinary factors also come into play in public-sector economics in terms of political considerations. Many other subfields of economics have ties to other disciplines – for example, defense economics and engineering, land economics and earth sciences, urban economics and civil engineering, and microeconomics and psychology. As economists endogenize more variables, such as tastes, there will be an increasing need to draw from other disciplines.

Although game theory has been identified as likely to experience less overall activity, important breakthroughs will result in more research on some game-theoretic issues. If learning can be modeled in a more interesting fashion, then there will be a tidal wave of activity in the study of games that embody learning. Thus far, uncertainty has been modeled in game representations using the von Neumann and Morgenstern (1944) axiomatic representation for expected utility.[5] Other modeling innovations for representing tastes under uncertainty that do not hinge on expected returns are likely to be incorporated into the game-theoretic analysis and may yield additional results. Innovative dynamic represen-

---

[5] Their axiomatic approach indicates, among others things, that any sure prospect can be expressed as an equivalent choice between two uncertain outcomes, even if one of the uncertain outcomes is a possibility of death. Of course, a small possibility of death must be joined with a high possibility of a large reward if the resulting gamble is going to equivalent to some certain outcome. Another requirement is that the probabilities attached to each outcome determine the expected utility and not how these probabilities are decided. Thus, the likelihood of the outcomes and not how the outcomes are presented is what is important. See von Neumann and Morgenstern (1944) for the other axioms of expected utility.

tations of game theory would also be a welcome advance that could lead to a flurry of activity.

I also envision more activity in macroeconomics, where an improved foundation must be engineered in terms of how to aggregate individual behavior. Macroeconomic models cannot remain blasé about how the behavior of the representative individual is aggregated to give an overall characterization of the economy. The fallacy of composition cautions that what might be true of a component of the economy may not hold for the entire economy. Advances begun in the last decades in establishing the microeconomic foundations of macroeconomics can be completed only when aggregation is addressed more carefully. In some situations, an aggregate approach, even without a microeconomic foundation, may be best. If macroecnomics is to continue to excite a new generation of economists, then a less nihilistic orientation toward policy is required. Policy must be designed to circumvent potential pitfalls. Actions taken by the Federal Reserve System in the United States to sustain the unprecedented expansion of the US economy with little inflation in the 1990s and beyond indicate that policy has a role to play.

Work on experimental economics is a good bet to remain an area of intense activity, provided that sources of funding through the National Science Foundation and other institutions remain available. Although a clever economist can, at times, design experiments that are inexpensive, many experiments are necessarily costly because subjects must be motivated by payoffs to take the experimental scenarios seriously. When empirical data either are not available or will take years or even decades to generate, experimental economics has much to offer. Experiments can serve as an important reality check on theoretical paradigms.

The need for further development of economic dynamics became clear after the fall of communist regimes in Eastern Europe. Economists were at a loss as to what to recommend, because they had never really thought about the transition from one economic system to another. The experiences of the last ten years are beginning to provide some results. Even in the case of economic development, which also involves a choice of pathways that will lead to changes in economic, social, and political variables over time, economists remain in a learning stage. In recent years, demonstrations against the World Bank and the International Monetary Fund indicate that not everyone views past practices as effective. Economic growth is influenced by a host of noneconomic factors that must be included in broader models; endogenous growth theory is an effort to move in this direction. Economists' past fixation on investment has not given enough answers regarding why some economies escape poverty and become viable industrial economies while others do not.

Evolutionary game theory is providing some novel results that help to explain how institutions and systems evolve. This technique is particularly adept at accounting for changes in both the composition of participants and their evolving set of strategic choices, factors that characterize real-world institutions. (I cannot recall any department of which I have been a member that had the same faculty two years running; departmental interactions would change every year.) Evolutionary game theory provides one means for introducing learning, an essential ingredient for understanding economic dynamics. In an evolutionary game-theoretic setting, learning takes the form of culling strategies with low payoffs and maintaining those with high payoffs.

IS THERE A CRISIS OF VISION?

In a provocative book, Heilbroner and Milberg (1995) attribute a crisis in modern economic theory to an absence of a widely held set of political and social principles that had directed macroeconomics over the previous few decades. These authors believe that such a vision was last offered by Keynesian economics and its faith in government policy as a means to overcome market failures from insufficient aggregate demand that arises from coordination failures under uncertainty (Heilbroner and Milberg 1995, p. 35). That is, industries lay off workers owing to insufficient demand to maintain current production levels. As workers become unemployed, aggregate demand declines still further, leading to worsening expectations. If industries could only coordinate with one another and jointly decide production plans, then their pessimism could be curtailed, as ample demand comes from the expectations of employed laborers spending their incomes and firms being one another's customers. Keynesian economics was real-world oriented, where the focus was to devise a set of economic principles that could guide government policy, a vision that goes back to the founding fathers of economics.

Although I agree with Heilbroner and Milberg that macroeconomics has divided into opposing camps with no defining unity or commonly accepted principles or purpose, I do not accept that a single vision for economics must come from macroeconomics. The marginalist vision of the latter nineteenth century was microeconomics-based and once served to unify the profession. Since the lack of a consensus in macroeconomics has become so deeply rooted, one must look toward microeconomics, where there have been so many recent developments.

There appear to be several shared microeconomic visions directing recent economic thought, rather than just one. Perhaps the most dominant vision has been the study of market failures, which has touched most of economics in some way. The associated focus on externalities reminds economists that even effective market economies possess imperfections that require attention. A second vision comes from the introduction of strategic behavior, which has influenced both macroeconomics and microeconomics. With strategic considerations, economic thought has fundamentally changed, because the behavior of an isolated firm or individual is no longer of much interest when the anticipated actions and reactions of others can influence its choices and payoffs. For example, economists can no longer hypothesize the entry decisions of a firm without accounting for the likely responses of other firms. Game theory has provided a whole new vocabulary for the study of economics and has altered the graduate curriculum over the last decade. Strategic thinking takes rational action to a heightened awareness. When strategic considerations are included, theoretical predictions can be counterintuitive unless one becomes accustomed to such thinking.

Another current vision comes from the endogeneity of additional variables – a theme shared by the concepts in many of the chapters here. From institutional design to endogenous growth, economists are taking fewer factors as given and beyond economic analysis. This increased endogeneity marks an important break with economic analysis prior to the 1960s, and brings economics into closer contact with other disciplines. For habit and taste formation, economic analysis must incorporate insights and techniques from psychology. As any discipline matures, it is desirable that it expand its boundaries of study, thus limiting the constraints by which it operates.

Economics is widening its reach, not only in terms of assuming less as given, but also in terms of the topics to which economic methods are applied. These efforts to employ economic applications on untraditional topics constitute another shared vision during the last several decades. For sociological topics, economists have explained decisions within a family, the formation of groups, and the appearance of herd behavior. Economic analysis of civil wars, insurgencies, terrorism, voting behavior, and party politics involve topics once the domain of political scientists. Economics has been applied to diverse topics such as risk assessment, outer space resources, demography, location decisions, disarmament, the causes of war, network design, genetic engineering, and the internet. A relatively new field has joined law and economics to investigate such issues as liability assignment, the deterrent effects of capital punishment, the optimal number of prisons, and the effects of police on crime. Another new field of economics has focused on culture and the arts, while yet another has evaluated various economic aspects of health care.

A final shared vision involves the importance of information in economic analysis.[6] Once assumed complete and costless, information now plays a much greater role in economic studies. Information is an important consideration in game theory, the study of institutions, interdisciplinary studies, intergenerational economics, rational expectations, asymmetric information, market failures, and public-sector economics. Even laboratory economics lends itself to the study of the impact of information on different economic scenarios. With the focus on information comes the need to understand learning and the transaction costs associated with the acquisition of information.

Thus, modern economics is guided by a number of important visions that influence both macroeconomics and microeconomics. There is hope that with economics' broader range that it will become more policy-oriented and socially oriented. Certainly, recent activity gives this impression. If one looks to modern-day macroeconomics with its opposing schools of thought for a single vision, as Heilbroner and Milberg have done, no unified view is apparent. Nevertheless, modern concepts of economics demonstrate that economists continue to share common values. I am sanguine about the future of economics and what it can contribute to a changing, complex world. With its varied concerns, economics must reflect multiple complementary visions if it is to succeed. The days when a single view could serve to guide a discipline with so many issues of social and political significance are gone. Stabilization of employment and the price level, although important, is just one concern of economics. Income inequality, financial stability, environmental preservation, and sustainable growth are a few of the other essential problems. Economics will continue to branch out and develop new paradigms and interests as it contributes to a society of increasing complexity.

---

[6] Stiglitz (1996) also holds this view of the importance of information in modern economic thought.

References

Aghion, Philippe, Eve Caroli, and Cecilia Garcia-Peñalosa (1999), "Inequality and Economic Growth: The Perspective of the New Growth Theories," *Journal of Economic Literature*, 37(4), 1615–60.

Aghion, Philippe and Peter Howitt (1998), *Endogenous Growth Theory* (Cambridge, MA: MIT Press).

Akerlof, George A. (1970), "The Market for 'Lemons': Quality Uncertainty and the Market Mechanism," *Quarterly Journal of Economics*, 84(3), 488–500.

Alchian, Armen A. and Harold Demsetz (1972), "Production, Information Costs, and Economic Organization," *American Economic Review*, 62(5), 777–95.

Alesina, Alberto and Dani Rodrik (1994), "Distributive Politics and Economic Growth," *Quarterly Journal of Economics*, 109(2), 465–90.

Alley, Richard B. and Michael L. Bender (1998), "Greenland Ice Cores: Frozen in Time," *Scientific American*, 278(2), 80–5.

Andreoni, James (1990), "Impure Altruism and Donations to Public Goods: A Theory of Warm-Glow Giving," *Economic Journal*, 100(3), 464–77.

——— (1995), "Warm-Glow versus Cold-Prickle: The Effects of Positive and Negative Framing on Cooperation in Experiments," *Quarterly Journal of Economics*, 110(1), 1–21.

Anselin, Luc (1988), *Spatial Econometrics: Methods and Models* (Dordrecht, Netherlands: Kluwer Academic).

Aoki, Masahiko (1984), *The Co-operative Game Theory of the Firm* (Oxford: Oxford University Press).

Arce M., Daniel G. (1997), "Correlated Strategies as Institutions," *Theory and Decision*, 42(3), 271–85.

Arce M., Daniel G. and Todd Sandler (2001), "Transnational Public Goods: Strategies and Institutions," *European Journal of Political Economy*, 17, forthcoming.

Arrow, Kenneth J. (1951), "An Extension of the Basic Theorems of Classical Welfare Economics," in Jerzy Neyman (ed.), *Proceedings of the Second Berkeley Symposium on Mathematical Statistics and Probability* (Berkeley, CA: University of California Press), 507–32.

——— (1963), *Social Choice and Individual Values*, rev. ed. (New York: John Wiley and Sons).

(1970), "The Organization of Economic Activity: Issues Pertinent to the Choice of Market versus Non-Market Allocation," in Robert H. Haveman and John Margolis (eds.), *Public Expenditures and Policy Analysis* (Chicago: Markham), 59–73.

(1974a), "General Economic Equilibrium: Purpose, Analytic Techniques, Collective Choice," *American Economic Review*, 64(3), 253–72.

(1974b), *The Limits of Organization* (New York: Norton).

(1978), "The Future and the Present in Economic Life," *Economic Inquiry*, 16(2), 157–69.

(1999), "Discounting, Morality, and Gaming," in Paul R. Portney and John P. Weyant (eds.), *Discounting and Intergenerational Equity* (Washington, DC: Resources for the Future), 13–21.

Arrow, Kenneth J. and Gerard Debreu (1954), "Existence of an Equilibrium for a Competitive Economy," *Econometrica*, 22(3), 265–90.

Atkinson, Anthony B. and N. H. Stern (1974), "Pigou, Taxation, and Public Goods," *Review of Economic Studies*, 41(1), 119–28.

Aumann, Robert J. (1974), "Subjectivity and Correlation in Randomized Strategies," *Journal of Mathematical Economics*, 1(1), 67–97.

(1987), "Correlated Equilibria as an Expression of Bayesian Rationality," *Econometrica*, 55(1), 1–18.

Axelrod, Robert (1984), *The Evolution of Cooperation* (New York: Basic Books).

Barrett, Scott A. (1993), *Convention on Climate Change: Economic Aspects of Negotiations* (Paris: Organisation for Economic Co-operation and Development).

(1994), "Self-Enforcing International Environmental Agreements," *Oxford Economic Papers*, 46(4), 878–94.

(1998), "On the Theory and Diplomacy of Environmental Treaty-Making," *Environmental and Resource Economics*, 11(3–4), 317–33.

(1999), "Montreal versus Kyoto: International Cooperation and the Global Environment," in Inge Kaul, Isabelle Grunberg, and Marc A. Stern (eds.), *Global Public Goods: International Cooperation in the 21st Century* (New York: Oxford University Press), 192–219.

Barro, Robert J. (1991), "Economic Growth in a Cross Section of Countries," *Quarterly Journal of Economics*, 106(2), 407–43.

Barro, Robert J. and Xavier Sala-i-Martin (1992), "Convergence," *Journal of Political Economy*, 100(2), 223–51.

Baumol, William J. (2000), "What Marshall Didn't Know: On the Twentieth Century's Contributions to Economics," *Quarterly Journal of Economics*, 115(1), 1–44.

Bazerman, Max H. and William F. Samuelson (1983), "I Won the Auction but Don't Want the Prize," *Journal of Conflict Resolution*, 27(4), 618–34.

Becker, Gary S. (1996), *Accounting for Tastes* (Cambridge, MA: Harvard University Press).

Becker, Gary S. and Casey B. Mulligan (1997), "The Endogenous Determination of Time Preference," *Quarterly Journal of Economics*, 112(3), 729–58.

Benedick, Richard E. (1991), *Ozone Diplomacy* (Cambridge, MA: Harvard University Press).

Bergstrom, Theodore C. (1995), "On the Evolution of Altruistic Ethical Rules for Siblings," *American Economic Review*, 85(1), 58–80.

Bergstrom, Theodore C. and Robert P. Goodman (1973), "Private Demands for Public Goods," *American Economic Review*, 63(3), 280–96.

Bergstrom, Theodore C. and Oded Stark (1993), "How Altruism Can Prevail in an Evolutionary Environment," *American Economic Review*, 83(2), 149–55.

Bhagwati, Jagdish N. and T. N. Srinivasan (1980), "Revenue Seeking: A Generalization of the Theory of Tariffs," *Journal of Political Economy*, 88(6), 1069–87.

Binmore, Ken (1992), *Fun and Games* (Lexington, MA: D. C. Heath).

Black, Duncan (1958), *The Theory of Committees and Elections* (Cambridge: Cambridge University Press).

Blaug, Mark (1997), *Economic Theory in Retrospect*, 5th ed. (Cambridge: Cambridge University Press).

Boadway, Robin W. and Neil Bruce (1984), *Welfare Economics* (Oxford: Basil Blackwell).

Bohm, Peter (1972), "Estimating Demand for Public Goods: An Experiment," *European Economic Review*, 3(2), 111–30.

(1984), "Revealing Demand for an Actual Public Good," *Journal of Public Economics*, 24(2), 131–51.

Borcherding, Thomas E. and Robert T. Deacon (1972), "The Demand for the Services of Non-Federal Governments," *American Economic Review*, 62(5), 891–901.

Brada, Josef C. (1996), "Privatization Is Transition – Or Is It?," *Journal of Economic Perspectives*, 10(2), 67–86.

Bruce, Neil (2001), *Public Finance and the American Economy*, 2nd ed. (Reading, MA: Addison-Wesley).

Buchanan, James M. (1965), "An Economic Theory of Clubs," *Economica* 32(1), 1–14.

Buchanan, James M., Robert D. Tollison, and Gordon Tullock (eds.) (1980), *Toward a Theory of the Rent-Seeking Society* (College Station, TX: Texas A & M Press).

Buchanan, James M. and Gordon Tullock (1962), *The Calculus of Consent* (Ann Arbor: University of Michigan Press).

Buchholz, Wolfgang, Christian Haslbeck, and Todd Sandler (1998), "When Does Partial Cooperation Pay?," *Finanzarchiv*, 55(1), 1–20.

Bush, William C. and Lawrence S. Mayer (1974), "Some Implications of Anarchy for the Distribution of Property," *Journal of Economic Theory*, 8(4), 401–12.

Cauley, Jon, Richard Cornes, and Todd Sandler (1999), "Stakeholder Incentives and Reforms in China's State-Owned Enterprises: A Common-Property Theory," *China Economic Review*, 10(2), 191–206.

Cauley, Jon and Todd Sandler (1992), "Agency Theory and the Chinese Enterprise under Reform," *China Economic Review*, 3(1), 39–56.

Cauley, Jon, Todd Sandler, and Richard Cornes (1986), "Nonmarket Institutional Structures: Conjectures, Distribution, and Efficiency," *Public Finance*, 41(2), 153–72.

Chari, V. V. (1998), "Nobel Laureate Robert E. Lucas, Jr.: Architect of Modern Macroeconomics," *Journal of Economic Perspectives*, 12(1), 171–86.

Choi, Kwang (1983), "A Statistical Test of Olson's Model," in Dennis C. Mueller (ed.), *The Political Economy of Growth* (New Haven, CT: Yale University Press), 57–78.

Cicchetti, Charles J., Anthony C. Fisher, and V. Kerry Smith (1976), "An Econometric Evaluation of a Generalized Consumer Surplus Measure: The Mineral King Controversy," *Econometrica*, 44(6), 1259–87.

Clark, Colin W. (1985), *Bioeconomic Modelling and Fisheries Management* (New York: Wiley).

Clarke, Edward H. (1977), "Some Aspects of the Demand-Revealing Process," *Public Choice*, 29 (supplement), 37–49.

Coase, Ronald H. (1937), "The Nature of the Firm," *Economica*, 4(4), 386–405.
  (1960), "The Problem of Social Cost," *Journal of Law and Economics*, 3(1), 1–44.
  (1992), "The Institutional Structure of Production," *American Economic Review*, 82(4), 713–19.
  (1998), "The New Institutional Economics," *American Economic Review*, 88(2), 72–4.

Coe, David T. and Elhanan Helpman (1995), "International R & D Spillovers," *European Economic Review*, 39(5), 859–87.

Collier, Paul and Anke E. Hoeffler (1998), "On the Economic Causes of Civil Wars," *Oxford Economic Papers*, 50(4), 563–73.
  (2000), "Greed and Grievance in Civil War," unpublished manuscript, World Bank, Washington, DC.

Commons, John R. (1934), *Institutional Economics* (Madison, WI: University of Wisconsin Press).

Congleton, Roger D. (1992), "Political Institutions and Pollution Control," *Review of Economics and Statistics*, 74(3), 412–21.

Conrad, Jon M. (1995), "Bioeconomic Models of Fishery," in Daniel W. Bromley (ed.), *The Handbook of Environmental Economics* (Oxford: Blackwell, 1995), 405–33.

Cornes, Richard and Todd Sandler (1983), "On Commons and Tragedies," *American Economic Review*, 73(4), 787–92.
  (1985), "The Simple Analytics of Pure Public Good Provision," *Economica*, 52(1), 103–16.
  (1996), *The Theory of Externalities, Public Goods, and Club Goods*, 2nd ed. (Cambridge: Cambridge University Press).

Costanza, Robert, Charles Perrings, and Cutler J. Cleveland (eds.) (1995), *The Development of Ecological Economics* (Cheltenham, UK: Edward Elgar).

Cournot, Augustin (1838), *Recherches sur les Principes Mathématiques de la Théorie des Richesses* (Paris: Hachette). English translation by N. T. Bacon (1927), *Researches into the Mathematical Principles of the Theory of Wealth* (New York: Macmillan).

Craven, John (1992), *Social Choice: A Framework for Collective Decisions and Individual Judgements* (Cambridge: Cambridge University Press).

Cressie, Noel (1993), *Statistics for Spatial Data*, rev. ed. (New York: John Wiley).

Cummings, Ronald G., David S. Brookshire, and William D. Schulze (eds.) (1986), *Valuing Public Goods: A State of the Arts Assessment of the Contingent Valuation Method* (Totowa, NJ: Rowman and Allanheld).

Cummins, J. Michael (1977), "Incentive Contracting for National Defense: A Problem of Optimal Risk Sharing," *Bell Journal of Economics*, 8(1), 168–85.

Davis, Otto A. and Anthony B. Whinston (1965), "Welfare Economics and the Theory of Second Best," *Review of Economic Studies*, 32(1), 1–14.

(1967a), "On the Distinction between Public and Private Goods," *American Economic Review*, 57(2), 360–73.

(1967b), "Piecemeal Policy in the Theory of Second Best," *Review of Economic Studies*, 34(3), 323–31.

Debreu, Gerard (1959), *Theory of Value* (New York: Wiley).

de Gruijl, Frank R. (1995), "Impacts of a Projected Depletion of the Ozone Layer," *Consequences: The Nature & Implications of Environmental Change*, 1(2), 13–21.

Demsetz, Harold (1964), "The Exchange and Enforcement of Property Rights," *Journal of Law and Economics*, 7(2), 11–26.

(1967), "Toward a Theory of Property Rights," *American Economic Review*, 57(2), 347–59.

(1968), "The Cost of Transacting," *Quarterly Journal of Economics*, 82(1), 33–53.

DeSoto, Hernando (2000), *The Mystery of Capital: Why Capitalism Triumphs in the West and Fails Everywhere Else* (New York: Basic Books).

Dixit, Avinash K. (1998), *The Making of Economic Policy: A Transaction-Cost Politics Perspective* (Cambridge, MA: MIT Press).

Dixit, Avinash and Susan Skeath (1999), *Games of Strategy* (New York: Norton).

Doeleman, Jacobus A. and Todd Sandler (1998), "The Intergenerational Case of Missing Markets and Missing Voters," *Land Economics*, 74(1), 1–15.

Downs, Anthony (1957), *An Economic Theory of Democracy* (New York: Harper and Row).

Dusansky, Richard and John Walsh (1976), "Separability, Welfare Economics and the Theory of Second Best," *Review of Economic Studies*, 43(1), 49–51.

Edelson, Burton (1977), "Global Satellite Communications," *Scientific American*, 236(2), 58–73.

Edgeworth, F. Y. (1881), *Mathematical Psychics* (London: C. Kegan Paul).

Eggertson, Thrainn (1990), *Economic Behavior and Organizations* (New York: Cambridge University Press).

Eichberger, Jürgen (1993), *Game Theory for Economists* (San Diego: Academic Press).

Eliassen, Anton and Jørgen Saltbones (1983), "Modelling of Long-Range Transport of Sulphur over Europe: A Two-Year Model Run and Some Model Experiments," *Atmospheric Environment*, 17(8), 1457–73.

Enders, Walter and Todd Sandler (1993), "The Effectiveness of Antiterrorism Policies: A Vector-Autoregression-Intervention Analysis," *American Political Science Review*, 87(4), 829–44.

(1996), "Terrorism and Foreign Direct Investment in Spain and Greece," *KYKLOS*, 49(3), 331–52.

Environmental Protection Agency (1987a), *Assessing the Risks of Trace Gases That Can Modify the Stratosphere*, 7 vols. (Washington, DC: Environmental Protection Agency).

(1987b), *Regulatory Impact Analysis: Protection of Stratospheric Ozone*, 3 vols. (Washington, DC: Environmental Protection Agency).

Ericson, Richard E. (1991), "The Classical Soviet-Type Economy: Nature of the System and Implementations for Reform," *Journal of Economic Perspectives*, 5(4), 11–27.

Faden, Arnold M. (1977), *Economics of Space and Time: The Measure-Theoretic Foundations of Social Science* (Ames, IA: Iowa State University Press).

Fischer, Stanley and Alan Gelb (1991), "The Process of Socialist Economic Transition," *Journal of Economic Perspectives*, 5(4), 91–105.

Fischer, Stanley, Ratna Sahay, and Carlos A. Végh (1996), "Stabilization and Growth in Transition Economies: The Early Experience," *Journal of Economic Perspectives*, 10(2), 45–66.

Frankel, Jeffrey A. and David Romer (1999), "Does Trade Cause Growth?" *American Economic Review*, 89(3), 379–99.

Frankel, Marvin (1962), "The Production Function in Allocation and Growth: A Synthesis," *American Economic Review*, 52(5), 995–1022.

Fréchet, Maurice (1953), "Emile Borel, Initiator of the Theory of Psychological Games and Its Application," *Econometrica*, 21(1), 95–124.

Friedman, Milton (1968), "The Role of Monetary Policy," *American Economic Review*, 58(1), 1–17.

Gardner, Roy (1995), *Games for Business and Economics* (New York: Wiley).

Gardner, Roy and Elinor Ostrom (1991), "Rules and Games," *Public Choice*, 70(2), 121–49.

Gordon, H. Scott (1954), "The Economic Theory of a Common Property Resource: The Fishery," *Journal of Political Economy*, 62(2), 124–42.

Grief, Avner (1998), "Historical and Comparative Institutional Analysis," *American Economic Review*, 88(2), 80–4.

Grossman, Gene M. and Alan B. Krueger (1995), "Economic Growth and the Environment," *Quarterly Journal of Economics*, 110(2), 45–66.

Grossman, Herschel I. (1991), "A General Equilibrium Model of Insurrections," *American Economic Review*, 81(4), 912–21.

(1995), "Insurrections," in Keith Hartley and Todd Sandler (eds.), *Handbook of Defense Economics* (Amsterdam: North Holland), 191–212.

Groves, Theodore and John O. Ledyard (1977), "Optimal Allocation of Public Goods: A Solution to the 'Free Rider' Problem," *Econometrica*, 45(4), 783–809.

Gwin, Catherine and Joan M. Nelson (eds.) (1997), *Perspectives on Aid and Development*, Overseas Development Council Policy Essay No. 22 (Washington, DC: Overseas Development Council).

Hall, Robert E. (1978), "Stochastic Implications of the Life Cycle–Permanent Income Hypothesis: Theory and Evidence," *Journal of Political Economy*, 86(6), 971–87.

Hardin, Garrett (1968), "The Tragedy of the Commons," *Science*, 162, 1243–8.
Hardin, Russell (1982), *Collective Action* (Baltimore, MD: Johns Hopkins University Press).
Hay, D., D. Morris, D. Liu, and S. Yao (1994), *Economic Reform and State-Owned Enterprises in China, 1979–1987* (Oxford: Clarendon).
Heal, Geoffrey (1997), "Valuing Our Future: Cost-Benefit Analysis and Sustainability," Discussion Papers Series, United Nations Development Program, Office of Development Studies, New York.
Heckathorn, Douglas D. (1989), "Collective Action and the Second-Order Free-Rider Problem," *Rationality and Society*, 1(1), 78–100.
Heilbroner, Robert (1986), *The Worldly Philosophers: The Lives, Times, and Ideas of the Great Economic Thinkers*, 6th ed. (New York: Simon & Schuster).
Heilbroner, Robert and William Milberg (1995), *The Crisis of Vision in Modern Economic Thought* (Cambridge: Cambridge University Press).
Heller, W. P. and David A. Starrett (1976), "On the Nature of Externalities," in S. A. Y. Lin (ed.), *Theory and Measurement of Economic Externalities* (New York: Academic Press), 9–21.
Helm, Dieter (ed.) (1991), *Economic Policy towards the Environment* (Oxford: Blackwell).
Henderson, James M. and Richard E. Quandt (1980), *Microeconomic Theory: A Mathematical Approach*, 3rd ed. (New York: McGraw-Hill).
Hicks, John R. (1939), *Value and Capital* (Oxford: Clarendon Press).
Hinich, Melvin J. and Michael C. Munger (1997), *Analytical Politics* (Cambridge: Cambridge University Press).
Holmström, Bengt (1982), "Moral Hazard in Teams," *Bell Journal of Economics* 13(3), 324–40.
Hotelling, Harold (1929), "Stability in Competition," *Economic Journal*, 39(1), 41–57.
(1931), "The Economics of Exhaustible Resources," *Journal of Political Economy*, 39(2), 137–75.
Howarth, Richard B. (1995), "Sustainability under Uncertainty: A Deontological Approach," *Land Economics*, 71(4), 417–27.
Howarth, Richard B. and Richard B. Norgaard (1992), "Environmental Valuation under Sustainable Development," *American Economic Review*, 82(2), 473–77.
Hurwicz, Leonid (1973), "The Design of Mechanisms for Resource Allocation," *American Economic Review*, 63(2), 1–30.
(1999), "Revisiting Externalities," *Journal of Public Economic Theory*, 1(2), 225–45.
INTELSAT (1995), *INTELSAT in the '90s* (Washington, DC: INTELSAT).
James, Patrick, Eric Solberg, and Murray Wolfson (1999), "An Identified Systemic Model of the Democracy-Peace Model," *Defence and Peace Economics*, 10(1), 1–37.
Johansen, Leif (1977), "The Theory of Public Goods: Misplaced Emphasis?" *Journal of Public Economics* 7(1), 147–52.
Johansson, Per-Olov (1991), *An Introduction to Modern Welfare Economics* (Cambridge: Cambridge University Press).

John, A. Andrew and Rowena A. Pecchenino (1997), "International and Intergenerational Environmental Externalities," *Scandinavian Journal of Economics*, 99(3), 371–87.

Kagel, John H., Raymond C. Battalio, Howard Rachlin, Leonard Green, Robert L. Basmann, and W. R. Klemm (1975), "Experimental Studies of Consumer Demand Behavior Using Laboratory Animals," *Economic Inquiry*, 13(1), 22–38.

Kagel, John H. and Dan Levin (1986), "The Winner's Curse and Public Information in Common Value Auctions," *American Economic Review*, 76(5), 894–920.

Kagel, John H. and Alvin E. Roth (eds.) (1995), *The Handbook of Experimental Economics* (Princeton, NJ: Princeton University Press).

Kahneman, Daniel and Amos Tversky (1979), "Prospect Theory: An Analysis of Decision under Risk," *Econometrica*, 47(2), 263–91.

Kanbur, Ravi, Todd Sandler, and Kevin Morrison (1999), *The Future of Development Assistance: Common Pools and International Public Goods*, Overseas Development Council Policy Essay No. 25 (Washington, DC: Overseas Development Council).

Kantor, Brian (1979), "Rational Expectations and Economic Thought," *Journal of Economic Literature*, 17(4), 1422–41.

Kaul, Inge, Isabelle Grunberg, and Marc A. Stern (eds.) (1999), *Global Public Goods: International Cooperation in the 21st Century* (New York: Oxford University Press).

Kelly, Jerry S. (1988), *Social Choice Theory: An Introduction* (Berlin: Springer-Verlag).

Kim, Oliver and Mark Walker (1984), "The Free Rider Problem: Experimental Evidence," *Public Choice*, 43(1), 3–24.

Kovacic, William E. (1991), "Commitment in Regulation: Defense Contracting and Extensions to Price Caps," *Journal of Regulatory Economics*, 3(3), 219–40.

Kreps, David M. (1990a), *Game Theory and Economic Modelling* (Oxford: Clarendon Press).

(1990b), *A Course in Microeconomic Theory* (Princeton, NJ: Princeton University Press).

Krueger, Anne O. (1974), "The Political Economy of Rent-Seeking Society," *American Economic Review*, 64(3), 291–303.

Krutilla, John V. and Anthony C. Fisher (1975), *The Economics of Natural Environments: Studies in the Valuation of Commodity and Amenity Resources* (Baltimore, MD: Johns Hopkins University Press for Resources for the Future).

Laffont, Jean-Jacques and Jean Tirole (1986), "Using Cost Observation to Regulate Firms," *Journal of Political Economy*, 94(3), 614–41.

(1990), "The Regulation of Multiproduct Firms: Part I: Theory," *Journal of Public Economics*, 43(1), 1–36.

(1993), *A Theory of Incentives in Procurement and Regulation* (Cambridge, MA: MIT Press).

Langlois, Richard N. and Nicolai J. Foss (1999), "Capabilities and Governance: The Rebirth of Production in the Theory of Economic Organizations," *KYKLOS*, 52(2), 201–18.

Lapan, Harvey E. and Todd Sandler (1988), "To Bargain or Not to Bargain: That Is the Question," *American Economic Review*, 78(2), 16–20.

(1993), "Terrorism and Signalling," *European Journal of Political Economy*, 9(3), 383–97.

Lazear, Edward P. (2000), "Economic Imperialism," *Quarterly Journal of Economics*, 115(1), 99–146.

Ledyard, John O. (1995), "Public Goods: A Survey of Experimental Research," in John H. Kagel and Alvin E. Roth (eds.), *The Handbook of Experimental Economics* (Princeton, NJ: Princeton University Press), 111–94.

Lee, K. (1991), *Chinese Firms and the State in Transition: Property Rights and Agency Problems in the Reform Era* (Armonk, NY: M. E. Sharpe).

Leijonhufvud, Axel (1968), *On Keynesian Economics and the Economics of Keynes: A Study in Monetary Theory* (New York: Oxford University Press).

Lewis, Tracy (1996), "Protecting the Environment When Costs and Benefits Are Privately Known," *RAND Journal of Economics*, 27(4), 819–47.

Libecap, Gary D. (1989), *Contracting for Property Rights* (Cambridge: Cambridge University Press).

Lipsey, Richard G. and Kevin Lancaster (1956–7), "The General Theory of Second Best," *Review of Economic Studies*, 24(1), 11–32.

Lucas, Robert E., Jr. (1972), "Expectations and the Neutrality of Money," *Journal of Economic Theory*, 4(2), 102–24.

(1973), "Some International Evidence on Output-Inflation Trade-offs," *American Economic Review*, 63(3), 326–34.

(1996), "Nobel Lecture: Monetary Neutrality," *Journal of Political Economy*, 104(4), 661–82.

Luce, R. Duncan and Howard Raiffa (1957), *Games and Decisions* (New York: Wiley).

Lueck, Dean (1993), "Contracting into the Commons," in Terry L. Anderson and Randy T. Simmons (eds.), *The Political Economy of Customs and Culture: Informal Solutions to the Commons Problem* (Lanham, MD: Rowman and Littlefield), 43–59.

MacDonald, Glenn (1984), "New Directions in the Economic Theory of Agency," *Canadian Journal of Economics*, 17(3), 415–40.

Maddock, Rodney and Michael Carter (1982), "A Child's Guide to Rational Expectations," *Journal of Economic Literature*, 20(1), 39–51.

Mäler, Karl-Goran (1989), "The Acid Rain Game," in H. Folmer and E. van Ierland (eds.), *Valuation Methods and Policy Making in Environmental Economics* (Amsterdam: Elsevier Science), 231–52.

Mankiw, N. Gregory, David Romer, and David N. Weil (1992), "A Contribution to the Empirics of Economic Growth," *Quarterly Journal of Economics*, 107(2), 407–37.

March, James G. and Herbert A. Simon (1958), *Organizations* (New York: Wiley).

Margolis, Julius (1955), "A Comment on the Pure Theory of Public Expenditure," *Review of Economics and Statistics*, 37(4), 347–9.

Marshall, Alfred (1890), *Principles of Economics* (London: MacMillan & Co.).

Marwell, Gerald and Ruth E. Ames (1981), "Economists Free Ride, Does Anyone Else? Experiments on the Provision of Public Goods, IV," *Journal of Public Economics*, 15(3), 295–310.

Maynard Smith, John (1982), *Evolution and the Theory of Games* (New York: Cambridge University Press).

McAfee, R. Preston and John McMillan (1986), "Bidding for Contracts: A Principal-Agent Analysis," *Rand Journal of Economics*, 17(3), 326–38.

McGuire, Martin C. and Carl H. Groth (1985), "A Method for Identifying the Public Good Allocation Process within a Group," *Quarterly Journal of Economics*, 100 (supplement), 915–34.

McKenzie, Lionel W. (1959), "On the Existence of General Equilibrium for a Competitive Market," *Econometrica*, 27(1), 54–71.

McMillan, John (1986), *Game Theory in International Economics* (London: Harwood Academic Publishers).

Meltzer, Allan H. and Scott F. Richard (1981), "A Rational Theory of the Size of Government," *Journal of Political Economy*, 89(5), 914–27.

(1983), "Tests of a Rational Theory of the Size of Government," *Public Choice*, 41(3), 403–18.

Messinis, George (1999), "Habit Formation and the Theory of Addiction," *Journal of Economic Surveys*, 13(4), 417–42.

Meyer, Charles W. and Nancy Wolff (1993), *Social Security and Individual Equity: Evolving Standards of Equity and Adequacy* (Westport, CT: Greenwood Press).

Mishan, Erza J. (1971), "The Postwar Literature on Externalities: An Interpretative Essay," *Journal of Economic Literature*, 9(1), 1–28.

Morrow, James D. (1991), "Alliances and Asymmetry: An Alternative to the Capability Aggregation Model of Alliances," *American Journal of Political Science*, 35(4), 904–13.

Mosteller, Frederick and Philip Nogee (1951), "An Experimental Measurement of Utility," *Journal of Political Economy*, 59(5), 371–404.

Mueller, Dennis C. (1989), *Public Choice II* (Cambridge: Cambridge University Press).

Murdoch, James C. and Todd Sandler (1982), "A Theoretical and Empirical Analysis of NATO," *Journal of Conflict Resolution*, 26(2), 237–63.

(1984), "Complementarity, Free Riding, and the Military Expenditures of NATO Allies," *Journal of Public Economics*, 25(1–2), 83–101.

(1997), "The Voluntary Provision of a Pure Public Good: The Case of Reduced CFC Emissions and the Montreal Protocol," *Journal of Public Economics*, 63(2), 331–49.

Murdoch, James C., Todd Sandler, and Keith Sargent (1997), "A Tale of Two Collectives: Sulphur versus Nitrogen Oxides Emission Reduction in Europe," *Economica*, 64(2), 281–301.

Murrell, Peter (1996), "How Far Has the Transition Progressed?," *Journal of Economic Perspectives*, 10(2), 25–44.

Muth, John F. (1960), "Optimal Properties of Exponentially Weighted Forecasts," *Journal of the American Statistical Association*, 55(2), 299–306.

(1961), "Rational Expectations and the Theory of Price Movements," *Econometrica*, 29(3), 315–35.

Myerson, Roger G. (1999), "Nash Equilibrium and the History of Economic Theory," *Journal of Economic Literature*, 37(3), 1067–82.

Nasar, Sylvia (1998), *A Beautiful Mind* (New York: Simon & Schuster).

Nash, John F. (1951), "Noncooperative Games," *Annals of Mathematics*, 54(3), 289–95.

Nee, Victor (1998), "Norms and Networks in Economic and Organizational Performance," *American Economic Review*, 88(2), 85–9.

Newman, Philip C., Arthur D. Gayer, and Milton H. Spencer (eds.) (1954), *Source Readings in Economic Thought* (New York: Norton).

Niskanen, William A. (1971), *Bureaucracy and Representative Government* (Chicago: Aldine-Atherton).

North, Douglass C. (1961), *The Economic Growth of the United States, 1790–1860* (Englewood Cliffs, NJ: Prentice-Hall).

(1990), *Institutions, Institutional Change and Economic Performance* (Cambridge: Cambridge University Press).

(1994), "Economic Performance through Time," *American Economic Review*, 84(3), 359–68.

Nowell, Clifford and John T. Tschirhart (1993), "Testing Theories of Regulatory Behavior," *Review of Industrial Organization*, 8(6), 653–68.

Oakland, William H. (1972), "Congestion, Public Goods, and Welfare," *Journal of Public Economics*, 1(3–4), 339–57.

(1974), "Public Goods, Perfect Competition, and Underprovision," *Journal of Political Economy*, 82(5), 927–39.

Olson, Mancur (1965), *The Logic of Collective Action* (Cambridge, MA: Harvard University Press).

(1980), "Introduction," in Todd Sandler (ed.), *The Theory and Structures of International Political Economy* (Boulder, CO: Westview Press), 3–16.

(1982), *The Rise and Decline of Nations* (New Haven, CT: Yale University Press).

(1993), "Dictatorship, Democracy, and Development," *American Political Science Review*, 87(3), 567–76.

(2000), *Power and Prosperity: Outgrowing Communist and Capitalist Dictatorships* (New York: Basic Books).

Olson, Mancur and Richard Zeckhauser (1966), "An Economic Theory of Alliances," *Review of Economics and Statistics*, 48(3), 266–79.

Ordeshook, Peter C. (1986), *Game Theory and Political Theory: An Introduction* (Cambridge: Cambridge University Press).

Ostrom, Elinor (1990), *Governing the Commons: The Evolution of Institutions for Collective Action* (Cambridge: Cambridge University Press).

(1999), "Context and Collective Action: Four Interactive Building Blocks for a Family of Explanatory Theories," unpublished manuscript, Indiana University, Bloomington.

Ostrom, Elinor, Roy Gardner, and James Walker (1994), *Rules, Games, and Common-Pool Resources* (Ann Arbor: University of Michigan Press).

Page, Talbot (1977), "Discounting and Intergenerational Equity," *Futures*, 9(5), 377–82.

Pareto, Vilfredo (1909), *Manuel d'Économie Politique* (Paris: M. Giard).

Pauly, Mark V. (1967), "Clubs, Commonality, and the Core: An Integration of Game Theory and the Theory of Public Goods," *Economica*, 34(3), 314–24.

(1970), "Cores and Clubs," *Public Choice*, 9(1), 53–65.

Pearce, David and Giles Atkinson (1995), "Measuring Sustainable Development," in Daniel W. Bromley (ed.), *The Handbook of Environmental Economics* (Oxford: Blackwell), 166–81.

Peltzman, Sam (1980), "The Growth of Government," *Journal of Law and Economics*, 23(2), 209–88.

Phelps, Edmund S. (1968), "Money-Wage Dynamics and Labor-Market Equilibrium," *Journal of Political Economy*, 76(4), 678–711.

Phillips, A. W. (1958), "The Relation between Unemployment and the Rate of Change of Money Wage Rates in the United Kingdom, 1861–1957," *Economica*, 25(4), 283–99.

Pigou, A. C. (1920), *The Economics of Welfare* (London: Macmillan).

Plott, Charles R. and Michael E. Levine (1978), "A Model of Agenda Influence on Committee Decisions," *American Economic Review*, 68(1), 146–60.

Plott, Charles R. and Vernon L. Smith (1978), "An Experimental Examination of Two Exchange Institutions," *Review of Economic Studies*, 45(1), 133–53.

Portney, Paul R. and John P. Weyant (eds.) (1999), *Discounting and Intergenerational Equity* (Washington, DC: Resources for the Future).

Rabinovitch, Jonas and Josef Leitman (1996), "Urban Planning in Curitiba," *Scientific American*, 274(3), 46–53.

Ramsey, F. P. (1928), "A Mathematical Theory of Saving," *Economic Journal*, 38(4), 543–59.

Rapaczynski, Andrzej (1996), "The Roles of the State and the Market in Establishing Property Rights," *Journal of Economic Perspectives*, 10(2), 87–103.

Rapoport, Anatol and Melvin J. Guyer (1966), "A Taxonomy of 2 × 2 Games," *General Systems*, 11(2), 203–14.

Rawls, John (1971), *A Theory of Justice* (Cambridge, MA: Harvard University Press).

Riker, William (1962), *The Theory of Political Coalitions* (New Haven, CT: Yale University Press).

(1986), *The Art of Political Manipulation* (New Haven, CT: Yale University Press).

Rodrik, Dani (1999), *The New Global Economy and Developing Countries: Making Openness Work*, Overseas Development Council Policy Essay No. 24 (Washington, DC: Overseas Development Council).

Rogerson, William P. (1990), "Quality and Quantity in Military Procurement," *American Economic Review*, 80(1), 83–92.

(1991), "Excess Capacity in Weapons Production: An Empirical Analysis," *Defence Economics*, 2(3), 235–50.

Romer, Paul M. (1986), "Increasing Returns and Long Run Growth," *Journal of Political Economy*, 94(5), 1002–37.

Rose, Michael R. (1999), "Can Human Aging Be Postponed?," *Scientific American*, 281(6), 106–11.

Ross, Stephen A. (1973), "The Economic Theory of Agency: The Principal's Problem," *American Economic Review*, 63(2), 134–9.

Roth, Alvin E. (1995), "Introduction to Experimental Economics," in John H. Kagel and Alvin E. Roth (eds.), *The Handbook of Experimental Economics* (Princeton, NJ: Princeton University Press), 3–109.

Runge, C. Ford (1993), "International Public Goods, Export Subsidies, and the Harmonization of Environmental Regulations," in Matthew D. Shane and Harold von Witzke (eds.), *The Environment, Government Policies, and International Trade: A Proceedings* (Washington, DC: Economic Research Service, US Department of Agriculture), 24–44.

Russett, Bruce (1993), *Grasping the Democratic Peace* (Princeton, NJ: Princeton University Press).

Safina, Carl (1995), "The World's Imperiled Fish," *Scientific American*, 273(5), 46–53.

Sah, Raaj K. and Joseph E. Stiglitz (1986), "The Architecture of Economic Systems: Hierarchies and Polyarchies," *American Economic Review*, 76(4), 716–27.

Samuelson, Paul A. (1954), "The Pure Theory of Public Expenditure," *Review of Economics and Statistics*, 36(4), 387–9.

  (1955), "A Diagrammatic Exposition of a Theory of Public Expenditure," *Review of Economics and Statistics*, 37(4), 350–6.

Sandler, Todd (1977), "Impurity of Defense: An Application to the Economics of Alliances," *KYKLOS*, 30(3), 443–60.

  (1978a), "Public Goods and the Theory of Second Best," *Public Finance*, 33(3), 330–44.

  (1978b), "Interregional and Intergenerational Spillover Awareness," *Scottish Journal of Political Economy*, 25(3), 273–84.

  (1982), "A Theory of Intergenerational Clubs," *Economic Inquiry*, 20(2), 191–208.

  (1992), *Collective Action: Theory and Applications* (Ann Arbor: University of Michigan Press).

  (1997), *Global Challenges: An Approach to Environmental, Political, and Economic Problems* (Cambridge: Cambridge University Press).

  (1998), "Global and Regional Public Goods: A Prognosis for Collective Action," *Fiscal Studies*, 19(3), 221–47.

  (1999), "Intergenerational Public Goods: Strategies, Efficiency, and Institutions," in Inge Kaul, Isabelle Grunberg, and Marc A. Stern (eds.), *Global Public Goods: International Cooperation in the 21st Century* (New York: Oxford University Press for United Nations Development Program), 20–50.

  (2000), "Global Challenges and the Need for Supranational Infrastructure," unpublished manuscript, Iowa State University, Ames.

Sandler, Todd and Jon Cauley (1977), "The Design of Supranational Structures: An Economic Perspective," *International Studies Quarterly*, 21(2), 251–76.

(1980), "A Hierarchical Theory of the Firm," *Scottish Journal of Political Economy*, 27(1), 17–29.

Sandler, Todd, Jon Cauley, and John T. Tschirhart (1983), "Toward a Unified Theory of Nonmarket Institutional Structures," *Australian Economic Papers*, 22(1), 233–54.

Sandler, Todd and Keith Hartley (1995), *The Economics of Defense* (Cambridge: Cambridge University Press).

(1999), *The Political Economy of NATO: Past, Present, and into the 21st Century* (Cambridge: Cambridge University Press).

Sandler, Todd and Harvey E. Lapan (1988), "The Calculus of Dissent: An Analysis of Terrorists' Choice of Targets," *Synthese*, 76(2), 245–61.

Sandler, Todd and James C. Murdoch (1990), "Nash-Cournot or Lindahl Behavior?: An Empirical Test for the NATO Allies," *Quarterly Journal of Economics*, 105(4), 875–94.

Sandler, Todd and Keith Sargent (1995), "Management of Transnational Commons: Coordination, Publicness, and Treaty Formation," *Land Economics*, 71(2), 145–62.

Sandler, Todd and William D. Schulze (1981), "The Economics of Outer Space," *Natural Resources Journal*, 21(2), 371–93.

(1985), "Outer Space: The New Market Frontier," *Economic Affairs*, 5(4), 6–10.

Sandler, Todd and V. Kerry Smith (1976), "Intertemporal and Intergenerational Pareto Efficiency," *Journal of Environmental Economics and Management*, 2(3), 151–9.

Sandler, Todd and John T. Tschirhart (1980), "The Economic Theory of Clubs: An Evaluative Survey," *Journal of Economic Literature*, 18(4), 1481–521.

(1997), "Club Theory: Thirty Years Later," *Public Choice*, 93(3–4), 335–55.

Sandnes, Hilde (1993), *Calculated Budgets for Airborne Acidifying Components in Europe, 1985, 1987, 1989, 1990, 1991, and 1992*, EMEP/MSC-W Report 1/93 (Oslo: Norske Meterologiske Institutt).

Schaefer, M. B. (1954), "Some Aspects of the Dynamics of Populations Important to the Management of Commercial Marine Fisheries," *Bulletin of the Inter-American Tropical Tuna Commission*, 1(1), 25–56.

Schelling, Thomas C. (1960), *The Strategy of Conflict* (Cambridge, MA: Harvard University Press).

Schotter, Andrew (1994a), "Social Institutions and Game Theory," in Peter J. Boettke (ed.), *The Elgar Companion to Austrian Economics* (Aldershot, UK: Elgar), 556–64.

(1994b), *Microeconomics: A Modern Approach* (New York: HarperCollins College Publishers).

Schulze, William D., David S. Brookshire, and Todd Sandler (1981), "The Social Rate of Discount for Nuclear Waste Storage: Economics or Ethics?," *Natural Resources Journal*, 2(4), 811–32.

Schumpeter, Joseph A. (1934), *The Theory of Economic Development* (Cambridge, MA: Harvard University Press).

Selten, Reinhard (1965), "Spieltheoretische Behandlung eines Oligopolmodells mit Nachfragetragheit," *Zeitschrift für die gesamte Staatswissenschaft*, 12(2), 301–24.

(1975), "Reexamination of the Perfectness Concept for Equilibrium Points in Extensive Games," *International Journal of Game Theory*, 4(1), 25–55.

Sen, Amartra K. (1979), *Collective Choice and Social Welfare* (Amsterdam: North-Holland).

Silver, Morris (1980), *Affluence, Altruism, and Atrophy: The Decline of Welfare States* (New York: New York University Press).

Skyrms, Brian (1996), *Evolution of the Social Contract* (Cambridge: Cambridge University Press).

Smith, Vernon L. (1962), "An Experimental Study of Competitive Market Behavior," *Journal of Political Economy*, 70(2), 111–37.

(1980), "Experiments with a Decentralized Mechanism for Public Good Decisions," *American Economic Review*, 70(4), 584–99.

(1982), "Competitive Market Institutions: Double Auctions versus Sealed Bid-Offer Auctions, *American Economic Review*, 72(1), 58–77.

Solow, Robert M. (1957), "Technical Change and the Aggregate Production Function," *Review of Economics and Statistics*, 39(3), 312–20.

(1986), "On the Intergenerational Allocation of Natural Resources," *Scandinavian Journal of Economics*, 88(1), 141–49.

Spence, A. Michael (1973), "Job Market Signaling," *Quarterly Journal of Economics*, 87(3), 355–74.

Starr, Ross M. (1997), *General Equilibrium Theory: An Introduction* (Cambridge: Cambridge University Press).

Stigler, George J. (1968), *The Organization of Industry* (Homewood, IL: Richard D. Irwin).

Stiglitz, Joseph E. (1974), "Risk Sharing and Incentives in Sharecropping," *Review of Economic Studies*, 61(2), 219–56.

(1996), *Whither Socialism?* (Cambridge, MA: MIT Press).

(1999), "Knowledge as a Global Public Good," in Inge Kaul, Isabelle Grunberg, and Marc A. Stern (eds.), *Global Public Goods: International Cooperation in the 21st Century* (New York: Oxford University Press), 308–25.

Thurstone, L. L. (1931), "The Indifference Function," *Journal of Social Psychology*, 2(2), 139–67.

Tideman, T. Nicholaus and Gordon Tullock (1976), "A New and Superior Process for Making Social Choices," *Journal of Political Economy*, 84(6), 1145–59.

Tiebout, Charles M. (1956), "A Pure Theory of Local Expenditures," *Journal of Political Economy*, 64(4), 416–24.

Tirole, Jean (1986), "Procurement and Renegotiation," *Journal of Political Economy*, 94(2), 235–59.

Toman, Michael A. (1994), "Economics and 'Sustainability': Balancing Trade-offs and Imperatives," *Land Economics*, 70(4), 399–413.

Toman, Michael A., John Pezzey, and Jeffrey Krautkraemer (1995), "Neoclassical Economic Growth Theory and 'Sustainability,'" in Daniel W. Bromley (ed.), *The Handbook of Environmental Economics* (Oxford: Blackwell), 139–65.

Toon, Owen R. and Richard P. Turco (1991), "Polar Stratospheric Clouds and Ozone Depletion," *Scientific American*, 264(1), 68–74.

Tschirhart, John T. (2000), "General Equilibrium of an Ecosystem," *Journal of Theoretical Biology*, 203(1), 13–32.

Tullock, Gordon (1967), "The Welfare Costs of Tariffs, Monopolies, and Theft," *Western Economic Journal*, 5(2), 224–32.

United Nations Development Program (1999), *Human Development Report 1999* (New York: Oxford University Press).

United Nations Population Fund (1994), *The State of World Population 1994: Choices and Responsibilities* (New York: UN Population Fund).

van de Walle, Nicholas and Timothy A. Johnston (1996), *Improving Aid to Africa*, Overseas Development Council Policy Essay No. 21 (Washington, DC: Overseas Development Council).

van den Bergh, Jeroen C. J. M. and Jan van der Straaten (eds.) (1997), *Economy and Ecosystems in Change: Analytical and Historical Approaches* (Cheltenham, UK: Edward Elgar).

Varian, Hal R. (1993), *Intermediate Microeconomics: A Modern Approach*, 3rd ed. (New York: Norton).

Vega-Redondo, Fernando (1996), *Evolution, Games, and Economic Behavior* (Oxford: Oxford University Press).

Vickrey, William S. (1961), "Counterspeculation, Auctions, and Competitive Sealed Tenders," *Journal of Finance*, 16(1), 8–37.

  (1969), "Congestion Theory and Transport Investment," *American Economic Review*, 59(2), 251–60.

Vonnegut, Kurt, Jr. (1970), "Harrison Bergeron," in Kurt Vonnegut, Jr. (ed.), *Welcome to the Monkey House* (New York: Dell).

von Neumann, John (1928), "Zur Theories der Gessellschaftsspiele," *Mathematische Annalen*, 100, 295–320. English translation by S. Bergmann in R. Duncan Luce and Albert W. Tucker (eds.) (1959), *Contributions to the Theory of Games IV* (Princeton, NJ: Princeton University Press), 13–42.

von Neumann, John (1937), "Uber ein Ökonomisches Gleichungssytem und eine Verallgemeinerung des Brouwerschen Fixpunktsatzes," *Ergebnisse eines Mathematik Kolloquiums*, 8(1), 73–83.

von Neumann, John and Oscar Morgenstern (1944), *The Theory of Games and Economic Behavior* (Princeton, NJ: Princeton University Press).

Wallis, W. Allen and Milton Friedman (1942), "The Empirical Derivation of Indifference Functions," in Oscar Lange, Francis McIntyre, and Theodore O. Yntema (eds.), *Studies in Mathematical Economics and Econometrics in Memory of Henry Schultz* (Chicago: University of Chicago Press), 175–89.

Walras, Leon (1874), *Elements d'Economie Politique Pure* (Lausanne: L. Corbanz). Translated by William Jaffe as *Elements of Pure Economics* (Homewood, IL: Richard D. Irwin, 1954).

Wan, Henry Y. (1971), *Economic Growth* (New York: Harcourt Brace Jovanovich).

Warr, Peter G. (1983), "The Private Provision of a Public Good Is Independent of the Distribution of Income," *Economics Letters*, 13(2), 207–11.

Weibull, Jörgen W. (1995), *Evolutionary Game Theory* (Boston: MIT Press).

Weisbrod, Burton (1988), *The Nonprofit Economy* (Cambridge, MA: Harvard University Press).

Weitzman, Martin L. (1999), "Just Keeping Discounting, But . . . ," in Paul R. Portney and John P. Weyant (eds.), *Discounting and Intergenerational Equity* (Washington, DC: Resources for the Future), 23–9.

Wihlborg, Clas G. and Per Magnus Wijkman (1981), "Outer Space Resources in Efficient and Equitable Use: New Frontiers for Old Principles," *Journal of Law and Economics*, 24(1), 23–43.

Williamson, Oliver E. (1967), "Hierarchical Control and Optimum Firm Size," *Journal of Political Economy*, 75(2), 123–38.

(1975), *Markets and Hierarchies: Analysis and Antitrust Implications: A Study in the Economics of Internal Organization* (New York: The Free Press).

(1998), "The Institutions of Governance," *American Economic Review*, 88(2), 75–9.

(2000), "The New Industrial Economics: Taking Stock, Looking Ahead," *Journal of Economic Literature*, 38(3), 595–613.

Wiseman, Jack (1957), "The Theory of Public Utility Price – An Empty Box," *Oxford Economic Papers*, 9(1), 56–74.

Wolf, Thomas A. (1991), "The Lessons of Limited Market-Oriented Reform," *Journal of Economic Perspectives*, 5(4), 45–58.

World Bank (1998), *Assessing Aid: What Works, What Doesn't, and Why* (New York: Oxford University Press).

World Commission on Environment and Development (Brundtland Report) (1987), *Our Common Future* (New York: Oxford University Press).

Yang, Xiaokai (1993), "Theories of Property Rights and China's Reforms," *China Economic Review*, 4(2), 195–212.

Author Index

Subject Index